# THE END OF TECHNOPHOBIA

## A practical guide to digitising your business

## TRACY SHEEN

'My over 20-year career of assisting Australian and international businesses to start, innovate, grow and prosper has identified that a key ingredient to small business success and sustainability is "confidence" – especially in our ever-changing digital world of globalisation. Having worked with Tracy in her capacity as an expert digital business adviser and mentor under the Australian Small Business Advisory Services Digital Solutions government program, I have witnessed Tracy's passion for and commitment to helping regional small businesses embrace digital technologies – working both directly and through stakeholder engagement. As an experienced, expert workshop creator, presenter and facilitator, Tracy has a rare talent to easily connect with people and deliver content in an easy-to-understand and practical way. Through both her extensive client work and especially this new book, Tracy engenders businesses with the confidence to "go digital" to more efficiently connect, collaborate, expand their brand to reach new customers, conduct business in broader markets, and get ahead of their competitors. I thoroughly recommend Tracy and *The End of Technophobia – A Practical Guide to Digitising Your Business* as key ingredients to the recipe of small business success.'

*Rowena Ryan – AusIndustry (Australian Department of Industry, Science, Energy & Resources)*
*www.business.gov.au*


'I have been blessed to work with Tracy over the last three years, referring many small businesses to one of her engaging workshops or advisory sessions. Many a technology challenged regionally based business has found a new love for all things tech thanks to Tracy Sheen. I personally thank you for your commitment to businesses across regional and rural Queensland. Your ability to deliver content in an easily digestible way has resulted in business owners being able to sell their products and engage worldwide, and for that Regional Development Australia Darling Downs and South West will be forever grateful.'

*Trudi Bartlett*
*Director, Regional Development Australia Darling Downs and South West QLD*
*www.rda-ddsw.org.au*

'Greater Springfield Chamber of Commerce (GSCC) had the privilege of having Tracy sit on our board for a number of years. Tracy came to us at a huge time of change for the Chamber and helped us achieve so many goals.

'During 2017 Tracy helped us rebrand and provided the content for our new website; today this is still the hub of everything we do.

'Her commitment to small businesses, especially those in more regional and rural areas, is amazing; her desire to see them succeed is shown in the work and enthusiasm she has when working with them. We have been lucky enough to utilise all Tracy's amazing abilities – she has helped the Chamber provide educational training through being an ASBAS advisor. Her programs are easy to understand, practical and most importantly easy to implement in your own business. The chamber has often asked Tracy to create and present workshops to our members as we know she provides invaluable advice and real-life experience when wishing to grow your business.

'Tracy helped us to bring one of our much wanted events to reality: our International Women's Day Luncheon is now one of our stand out events of the year which Tracy has always MC'd for us.

'We cannot recommend Tracy's abilities as a presenter, educator and MC enough and we look forward to our continued relationship with her.'

*Leila Stewart, Executive Assistant*
*Greater Springfield Chamber of Commerce QLD*
*www.gscc.com.au*

'Tracy is a fabulously knowledgeable and helpful business and digital coach. Our paddock to plate business prides itself on having good customer connections and Tracy has helped me to further develop my customer community through social media and online streams in a way that fits with my business ethos. I am excited to read Tracy's book and see what other tips and technologies I can incorporate into my business and personal life.'

*Skye Douglass, HighBrit Beef and The Farm Crate*
*www.highbritbeef.com.au*

'I've known Tracy for several years now. Her commitment to helping small businesses not only survive, but thrive is inspiring. She seems to have an endless amount of knowledge in digital marketing. It's not surprising that she is an advisor for ASBAS. Tracy has an uncanny ability to explain complex concepts in simple terms.

'She has helped me to simplify my business, making it easier for me to communicate what it is I do with my clients. Tracy has drawn out information that I didn't even know I had about my business and restructured it in a way that I simply would not have been able to connect without her. I've always found her presentations engaging and interesting, even the dry topics. She has this ability to introduce new life to old concepts and present them in a new light.

'I would recommend you read this book and consume any content that Tracy produces and has produced. You're guaranteed to learn something new.'

*Steven Jaenke*
*Digimark Australia*
*www.digimark.com.au*


'Tracy's mentorship and coaching helped transform my gin podcast ideas into reality. Her support, guidance and constructive feedback were crucial to making this happen.

'To see the outcomes from our hands-on strategy session manifest themselves practically as 3 seasons and 30 episodes in 6 months, still staggers me.

'Tracy's belief in me and the project were unwavering, culminating in an on-time launch for World Gin Day 2020.

'Thanks Tracy, you've well and truly earned a Martini or two!'

*Marcel Thompson, Distiller and author of Still Magic*
*www.stillmagic.net*

'I have had the pleasure of working with Tracy on a number of digital items. She has supported us in our business in transitioning to a CRM program, along with providing a getting started training module delivered over Zoom. This was very helpful as I found her to be systematic and concise in her approach. It was a great leap to launching a new program into our business. We have engaged her to help with website reviews, copy reviews and various advice on a number of other digital solutions which we required to support the growth in our business. I have also attended some of her online training and always go back for more. She is very professional in her approach with businesses, her knowledge in the digital space of all things geeky is quite incredible. If I need advice or would like options to consider to implement in our business Tracy is my "go-to person". I've found her to be honest and direct, which is how I prefer to do business.'

*Kylie Martin Hollonds*
*Managing Director, GF Oats Australia*
*www.gfoats.com.au*

**CATCH MY DRIFT!**

Remember the very nature of technology means things are constantly changing. While everything in this book is correct and current as of January 2021, things may have changed by the time you read this book. The lessons and foundations will remain solid though, even if the screen looks slightly different.

Everyone has dreamed about their Oscar acceptance speech (haven't they?). With that in mind I do have a few people I'd like to acknowledge, thank or otherwise share my appreciation for. And so, in no particular order (because you're all important to me).

Peter. Thank you for bringing me coffee, keeping me fed and watered and always being proud of what we achieve together. I still don't know what I ever did to get so lucky, but I thank the Gods every day that you're my person. Can't wait for what happens next.

AG. Without you I can honestly say this book would not have happened. Thank you for pushing me for better outcomes and playing a lead role in this chapter of my journey. Thank you for being there to talk me down from the metaphorical ledge and for believing the Digital Guide is a project that needed to find its voice. You really are a good egg.

Mum, Dad and my family. Thank you for believing I could be an author... I wonder what Charmaine would have to say.

To every single one of the small business owners I've worked with. You have each contributed something to this book. Thank you for daring to build your own future, being so willing to overcome your technophobia and embrace your inner geek.

To my broader support team. Drew, Wendy, Simone, Geoff, Leila et al, thank you for listening to the rants and keeping me focused when it all felt too much.

And finally, Obi and Watson... for reminding me there is always time for play, time for cuddles and time for naps.

Oh... and I cannot forget you, my fabulous reader. Without you this book would be nothing but a paperweight.

Big hugs... Tracy.

First published in 2021 by Tracy Sheen

A catalogue entry for this book is available from the National Library of Australia.

ISBN: 978-1-922391-96-4

Printed in Australia by McPherson's Printing
Project management and text design by Publish Central
Cover design by Peter Reardon
Illustrations by Jane D Thornton e: jdt@charactergirl.com

The paper this book is printed on is certified as environmentally friendly.

**Disclaimer:** The material in this publication is of the nature of general comment only, and does not represent professional advice. It is not intended to provide specific guidance for particular circumstances and it should not be relied on as the basis for any decision to take action or not take action on any matter which it covers. Readers should obtain professional advice where appropriate, before making any such decision. To the maximum extent permitted by law, the author and publisher disclaim all responsibility and liability to any person, arising directly or indirectly from any person taking or not taking action based on the information in this publication.

# CONTENTS

# FOREWORD

*by Andrew Griffiths – Bestselling Author, Speaker & Entrepreneurial Futurist*

What a weird and wonderful world we find ourselves in, one filled with previously unimaginable technology, all available at our fingertips, 24 hours a day. Things have become so much easier, haven't they? Because you're reading this book, I'm pretty certain the transition from technophobe to techno geek hasn't been a smooth one. And all I can say is thank you Tracy Sheen for being our guide on this perilous journey.

There is no doubt that technology is an incredible tool. If you can remember, think back to the dark ages when you had to get up and walk over to your television to change channels. Imagine life without a remote? Or having to have to go into a bank to withdraw money? Oh the horror. And whilst these are examples of tech that we've all hopefully mastered, there is a constant and never-ending barrage of new tech that we have to deal with. And nowhere is this more relevant than in the world of business.

As a business owner you know you need to be doing things smarter. In the words of Alvin Toffler, author of the famous book *Future Shock*, "the illiterate of the 21st century won't be those who can't read or write but those who can't learn, unlearn and relearn". And never has there been a statement that is more relevant than this. We are in a constant state of learning, unlearning and relearning, often just to keep up.

It's easy to fall behind, to struggle to embrace new apps, new software, new machines, new platforms. And we can often get to a stage where we are so far behind that catching up seems impossible. To be honest, that's a scary feeling for a business owner.

It's OK to have a little technophobia. Don't beat yourself up – we all do. That's why we need people like Tracy Sheen to come along and take what looks like the overwhelmingly complex and impossible, and show us a path through. And Tracy goes to great lengths in this book to make this process simple, easy to understand, fun and most importantly doable.

As I was reading *The End of Technophobia* I kept getting lost in the content. I started a list of things to do, I opened my phone and played with apps and setttings, I went onto platforms that I was scared of and figured stuff out, all the time being gently guided and coerced by Tracy's reassuring 'just do this' narrative.

There really is a big reward for working your way through *The End of Technophobia*. You will have a renewed sense of being in control of the tech in your business as opposed to being in fear of it. This control will translate into greater efficiency, improved profitability, stronger customer relationships, more customers and more time for you to do the things that matter in your business. And in the highly competitive world we live in, who doesn't want all of this?

If you invest the time to use this book wisely, I guarantee you will get great results – some expected, many unexpected. I think it's time to begin the journey and to put an end to technophobia, once and for all.

# HOW TO READ THIS BOOK

I'm going to take a wild guess here: you picked up this book because you're overwhelmed by technology, or maybe you *just don't get it*. You suffer from Technophobia.

Whatever your reason, I'm mindful that the sheer size and weight of *The End of Technophobia* may in itself be adding to your stress levels. So, let me lessen those levels straight off the bat.

You don't need to read this book cover to cover.

I've designed it in such a way that you can flick to a section you'd like more information on and get what you need. You'll find each section stands on its own. If I do reference something which you're not familiar with I'll let you know the section – you'll be able to find background or additional information. In saying that, I do suggest everyone reads the first three chapters before deciding which area of the business to focus on first.

Everyone will come to this book with different priorities. That's perfectly okay. Focus on what you need and access the rest when you need it.

There's also a glossary at the back of the book to give you the really quick answer to your 'what the hell does that acronym mean?' questions. The glossary can also be found on my website, where it will remain updated as new information becomes available.

The main thing I'd like you to know about what you're going to read though is this: I've designed this book to be a practical and educational resource. Something, hopefully, you'll pick up over and over again to learn something new about how digitising your business can change the way you look at everything (including your personal life). The first thing you'll notice as you flick through the book is the inclusion of loads of screenshots. I have included these because

I've found that images will often help us absorb information. These screenshots have not been edited or changed in any way (except to remove personal information where applicable). Remember though the very nature of technology means things are constantly changing. While everything is correct and current as of January 2021, things may have changed by the time you read this book. The lessons and foundations will remain solid though even if the screen looks slightly different.

The nature of this book means I'm going to suggest you pause and reflect as you finish each section. Take notes of things you need more information on. Create an action plan, so once you reach the end of the book you have your to-do list of the things to follow up, implement or change within your business.

My final thoughts ... Stay hydrated and chunk the reading down. If tech isn't your 'thing' then some of it might feel like I'm cracking your head open to pour information in. Staying hydrated will help you to take the information in, and allocating time to read a section at a time will mean you're more likely to absorb what you are reading.

## Egon in the room alert

Meet Egon (named after the Harold Ramis character of the same name in *Ghostbusters*). Throughout the book you'll come across Egon whenever there is a need for an 'elephant in the room' alert. He'll appear when I think we're hitting on something that may seem bleedingly obvious but would otherwise be ignored ... Or, when we're about to cover something that may be controversial but needs to be stated.

The first elephant in the room I want to address is the fact that I've written *a book* about technology.

At first glance it kinda feels like an oxymoron. Shouldn't I have just put all this info onto a website, blogs, videos or a podcast?

Well, sure. I've got some of this information out on my website and other places, but here's the thing. Most of the folks reading this are completely overwhelmed by technology and unsure where to start. I felt giving them yet another piece of tech to deal with to solve their problems was just downright mean.

And so, I've collated my 30 years hanging around and working in tech and small business and put pen to paper. Hopefully you'll find this a much easier way to digest the information you need in a way that makes sense and is familiar.

I have created additional resources which you can access at any time by visiting my website. These will stay updated and allow you to work through some of the content at your own pace. I'll include the link or a QR code (Quick Response) to the resource page at the end of each section that has additional resources. To access the QR code simply open the camera on your phone and point it at the code, you'll then be redirected to the website page with all the information.

If you choose to only read this book though, and not access any additional resources, you'll still be much further down the digital road than you are now.

Good luck ... you got this.

Now, let's get started ...

# 1. UNDERSTANDING YOUR BUSINESS FIRST

The decision I made to write this book came down to a conversation I had with my business coach in 2019. We were chatting various things through (as you do) when I made a throwaway comment about Apple News now including a wide variety of magazines available to download each month for a small monthly subscription fee. I continued talking and noticed he was just staring at me.

'Back up for a minute,' he said, 'What's that about the magazines?' I gave him a look that indicated my amusement that he didn't already know about this, to which he replied, 'You work in this area. You're always reading, listening and watching the latest digital and tech updates. Most business owners have no idea about this stuff, and you take it for granted. You need to harness that info and share it with your community.'

I thought about that for a long time and realised it's something we all do: downplay our own knowledge. We tend to think, 'surely everyone already knows that'. I figured out in that one conversation though, they don't, and so ... here we are.

In fact, I've found typically the digital landscape is something that creates a bit of a dividing camp for small business owners. You're either all in, trialling every new app or software service that hits the airwaves or you're someone who doesn't typically update your laptop or smartphone until the chargers are no longer working and the response time is so slow you could chisel an email to your client quicker than your device will create it.

I clearly sit firmly on the side of the divide where devices are updated every 12 to 18 months, apps are constantly being downloaded and tested, and software is something I set aside to learn and integrate.

As with anything new I do have a few things I would urge you to consider before we dive headfirst into the digital world. It's important for you to pause and take stock of your own business... *all areas* of your business. You see, once you dive down the digital rabbit hole, you'll quickly learn that embracing technology can assist you across all areas of your business (and personal life). From productivity to HR, accounting to marketing, once you start down the path there are a multitude of areas you can branch off and explore. This can really quickly lead to overwhelm and time wasting, which is not the outcome we want for anyone.

The tech world (you'll notice I'll use digital and tech interchangeably throughout the book) is changing almost daily. The stuff I rely upon in my business is possibly irrelevant to what you do, and vice versa. The single biggest mistake I see business owners make when they start investigating some kind of digital solution is they don't actually understand the problem they are trying to solve with tech to begin with.

So, before you really start your journey, I'm going to challenge you to take a really good look at your business. Understand where you are, where you're going and what you're looking for as an end result. There are a plethora of tech solutions on offer that will do a multitude of different tasks, but if you don't know what you're looking to achieve you'll waste a tonne of time, a bucketload of cash and you'll end up frustrated and annoyed that tech didn't solve your problem.

To help you get a good handle on what I mean by understanding your business here's a few questions to kick you off.

Take your time to put some thought into the below – by answering these questions carefully now you will save yourself a lot of heartache over the coming weeks, months and years. It will also give you a really good idea of which part of the book you will get the most benefit from immediately.

- How long has your business been in operation?

- Who do you service?

- What are the products or services you offer?

- How do you deliver these products or services? Is it online? Face to face? A mix?

- Do you have a supply chain? How do you follow and update your team/clients about supply updates?

- Do you have staff? What are their roles? Are they 'virtual' or 'in person'?

- What software systems or other tools do they have to perform their roles?

- Do you have policies and procedures in place? If so, where do you store them? How often are they updated? Do your team know where and how to find them?

- Do you have premises you work from?

- How do you find new clients?

- Where are they typically based? City? Regional? Rural? Domestic? International?

- What does it cost you to acquire a new client? Time? Money? Both?

- What is a new client worth to your business, dollar wise?

- How long do you typically keep a client?

- What is the lifetime value of a client to you, dollar wise?

- How do you communicate with your clients? Email? Phone? Online? In Person? Newsletters? A mix?

- Do you have and use a CRM (Customer Relationship Manager)?

- Do you track any issues or complaints from your clients?

- How do you communicate with your team? What about suppliers?

- How frequently are you talking to your clients?

Okay, good job. Hopefully that wasn't too painful. Now you have a good idea of what makes your business tick. The next chapter about creating your digital baseline will make a lot more sense now. Now, go grab a coffee... things are about to kick off.

# 2. YOUR DIGITAL BASELINE

Right. You've completed the questions from the first chapter (if you haven't, I strongly suggest you go back and do that first). Before we dive head-first into the world of technology or learn all about the latest cool app, it's important to get an understanding of what I call your 'digital baseline'.

Just like starting at a new gym, chances are your PT will want to check a few basic measurements before getting you on the tread-mill. What's your weight, your height, your fat percentage? And so on.

Doing these basic measurements at the start of your journey is a great way to show your progression in real time. They are the hard measurements you can look back on in one month, three months, twelve months to see the real results of your hard work.

Leaning into the digital landscape is no different. Often when we adopt a new software application or download a new app for our phones it feels like nothing has been gained. Having a few basic benchmarks to measure your digital progress can provide you with the boost to keep going when it feels like you're wasting your time, money or energy.

But how do you choose what to measure?

It's a great question. I have found over the years just like your own physical fitness there are a few basic indicators every business owner can track to ensure they're headed in the right direction.

Take a stocktake of what technology you currently have in place. Do you own a laptop? A desktop computer? What about a smartphone? A tablet? Make a list of everything you have and put a date (or year) of purchase beside each item. It's true that technology outdates itself pretty quickly, so having a running inventory of what you have and when you got it can be the first (and biggest) wakeup call your business has.

The next is to check in with the biggest pain point your business has currently. Is it onboarding new staff? Maybe it's having no way to track conversations with clients... Whatever it is, I guarantee you have one area in your business you've been wanting to overhaul or set up for a while. Now is the perfect time to check back in with the questions you answered in chapter one and give yourself a rating out of ten for each. Don't worry, unlike your PT, no one is going to be hovering over your shoulder asking you to dig deep for the last few questions. But if you really want to see tangible changes in your business you may as well be brutally honest with yourself. Look at any 12-step program and you'll see the idiom 'we can't change what we don't acknowledge'.

The third area you'll be checking in with is your business growth priorities. Hopefully you have an idea of the area(s) you'd like your business to grow. The 'how' might be a little fuzzy (and that's okay), but having a clear idea of where you want your business to get to will be one of those areas you'll be able to quickly check in with in months to come and assess your progress.

The final area I'd like you to review is your overarching business strategy. How are you documenting this? Are you working with anyone to help you achieve your goals? What mechanisms have you got in place to track your goals, successes, obstacles and pain points.

Over the years working with clients and taking them through various ways to track and capture information I've discovered people have a variety of coping mechanisms. Everything from 'I hold it all in my head' to sticky notes strewn across the office, to notes kept in old diaries or on a phone. Even audio files and whiteboards. The point is to identify how you're capturing and tracking the key metrics within your business so we can identify and implement strategies to streamline those areas within your business that require your attention.

There's no judgement here – just admiration that you're ready to end your technophobia.

I'll leave you to it. Once you've done this, you're ready to move on to the next chapter.

# 3. START WITH THE END IN MIND

A number of years ago, way before I went into business for myself, a friend gave me a copy of *The Seven Habits of Highly Effective People* by Stephen Covey. I'm not over exaggerating to say that book shaped the way I looked at life from that moment on. One principle in particular – 'Starting with the end in mind' – created a paradigm shift.

There is something so beautifully simple in the concept, so when you actually implement it into your thinking you immediately see a shift in thinking and actions.

That's why the next step on your digital journey is for you to 'Start with the end in mind'. Where does this exploration and adaptation of technology take you? Imagine it's 12 months from now, we're catching up for a coffee: how are things different in your business now compared to 12 months ago?

What about in five years' time? How is your business looking now? Are you capturing information about your clients, your numbers, your strategies the same way? What's changed? How are you feeling about technology now?

Having a clear end goal might seem a little like daydreaming, but having a clear vision and the ability to articulate it will assist you in many of the decisions you'll need to make around which pieces of technology to implement at what points and, almost as importantly, which pieces you can pass on altogether.

Take a moment now to put some thoughts to paper around what your business looks like in five years.

Do you still have staff or contractors? If so, how do you communicate with them? Do you incorporate software like Zoom or Skype (now known as Microsoft Teams)? Do you use collaboration tools that allow you to simultaneously work on the same project?

What about your client base? Has it grown? How are you finding new clients? Are you utilising platforms like Google Ads or social media to attract new clients? Are you communicating with them on a regular basis through automatic sequences of content?

If I asked you what your average client was worth to your business and how long they typically stayed as a client – could you find that information easily? Could you share a dashboard of your current cash position? What about your debtors?

Where are you working from these days? Is it in a cafe by the beach on your terms, or are you overseeing a number of offices and working a 'regular' work week? What about your productivity? Do you feel like you're achieving everything that you'd set out to do, or are you still running from project to project putting out fires?

There are no right or wrong answers. Just what's right for you and where you'd like your business and personal life to be within five years. I realise I've given you a lot of the heavy thinking to do before we get into the juicy stuff that you really came here for so again; I want to recognise the effort you're putting in upfront. I promise you it will make the remainder of the book more valuable to you as well as being immediately transferable to your business.

So, find yourself a journal and a pen (this won't be the only time through the book that I'll ask you to make some notes or jot your thoughts down). Your task now is to go for a walk outside. Find a beach, a river, a park somewhere away from your day to day and just sit. Stare out at your surroundings and allow your mind to think, dream and picture the five-year plan. You've earned a good dose of daydreaming.

Give yourself a good 30 to 60 minutes, at which point grab your journal and note down everything your brain came up with during your 'down time'. Don't judge it, just write down whatever comes up for you.

You'll be referring back to those dreams and 'end plans' through-out the book.

## It's not forever

One of the most frequent fears raised when I start working with any business owner around adapting technology into their business or personal life is the concern they will get it 'wrong'.

What if I pick the wrong system? The wrong phone? The wrong piece of software? The wrong app? What if I lose a bunch of time doing stuff and it's not 'right'?

Well, I've got some good news and bad news for you.

The nature of the digital landscape is transient. Things are chang-ing, adapting and growing every day (pretty much) so there will be times when you will make a misstep. There will be times you'll choose a piece of software and then discover it doesn't quite do what you thought it would, or, more likely, you'll figure out you needed it to do something slightly more or different than what you first thought. And that's okay.

The good news is, you'll reach a tipping point where you realise that the apps you've downloaded or that piece of software you've implemented has saved you (or the business) hours of time, has made a process better for your clients or the team, or saved you a bunch of cash.

Either way, by sticking with the process you will start to see little signposts along the way that you're on the right tech track.

## Your digital audit

This is all about getting a good understanding of where you're start-ing from. To have any hope of later measuring what you've learned, implemented or altered in your business as a result of the book, we need to know what's already in place.

You'll find the full audit available as a free downloadable from the website; for now though we're going to consider each of the sections in the book and review what you have in place as of today.

### Systems

*What are you using... Apple or PC?*

- Have you got a tablet or a smartphone?
- On a scale of 1 – 10, how well do you think you're using everything?

### Productivity

- Do you listen to podcasts or audiobooks on your commute?
- On a scale of 1 – 10 how productive do you think you are day to day?
- On a scale of 1 – 10 how productive is your team?
- Are there areas where you feel you could be more productive?
  - If so, where?

### Security

- On a scale of 1 – 10, how well do you understand online security implications in your business?
- What is your plan if your computer is hacked?
- Do you use two-factor authentications on your software?
- Do you use a password manager?

### Organising your life

- On a scale of 1 – 10 how organised do you feel in your business?
- On a scale of 1 – 10 how organised do you feel at home?
- Do you use a calendar?
- Does your family have a shared calendar for capturing everything?
- Can work access calendars for ease of team tracking?

### Money

- Have you got accounting software in place for your business?
- Do you have a process for capturing receipts and bills?
- Have you got a process for reimbursing expenses?

*Working remotely*

- On a scale of 1 – 10, how ready was your business to work remotely when COVID hit?
- Could you pick up tomorrow and work from anywhere?
- Where's your favourite place to work if you're not in the office?

*Marketing*

- On a scale of 1 – 10 how happy are you with your current marketing efforts?
- Have you got a digital marketing strategy in place?
- Do you understand your client personas? (While we go into a little more detail about these in the marketing section of the book, for now it might be useful to know that a client or buyer persona is a representation or archetype of a large section of your clients. Personas often include information like age, gender, location, as well as social and psychological information.)
- Have you got a content plan in place?
- Do you have Google Analytics in place?
- Are you reading insights on your social media?
- Have you got a CRM in place?
  - Are you using it?

*Sales*

- What does your sales process look like?
- Have you mapped your pipeline in your CRM?
- How long does an average sale take?
- How do you track it from lead to conversion?

*Customer experience*

- Have you segmented your data?
- What ways do you offer clients to connect?
- Are you collecting customer reviews?

*Health and wellness*

- Do you use any technology to track your health?
- Do you track your sleep?
- Do you monitor your daily steps or activity?

Remember, the full audit is available on the website; hopefully though these questions will get you thinking about what you currently have in place.

You'll hear me mention in the book that data is knowledge and knowledge is power. It's my aim that by the end of this book you'll be armed with considerable knowledge and understanding of how to use, implement and leverage technology in your business to really take control over the direction you want your business (and your life) to go.

## Choosing your system

In the '60s (I'm told) you were either a Beatles fan or a Rolling Stones fan. Sure, you could like both, but when push came to shove you pretty well came down on one side or the other.

As I was growing up it became a *Star Wars* vs *Star Trek* debate (in case you're interested, while I enjoy both, Jean-Luc Picard will always be my captain). My point is, one of the first big decisions you'll need to make for your business is whether you're going to fall into the Apple or the PC camp.

I'll state my allegiances up front. I'm firmly ensconced in the Apple camp. Our house is completely Apple, and I struggle to know how to navigate a PC, it's been that long since I used one (2009, when I left my corporate life).

It can become a passionate debate when chatting to people from either side of the technological divide, as they fervently put forward their best arguments as to why you should operate in one system over the other.

Both have their merits.

Potentially Apple has fewer security threats. It's a fact that there are fewer Malware programs designed with Mac in mind. In part (I think) because they hold the reins so tightly over their allowed componentry and what is allowed into their App store. The flip side of this depends on your industry; you may find software solutions more difficult to access for Mac, although this is becoming less and less of a concern as everything moves to cloud-based and SAAS (software as a service) based models.

If your business is design- or arts-based, then chances are you will fall naturally into the Mac camp. Apple has become synonymous over the years with the design world. So, if you're looking to do a lot of design work, editing (video or audio), CAD (Computer Assisted Design) work, etc. then Mac is probably the solution for you.

The PC world remains more customisable than Mac and significantly cheaper. You can pick up a PC laptop now for under $500 without really trying. If you're looking to kit out an office or a team of people, it's hard to go past PC in terms of value for money.

Ultimately what I see often determines people's allegiances is their choice of phone. If you're an iPhone or iPad user, then connecting and integrating your life becomes significantly easier if you are connecting directly to a Mac laptop or desktop.

If you're a Samsung Galaxy, Windows Android or any of the other android phone users then you'll probably naturally gravitate towards the PC camp.

And then in recent years we've had the emergence of the Google camp. Google Pixel users will swear by the Google Chromebook. To me there remain too many limitations with the Chromebook to consider it as a worthy opponent (yet) to the age-old PC vs Mac debate... but the thing with technology is it's fluid. Who knows what Google will come out with in the foreseeable future... It could turn everything on its head.

As we move more and more towards cloud-based computing solutions the debate over Mac or PC is becoming somewhat more redundant. You will notice throughout the book (and when you follow me on YouTube or Facebook) that my default is to talk about stuff as it appears in Apple.

This, at first, may cause you some confusion, but you'll soon realise what I show you on an Apple can be replicated on PC... you may just need to do a little clicking around to figure out the solution. There simply aren't enough pages in a book (or personal PC knowledge) for me to explain everything in both operating systems.

So... If you're at the point where you're considering Apple or Mac here are a few things to consider.

### Security

If security is a big concern for you then Mac still gets the nod as the system of choice. That's not to say it's impenetrable, but there are less designed security threats aimed at Mac.

### Gaming

If, after hours of course, you like to indulge in a little online gaming then PC is the way to go. Hands down, Mac doesn't even come close for this.

### Software

Less of a concern these days as most things are available as cloud-based solutions.

### Ecosystem

What sort of phone and/or tablet do you run? This could be the deciding factor in your solution.

### Maintenance

If you have any issue with a Mac you have only one place to turn, Apple. In saying that, their level of after-sales service is a sight to behold. If you have any issues with a PC, you can choose from dozens of folks probably operating in the same suburb as you to lean on for support.

\* \* \*

Whichever way you decide to go, you really can't lose. There are some excellent choices available to business owners now and it really is just about deciding which camp you want to land in.

## Needs vs wants

As you move through the book beware of the 'bright, shiny' digital options put before you. We can all easily get caught up in the thought of something saving us hundreds of hours or making us thousands of dollars.

Before you make any snap decisions though. Stop. Ask yourself, is this a need or a want? Have I got something in place in the business now that (kinda) does the same thing? If so, dust it off and give it a decent crack before you hand over your credit card for something new.

One of my roles as the digital guide is to try out a lot of these software solutions, apps and various other bibs and bobs. Every time you commit to purchasing a new piece of software or downloading an app, remember you're committing to hours and hours of learning and implementing.

Now learning new stuff is great... but go in with your eyes open.

Remember your digital audit. Think about what you already have in place, consider whether it's actually being used to its full potential, and ask yourself whether you're considering this as a distraction from doing other things in the business or whether it will actually serve a purpose. If you see a purpose for it, you also need to consider will it be scalable and could it potentially do away with something else to streamline a process? Your technology should always be pushing your business to greater things, not wasting your time trying to make something fit where it doesn't belong.

Contrary to what you may think, while I do love my technology, I love it when it serves a purpose and has a very clear reason for me installing, learning and embedding it.

Don't get caught up in the bright-and-shiny digital objects throughout the book because there are bound to be a lot of them.

## Final thought ...

### Egon in the room

As we prepare our descent into the digital rabbit hole, it's worth mentioning that we will be chatting about terms that may all seem a little like jargon ('cause let's face it, they are jargon). While I do my best to keep things as easy to understand as I can there may be times when it feels like you need a babel fish (or, interpreter: a little joke for my fellow Douglas Adams and *Hitchhiker's Guide to the Galaxy* fans) to understand. If that happens, you'll find a glossary of all the terms and jargon located at the back of the book. The glossary will also be located (and updated as new stuff comes on board) on my website. You can lean on this any time you need.

The last thing which you're probably thinking at this stage is, how long is it going to take to digitise my business?

That one is a little trickier to answer. I tend to liken it to when you start back at the gym after a long absence. You go to a pump class and sweat your a*se off for an hour in the hopes your jeans are a little less tight. You do the same thing week in and week out for six weeks and still don't feel like there's progress. But one day you put those jeans on and suddenly realise you're not sucking it all in to get them done up... Digitising your business is kinda like that.

It's a process. Sometimes you'll feel like you're getting nowhere, or you may even feel as though things are going backward. Don't despair – one day not too long from now you'll look up from your smartphone and realise that things are humming in the business and you finally get what all the fuss was about.

Stick with it... I promise we'll get you there.

\* \* \*

Okay... this is your final chance. Once you turn the page you can no longer refer to yourself as a luddite or a technophobe. There will be no more eye-rolling at technology and you must dive in with eyes wide open.

Best get yourself a drink of some description for this... it's going to be one hell of a ride.

# SECTION ONE

# PRODUCTIVITY

# Egon in the room

**I'M HOPELESS AT ORGANISING MY TIME.** I'm one of those people who, left to my own devices, will always underestimate that length of time a project will take me to complete and overestimate the number of clients or jobs I can complete in one day.

My natural tendency is to run at things full steam until I hit a wall and collapse from exhaustion. I'll take a few days to sleep and stare at a TV before getting back up and repeating the process over again. I've run this same pattern for as long as I can remember. Left unchecked it leads to stress, irritability and disappointing a bunch of people, including myself.

My hubby Peter, on the other hand, is meticulously planned. He runs his calendar like a logbook and can tell me where he was on any given day years back. He always seems to know exactly how long something will take to complete and rarely overextends himself in taking on new projects.

The difference between Pete and me (apart from the anatomical)? Peter embraced technology to assist with his productivity tracking long before I did.

Over the years I've tried and tested dozens of productivity-based digital solutions, each with varying levels of success. In this section, I'll lay bare the options available to you for tracking and improving your productivity along with some tips, tricks and avoids, helping you make the most of what's available.

# 4. HOW CAN TECHNOLOGY HELP YOU BE MORE PRODUCTIVE?

I mentioned in the introduction to this section my ongoing struggle with productivity; what I haven't mentioned before is that I have ADHD. One of the many tendencies of folks with ADHD is periods of intense focus. If I'm taken by a new project or topic, I can quite literally spend days immersed in learning absolutely everything I can about it. Obsessively reading, watching and purchasing materials to help me gain a rounded understanding until something else bright and shiny catches my eye. At which point I will drop the other topic like an unwanted toy to chase the latest thing.

How does this apply to the subject of technology and productivity I hear you ask?

Simply it's been in the adaptation of a few tools and the recognition of my predication to go down rabbit holes that has helped me soften the edges and recognise how I'm spending my time and allows me to make more informed decisions about what to do next.

Let me be clear though. Adopting a new app will not suddenly make you more productive. Often initially it's the reverse, you'll chew up additional time learning the app and implementing it across your business or your life. It's in the first couple of weeks of implementation that I see the biggest drop off. The best advice I can offer is to hang in there. Give it around three months. By then you'll have a good idea how the app works and whether it is helping you to achieve what you were looking for.

From that point, you should begin to see a marked improvement in the areas you were looking to track, monitor or change.

## Devices

One of the biggest decisions you'll make in your business is what sort of devices you want to operate from. Until this year I've been a laptop and smartphone girl. This gives me the flexibility to pick up at a moment's notice and head off wherever I need while keeping everything I could possibly want to know with me.

During COVID though spending more time operating from a single location, I realised that a laptop wasn't the best thing for me. I was starting to get back aches, neck strain and headaches. So, I dusted out my old Mac Pro desktop and set myself up 'ergonomically', and realised very quickly how much more productive that very small (but turns out quite significant) change has made to the quality and quantity of my work.

My desktop syncs with my laptop and phone so everything I need is always available to me on each device. And that's the thing with technology, once you've figured out the best way for you to work, you'll be able to ensure that everything you need is available to you at any time.

Peter, my hubby, runs his entire life from his iPad and his phone. He struggles to move back to a laptop now as he says it feels clunky. He's found solutions and workarounds for everything he needs to do, and only needing to carry an iPad has been a big win for him.

We're living in a time when you can decide how you want to run your business, and then find the technology you need to suit your requirements.

So, when it comes to deciding on your devices, ask yourself:

- How do I work now?
- How do I want to work?
- What are the main software platforms and apps I use?
    - Do they have solutions for the device(s) I'm considering?
- What's the battery life like on the device(s) I'm considering?
- What are my storage and expansion needs?

Providing you think through the way you want to work you'll find the solution that will best suit.

## What does productivity look like to you?

Before you jump on the productivity bandwagon, I think it's important to take a few moments to reflect on what productivity means to you and to your business.

For some folks, it means knowing where their time is going and on which tasks. For others it means understanding how long it actually takes to complete a project, for others still it's about identifying which tasks are taking away from the things they enjoy doing in their business in order to make some changes to the way the business is run.

For me, productivity is a mix of all of the above. Being able to track and monitor task duration means I've finally got a good handle on how long something takes to complete. So, when a client asks if I can have a 'quick' look at something, I know it'll actually take 60 minutes, which means I'm no longer dropping one thing to task switch to another. Instead, I'll schedule those 'quick tasks' into my calendar for later and maintain focus on the project at hand.

Understanding where my time is spent has also allowed me to see just how much effort I was spending doing things in my business that I didn't really enjoy. Let me give you an example. During the early part of COVID I began sharing a quick daily digital tip, showcasing an app or a piece of technology that could improve business. I loved recording these quick tips, but I found myself spending almost four times as long editing the tips before I could schedule them to my social platforms. By the time I'd written the content to go with the post, found an image and edited the tip a three-minute video was taking close to 45 minutes... not the best use of my time. So I found someone who could edit all the videos for me, leaving me to write and schedule the videos in batches, usually of an evening while I'm watching TV. That one small recognition allowed me to get around three hours of productive time back into my week.

So, before you go any further, let me encourage you to think about what productivity means to *you*. What is it you're interested in learning about or changing through an understanding of productivity in your life?

Do you want to:

· understand where your time is being spent?
· know how long tasks are taking to complete?
· streamline and gain time back in your day?
· understand what tasks chew time and could be allocated elsewhere?
· something different altogether?

With this lens, let's move forward and review just some of the applications available to you

## Productivity apps – what's out there

Open the app store on your device of choice and you'll see a great swathe of real estate devoted to apps to help your productivity. Some are free, some come with a price tag. All of them require learning.

Knowing what it is you want to achieve before choosing which app to download can save you a chunk of time, money and effort. So, as we review the following apps, keep in mind what it is you're looking to get out of a productivity app.

### For the list gatherers...

I love a good 'to do' list. There is something deeply satisfying about having a long list of stuff to achieve and being able to put a line through everything you've achieved. The downside of a to do list though is they never have an end. No sooner do you cross one thing off your list than another five pop up in their place.

However, when I find myself feeling overwhelmed by everything that needs to be done, I find the best place to start is to get everything out of my head into one long to do list. Then I can go back through and divide them into categories. Client work, admin, home stuff, personal stuff, aspirational stuff... you get the idea.

If you're someone who likes a good to do list, here are some options to check out. Now, by no means is this an exhaustive list, it's just some options that I've personally used over the years that tick all the to do list requirement boxes.

- Todoist
- Wunderlist (now owned by Microsoft)
- Google tasks
- Microsoft To Do
- Any.do
- ToodleDo.

| Product | Pros | Cons |
|---|---|---|
| **Todoist**<br>Available on:<br>iOS, Mac, Android, Windows and Desktop | – Email or SMS notifications and reminders<br>– Customisable filters to set focus tasks<br>– Task comments<br>– Easy sharing abilities<br>– Contact list integration<br>– Quick add<br>– Auto backup<br>– Real-time synchronisation<br>– Vast template library to adapt | – No meeting management<br>– No time tracking<br>– Sub tasks don't work well<br>– Customising is a little fiddly<br>– Doesn't really allow for advanced usage |
| **TeuxDeux**<br>*(pronounced 'To Do')*<br>Available on:<br>Web, iOS | – Drag and drop feature<br>– Text formatting<br>– Syncs across multiple devices<br>– Family sharing (up to 6 people)<br>– Auto task rollover to the next day for uncompleted tasks<br>– Calendar sync<br>– Easy to use | – Collaboration is clunky<br>– No time tracking<br>– No ongoing free version |

| Product | Pros | Cons |
|---|---|---|
| **Google tasks** <br><br>Available on:<br>Web, iOS, Android | – No frills <br>– Works great with other Google apps <br>– Great Google calendar view <br>– Clear completed tasks function | – No recurring tasks <br>– No organisation <br>– Doesn't play well with other platforms (Google users only) |
| **Microsoft To Do** <br><br>Download on:<br>iOS and Android | – Comes with Office 365 integration <br>– 'My Day' feature <br>– Task reminders <br>– Task prioritisation <br>– Outlook task integration <br>– Due date tracking <br>– List sharing <br>– Customisable task list colours and themes <br>– Daily task list <br>– Synchronises across multiple devices and platforms | – Best used in Microsoft Office as it won't integrate well across other platforms <br>– No recurring task management <br>– No tags or filters <br>– Can only integrate Outlook calendar <br>– Not great at collaboration |
| **Any.do** <br><br>Available on:<br>Desktop, iOS, Android, Chrome extension, Amazon Alexa | – Voice entry <br>– Easy to use <br>– Deadlines and reminders <br>– Notes within tasks <br>– Unlimited file attachment <br>– Recurring tasks <br>– Built-in calendar app | – Most of the features only available through premium |

| Product | Pros | Cons |
|---|---|---|
| **nTask**<br><br>Available on:<br><br>Web, iOS and Android | – Create, assign, prioritise tasks<br>– Create and schedule recurring tasks<br>– Schedule recurring meetings<br>– Connects with 'Slack' to convert comments to tasks<br>– Time tracking module<br>– To do list progress bar | – No team chat (though you can connect it to Slack)<br>– Messy third-party integrations<br>– Not for the novice. Takes some time and patience to set up |
| **ToodleDo**<br><br>Available on:<br><br>iOS, Android, Desktop | – Public and private lists<br>– Recurring tasks<br>– Task time tracking<br>– Location-based reminders<br>– Use of tags to customise<br>– Notes within tasks<br>– Habit tracking | – Collaboration only available on paid plans<br>– Advanced features only available on paid plans |

Essentially, they all do the same thing: provide a place for you to get thoughts out of your head and recorded in some kind of logical order. Some of them will have a steeper learning curve than others and, depending on the level of complexity you want your to do list to be able to cope with, you may need to pay to achieve what you want.

Bottom line though: if you are someone who likes jotting down the tasks that need completing and gain satisfaction in crossing things off your list, one of the above to do lists will bring you recurring joy for minimal effort. And, as a bonus, will help you to make sure everything is getting done.

## Project management productivity tools

There is a level of productivity players that I haven't yet mentioned. They fit into the to do list category, but they are so much more than that. Commonly referred to as project management tools, these guys take the humble to do list and throw a bunch of steroids down its neck.

If your business deals with a range of different clients at any one time and requires multiple tasks completed with various team members then there's a good chance you've at least heard of one of the following players.

Just like the to do lists, there are plenty of options on the market for those looking for something that provides a little more detail and complexity.

Over the last decade I've used quite a few of these platforms – the ones that consistently pop up with clients though are:

- Trello
- Asana
- Monday
- Basecamp

| Product | Pros | Cons |
|---------|------|------|
| **Trello** | – Super easy to use<br>– Easy to collaborate<br>– Drag and drop features<br>– Takes you from big picture down to micro level detail<br>– Labels, filters and search features make things easy to find<br>– Add or link to files or images<br>– Works across any industry on any size project<br>– Syncs across all devices<br>– Can 'plug in' other features | – Doesn't play well with other applications<br>– Takes a bit to set up<br>– No real support<br>– No communication portal. Team members must leave notes on individual tasks/cards<br>– No real reporting available |

| Product | Pros | Cons |
|---|---|---|
| **Asana** | – Easy to set up<br>– Drag and drop functionality<br>– User management – assign individual tasks within projects to team members<br>– Shared locations for notes and tasks | – Not great as a communication tool<br>– Not as visual as some of the others<br>– No place to track information<br>– No calendar option |
| **Monday** | – Good level of integrations<br>– Visual display of progress<br>– Clean interface | – Lots of advertising<br>– Mobile app not the easiest to use<br>– Need to pay for more functionality<br>– No team calendar<br>– Takes some setting up and understanding |
| **Basecamp** | – Dedicated messaging board<br>– Centralised place for all uploads<br>– Easy to collaborate | – Lacking good reporting<br>– A lot of email notifications<br>– Few integrations<br>– Difficult to edit uploaded files |

Personally, I've gone 'all in' with Trello. It suits the way my business runs, and I've taken the time to get to know the ins and outs of the platform. I like that I've managed to keep my usage free without feeling like I'm sacrificing functionality. The downside I've found with Trello is the ease with which you start setting up boards – this has led me to a recent Trello board purge.

## Time tracking and other productivity apps

I have many clients who want to be able to track where their time is going. This could be because they need to report back to clients on the time they've spent on a project, and in some instances it's because they are interested to know the apps or sites that are eating away their days. Because the nature of the two tracking requirements are different, we'll take a look at each in isolation.

### Time tracking

In case you haven't figured it out yet, there are a plethora of apps and websites on the market that will help you with just about any aspect of your business. Time tracking is no different.

Almost all of the time tracking apps will allow you to track your time in 'real time', meaning the clock will start running when you start and finish when you finish. If you're looking to use a tracking app to report back to clients, my best advice is to look for an app that will allow you to correct your time. This becomes really important when you've realised you left the clock running while you took that quick call or ducked away to make lunch. My next suggestion is to look for an app that will allow you to add a block of time after the fact. This is super important when that quick call from your client turns into a 30-minute consultation.

You may also want to consider whether you need to track time across a team. Personally, I tend to use a time tracker to see how long I've actually put into a project. This helps me check my pricing structure and make sure I'm on track with how long I 'think' a project takes vs how long a project 'actually' takes. Nothing like finding out you've been under quoting to deliver a piece of work!

Let's take a look at some of the time tracking software I (or my clients) have used. Again, not a complete or comprehensive list, but a good place for you to start. Figure out what's important to you and then do your research and make your decisions based on groundwork.

| Product | Pros | Cons | Compatible with |
|---------|------|------|-----------------|
| **Toggl** | – Has a great free version<br>– Little red button gives you a constant reminder of what you're tracking<br>– Can connect with Zapier for additional functionality<br>– Good Google Chrome browser extension gives functionality into Google suite | – Minimal reporting<br>– Free account members can't collaborate | – Mac iOS<br>– Android<br>– Web browser<br>– Browser extensions |
| **Everhour** | – Great option for team visibility<br>– Connects with Asana and other productivity apps<br>– Built-in invoicing | – Web timer doesn't work offline<br>– No mobile apps | – Web browser<br>– Browser extensions |
| **Timely** | – Great option if you currently use your calendar to chunk out your project time<br>– Gives a day-by-day view of time used<br>– Supports collaboration<br>– Connects with most calendars | – No free plan<br>– Takes time and effort to set up | – Mac iOS<br>– Android<br>– Web browser<br>– Browser extensions |
| **Timing** | – Great automatic tracking option for Mac users<br>– Works offline<br>– One-off payment (no monthly subscription)<br>– Manually add offline events | – Only works on Mac | – Mac OS |

If you're looking for something with more of a productivity focus, or 'where the hell did that day disappear to', then these are the apps I've tried or heard good things about from those I trust.

| Product | Pros | Cons | Compatible with |
|---|---|---|---|
| **Rescue Time** | – Set and forget<br>– Website blocker<br>– Free plan<br>– Set custom work hour | – Fiddly to set up (you have to define your categories and what you classify as productive)<br>– Alerts can get a little distracting | – Mac OS<br>– Android<br>– Windows<br>– Chrome<br>– Firefox |
| **Timeneye** | – Has some elements of a project management app to it<br>– Good for tracking projects rather than for invoicing<br>– Create clients, projects, tasks and view in calendar<br>– Connects to other productivity apps | – No invoicing<br>– No expenses | – Android<br>– iOS<br>– Web<br>– Apps via integration |
| **HourStack** | – Helps you to focus on planning your time ahead<br>– Create projects and tasks, also uses labels<br>– Has reasonable reporting capabilities | – No free plan<br>– Links with other productivity apps but you can't start the timer within the apps<br>– No invoicing | – Android<br>– iOS<br>– Web |

The important thing is to have a clear idea of what you'd like to track before choosing your software. Knowing whether you need (or want) to give clients a blow by blow of where and how your time was spent, whether you need invoicing or team collaboration or whether you're looking for something to give you an indication of where your days disappear.

Get clear on that ahead of choosing your software and you'll choose the best app based on your requirements.

## Internet browser extensions

An internet browser extension is like a small app that you add onto your internet browser of choice. Each browser will offer a range of extensions – the largest range I've found by far is available for users of Google Chrome.

To find them go to chrome.google.com/webstore – from there you'll be faced with the various options you can add. Some are free, some run offline, some work best with Android. The point is there are hundreds to choose from, including some of my favourites around productivity.

A quick note on security around extensions. Please read the terms and conditions carefully and be aware when adding an extension to your browser that you may be allowing collection and curation of data from your computer while accessing the tool. That's not always a bad thing as some apps will need this data to function, but it's definitely something to be mindful of.

### Productivity Owl

Need to stop yourself wasting time? Productivity Owl allows you a certain amount of time on a web page to find the information you need. After that it closes the page down.

You can set up 'free time' schedules and provide a list of sites to white label (Owl will give you a free pass on these).

The owl constantly flies around your pages reminding you that you only have a certain amount of time remaining. If you're not serious about being productive, or get annoyed by things distracting your peripheral vision, Productivity Owl may not be for you.

### Gyroscope

Provides you with a daily update of where you're spending your time and what sites you're working on.

Can connect with your devices to track steps and sleep and offers a real-time age counter… just in case you think about wasting time.

## Audiobooks and podcasts

If we're talking productivity, I would be remiss to not at least mention the value that audiobooks and podcasts have brought to our lives.

No longer are we beholden to the insistent rambling of talkback or inane chatter of radio hosts asking us to call in and 'talk about a time when…'. Thanks to the wider adoption of audiobooks and podcasts, our travel time can now be used to educate and amuse.

It wasn't that long ago the audiobooks were a rare commodity, solely for the consumption of those with visual impairments. Now thanks to the likes of Audible and our local libraries, the range of book titles and subjects is wide and varied.

Add to this mix the rise in popularity of podcasts and we no longer have an excuse to be channel surfing on road trips.

I'll talk a little more about the importance of considering a podcast as part of your overarching marketing strategy, as well as where they fit into your customer experience, later in the book. For now, though, it's sufficient to say that if you find yourself with travel downtime, consider putting it to good use by finding an audiobook or podcast to get some productivity into your commute.

# 5. THE INTERNET OF THINGS (IOT)

Over the last five years there has been an explosion in manufacturers scrambling to provide internet-connected versions of their appliances. Internet-connected devices are what has become referred to as the 'Internet of Things' (IOT for short).

What started as the 'smart home' novelty of connecting lights, doors and security now includes curtains, vacuum cleaners, air conditioning and lawn mowing... with the list growing weekly. So quickly in fact that former CISCO researcher David Evans calculates that roughly 127 new IOT devices are connecting each second!

Sensing the novelty of it all, companies began to incorporate some kind of connectivity into their devices, and very quickly this led to a tsunami of connected fridges that let us 'dial in' from the supermarket to check our supplies (or place an order for us when we run out); coffee machines that will update software overnight and warm your machine up for your early morning beverage, through to washing machines that will tell you exactly what your water and energy consumption will be for that particular wash as well as calculating the best time for the cycle to go ahead.

The explosion of IOT has led to significant advances in assisting those living with disabilities and the elderly, and started to significantly impact industries as far reaching as agriculture and transport infrastructure.

For many of us our first introduction to the IOT was through the 'smart assistants' developed on our mobiles. Siri, Google and Alexa quickly took up residence in our homes, finding many of us asking our invisible friend for recipes, to set timers, to play specific music or news, or even to remind us of the name of the band that sang a particular song.

The integration has been swift, and is becoming increasingly ubiquitous in our daily lives. At the close of 2019 the home market for IOT was worth over A$73 billion, and according to research by Business Insider the IOT industry is on track to grow to over $2.4 trillion and over 41 billion devices by 2027.

Living in an Apple universe as Peter and I do, our interactions with Siri on a daily basis usually go something like this:

On waking, we ask Siri to play a podcast while we make our coffee. Siri will usually choose a music playlist for background music while we work. If a parcel arrives Siri lets us know (via our Arlo security cameras) that something has been delivered. In the evening Siri turns our lights on and at 8:30pm Siri changes the colour of the lights to begin our wind-down sequence.

Currently we're looking at adding a front door keypad that will allow us to remotely open the door if needed, and connecting our front gate to open on arrival and the garage to remotely open as we approach.

During Christmas, we set up our village (yes, Peter and I build a Christmas village each year) to be completely powered via Siri. This means the lights, animation and music are all tied into voice control and 'smart switches'.

For the most part it all works great... except for the random 'Siri moments' when it will interrupt to play a song or try to answer a question that we haven't asked. Then again, Apple is known for their security, not their natural language capabilities.

So, let's take a look at a few of the areas within the IOT you may be interested in exploring for yourself to improve your productivity.

## Virtual 'home' assistants

Most people are now familiar with the concept of 'smart speakers'. Think Google Home (now known as the 'Google Nest') or the Apple

Home Pod. While there are dozens of different brands and styles to choose from now, essentially they all run via one of three virtual assistant services: Google, Apple or Amazon.

For the most part, choosing which smart speaker will suit your home or office will come down to budget and aesthetics – but keep in mind they will all come back to being driven by one of the three companies mentioned above.

In the short time since the introduction of our virtual home assistants, the list of things that you can ask of them has grown enormously from 'just' playing music. You can now task them with such commands as:

· read the news or news headlines

· set an alarm or timer

· take a note

· make a hands-free call

· provide updates on traffic conditions

· advise and manage your calendar

· read stories aloud

· provide weather updates and information

· answer trivia, music and fact-based questions

· play a move, TV show, music, radio or podcast

· provide recommendations on local services

· book tickets or a table at a restaurant

· interface with other smart home devices

So, let's take a look at the three big players and get an idea of what each can offer, and which one may be best suited to your requirements.

The first thing you need to know is that you can have more than one virtual assistant or smart speaker in your house. One of my good friends runs Google in the kitchen (they believe it's the best at reading and assisting with recipes), Siri in the media room for music and movies and has recently added Alexa to the family because they believe it has the best adaptability for connecting other third-party apps.

For a bit more of a detailed look through, let's start with Apple's Siri.

## Apple Siri

Without a doubt Siri is the best known of the virtual assistants. Launching in 2011 to mixed reviews, the system has undergone multiple iterations during its life.

Like everything in the Apple universe, Siri will only work on Apple devices. This means if you want to use Siri as a smart speaker in your house your only option is to look at the Home Pod. And like everything in the Apple universe, the Home Pod (or Home Pod mini if you're interested in the latest addition to the Apple home family) is extremely easy to set up and use, and, in my opinion, has phenomenal sound quality given the size of the device.

Given the Home Pod will only work within the Apple ecosystem, you can only play music from the Apple music store (sorry, no Spotify available), podcasts from Apple podcast and movies or TV from Apple TV. That doesn't mean you can't run Netflix, Disney, Stan or Prime, it just means they're all routed via the Apple TV.

Functionality on the Home Pod is quite limited too. If you go the route of the Home Pod you'll quickly get used to hearing 'I'm sorry I can't answer that on the Home Pod'.

It can however set timers, alarms, update you on the weather and connect in with other Apple smart devices. But, if you're looking for something to interact with in a natural conversation, it's probably not the device for you.

## Google Assistant

According to research released by Nielsen in September 2019, of the 2.9 million Aussies who have adopted home smart speakers 79% of them have chosen Google devices.

If yours is the type of household that likes asking for the best cafe near you or what time the cinema is running the movie you want to see then the Google Assistant could be the answer you're looking for.

Recently rebranded to Google 'Nest' to allow additional functionality around integration of other smart devices, the Google Assistant currently offers the best natural voice recognition.

Its ability to provide up-to-date information on local happenings comes down to just how much information Google is scraping from user devices every single day. A big pro of the Google Assistant is the number of add-ons it opens you up to across the market. The biggest drawback (and the reason I've chosen not to bring a Google Assistant into my home) is just how much data and how much listening the device actually does.

Overall if you're okay to trade the collection and curation of your data for easier use of a virtual assistant, I'd say go with the Google devices.

## Amazon Alexa

Alexa has made huge gains over the past couple of years with their natural language technology. So much so that in many aspects of searching it rivals or beats Google for responsiveness.

If entertainment is the driver for your virtual assistance and smart speaker consideration, then Alexa is possibly the best choice currently. From switching your TV off and on, controlling volume as well as launching shows, pausing, fast forwarding, etc. – all of these things are controlled most easily via Alexa.

The biggest downfall Alexa currently faces in Australia is connectivity. While there is a myriad of third-party apps and skills available, the list of those currently available in Australia is limited... This all comes down to what Amazon Australia has available to its Australian customers.

## Smart Homes

Out of all the questions I field around the internet of things, the number one is undoubtedly discussion around features available through what's become known as 'smart homes'.

At its core a smart home is a house that relies on technology to control or automate aspects within the house. People are looking to integrate aspects of smart technology into their home for a number of reasons, including:

- **Security:** Installing cameras, windows and door sensors, video doorbells, lighting, smart locks and smoke detectors offers homeowners peace of mind previously only available with a hefty price tag. Not to mention being able to track when your kids get home from school or allowing tradies to access your home at the press of a button, security has never been more attainable for the average homeowner. What's more, there are a lot of security options available for those people who rent and don't want things hardwired to their home.

- **Efficiency:** With increasing awareness of our carbon footprint and the rising cost of utilities, understanding when to operate devices and what devices are drawing the most power or water can save you thousands of dollars.

- **Convenience:** Having your air conditioner turn on 30 minutes before you arrive home or your garage door open as you approach are just a few of the conveniences available through smart home integration.

- **Comfort:** Temperature and lighting control set to your preferences and your favourite music or podcast at your voice command make comfort a big driver for those looking to integrate smart home appliances.

Your voice assistant discussed previously is your starting point when considering turning your home into a 'smart' home. Once you've decided on Apple, Amazon or Google, you'll begin to see the number of smart devices you can now connect to your assistant.

My suggestion when entering the world of smart devices... start slow. Take a look at the smart power points perhaps as a starting point and get your lights operating the way you'd like or begin with a video doorbell. Something you'll be able to install and monitor quickly to see how your adaption is affecting the family. We started with the Arlo security cameras (we opted for these because we were renting at the time and they didn't require any hard wiring) and then moved into the Phillips Hue lighting. My point is, one step at a time ... it's a never-ending project once you start.

\* \* \*

As we come to a close on all things productivity, it's time to take some action:

- Understand what you want to track and why.
- What are the areas in your life you would like to increase your productivity in?
- Find one app that you feel would add value, download it and diarise time to begin learning and implementing it.
- Commit to learning and implementing the app for the next 30 days, then make a judgement call on whether you need to delete and find an alternate solution.

Great work. Time to put the book down and take 10 minutes for yourself. Taking 5 to 10 minutes every hour to get up from your desk, stretch and stare out the window or talk to a friend who can keep you motivated to continue working for hours to come.

# SECTION TWO

## SECURITY

## Egon in the room

**OKAY, I GET IT** – security is not the sexiest (or most interesting) subject, but it is one of the most critical things to get right in your business. Very few people I work with ever want to have the security conversation (it's kinda like having 'the talk' with your kids) but I can't write a book around understanding and embracing technology in your life and business without addressing the security aspect.

At its core, 'cybersecurity' is a term used to describe the protection of your computer systems, data and networks from theft, manipulation or disruption.

We're all familiar in one way or another with the concept of cybersecurity. Most of us have received at some time emails that at first glance look legitimate but on closer inspection we realise they are indeed a scam. From impersonating the ATO to the major banks and telco companies, it's not hard for the scammers to create some very realistic-looking emails or text messages that lure even the most security conscious among us to click on a dodgy link or respond with some personal information.

The damage these security breaches cause to our business cannot just be measured in dollar terms, although that can be an eye-watering number. But also most damaging are data and information breeches. It's these information leaks that businesses often do not recover from.

Before we look at some of the risks our businesses face and what we can do to mitigate them, I think it's important to first look at the impact security breaches are having globally. I've pulled together a list of stats from a variety of sources to give you a bit of an idea of what we're actually facing:

- 4.1 billion. According to 'Risk Based Security', this is the number of data records exposed in 2019.

- $17,700. The amount of money lost every minute due to cybersecurity issues according to CSO Australia.

- Phishing attacks accounted for more than 80% of all reported security incidents according to CSO Australia.

- Attacks on IOT tripled in the first half of 2019 according to CSO Australia.

- 94% of all malware is delivered via email according to CSO Australia.

- According to the Australian small business and family enterprise ombudsman, 43% of all cyber attacks are aimed at small business.

- 60% of those small businesses that were attacked failed in the following six months.

- $276,323. The average cost to an Australian small business that experiences a cyber attack – according to the Australian small business and family enterprise ombudsman.

- 23 days. The average resolution time if your business suffers a cyber attack – according to the Australian small business and family enterprise ombudsman.

The Coronavirus pandemic also created a surge in cyber threats globally, with the FBI reporting that online crimes quadrupled from 1000 per day to 4000 per day from March 2020. This was in large part due to the number of people transitioning to work from their homes without time to plan for securing data on home WIFI networks. It's one thing for us all to consider the security of our business while on site, but we must also consider what our homes and appliances are exposing us, our businesses and our families to.

Now you have an understanding of the impact of cybersecurity, let's take some time to look at the various ways your business is potentially susceptible, and what you can do to protect yourself, your clients and your business reputation. I promise I'll do my best to make the whole thing less icky and more practical.

# 6. THE RISKS

As I mentioned earlier, there is every chance you have received at some point an email asking you to click on a link to update your information or download a file. These emails are made to look almost identical to emails from real companies we all deal with and are designed to catch out the unsuspecting. But it's not just cleverly created emails we need to be aware of, there is so much more lurking beneath the surface that, as business owners, we need to understand and mitigate.

If your business is subject to a security breach, there are a variety of ways you may be impacted including:

· loss of revenue
· loss of reputation
· loss of hours
· legal fees
· lost intellectual property
· compliance fines

Let's take a moment to look at some of the more common risks facing business owners today.

## Phishing (pronounced 'fishing')

According to the Ponemon Institute, 57% of companies experience phishing attacks. These are the fraudulent emails we are all so familiar with. Designed to mimic a company or person we interact with, these emails are looking to obtain information or other data. These emails are (usually) sent in bulk and are relatively easy for the scammer to execute.

According to Symantec's 2019 Internet Security Threat Report, the most common email subject headlines used in phishing attacks are:

- Urgent
- Request
- Important
- Payment
- Attention

In Q1 of 2020 according to 'Checkpoint', the most popular brands to impersonate in phishing scams were:

- Apple
- Netflix
- Yahoo
- WhatsApp
- PayPal
- Chase
- Facebook
- Microsoft
- eBay
- Amazon

When you consider all of the above brands and look for a common thread, you'll realise that each of these brands are in regular communication with clients. They have a high trust with their clients. Using this knowledge, scammers will request credit card information, passwords or addresses.

With COVID impacting Q2 2020, Zoom entered the top ten list as one of the most commonly impersonated brands in phishing attempts.

There are a couple of offshoots of the phishing emails which are also worth noting:

- **Spear phishing:** This is where emails are targeted to a particular person. These are far more detailed for the scammer to execute and will (usually) be looking for detailed information. It's usual that a spear phishing attempt will be aimed at the business owner or someone who has access to the finances.

- **Whale phishing:** Similar to spear phishing, the main difference being whale attacks are usually focused on larger companies where the target will be the CEO or CFO.

According to a study by Verizon, the main types of data usually attacked during a phishing expedition are:

- credentials (passwords, usernames, pin numbers)
- personal data (name, address, email address)
- internal data (sales projections, product roadmaps)
- medical data (treatment information, insurance claims)
- bank information (account numbers, credit card information).

So, how do we protect ourselves from phishing attacks?

- Education:
  - We can't stop the scammers sending these emails, but we can educate ourselves and our team to identify key characteristics of phishing emails and remind them to treat all emails with suspicion.
  - If you're not expecting an email from me and I send one with a link or file, don't just click on it. Instead, give me a call and double-check that I have indeed just sent you something.
  - If the email is from a 'trusted' company, check the email and URL by hovering over the link before clicking on anything. If you're in doubt, use Google to find the company URL and see if the email matches.
  - Block anything that is suspicious or doesn't meet company standards.
  - Beware of any URL redirections.
  - Legitimate companies (banks, professionals, etc.) will never ask for sensitive or confidential information via email.
- Consider virus software as an additional line of defence.
- Watch out for poor spelling and grammar.
- If something sounds too good to be true... delete and block!

- Avoid using public networks (unless using a VPN... more about that shortly).
- Beware of website pop-ups.

## Malware

Malware is often delivered via a phishing expedition, and can be described as any piece of software that has been intentionally designed to cause damage or disruption to your computer or networks. Malware is often referred to as a 'virus'.

There are many types of malware to be aware of. Some of the more notable ones are:

- **Trojan:** Disguises itself as 'good' code to infiltrate and disable the system.
- **Adware:** Will serve up unwanted advertisements.
- **Spyware:** Collects information from your computer without your knowledge.
- **Worms:** These will target vulnerabilities in your system and install themselves on a network. A worm will often be followed by a DDoS (distributed denial of service) attack or an attack to steal sensitive data.
- **Keyloggers:** These monitor what keys you are pressing on your keyboard. Some have practical applications (such as monitoring employee activity or ensuring children's security) while others can be used to steal passwords, banking details, etc.

Malware gets onto your computer in a variety of ways – some of the more common are:

- opening an email attachment that contains malware
- clicking on a fake error message or pop-up that contains malware
- visiting a website that is infected with malware
- downloading free software from the internet that contains malware.

Antivirus software company Kaspersky reported 24,610,126 'unique malicious objects' in 2019 and advised that around 20% of all internet users were subject to some type of Malware attack during 2019.

So, how do we protect against Malware?

- Keep your software and hardware up to date: Whether you're running Apple or Microsoft (or another operating system), your providers will offer regular updates. Making sure you're keeping on top of your updates goes a long way to helping protect your system.

- Be suspicious of all emails: If you're not expecting an email with an attachment or a link, do your due diligence before clicking.

- Limit your file sharing: Malware can be hidden behind images, games or videos. Think twice if someone sends you a video (even through social media) as it may contain Malware.

- Watch out for pop-ups on websites – particularly if they ask you to download something.

- Think twice before clicking on any links or downloading any attachments.

- Consider virus protection software.

- Educate yourself and your team around cybersecurity.

- Consider whether you need cybersecurity insurance.

## Ransomware

This is a type of malware which can encrypt your computer files or applications, preventing the owner from accessing them. You'll then be asked to pay a ransom for access to your own files. The average cost of a ransomware attack on a business according to Safe At Last is $133,000.

So, how do we protect against ransomware?

- Consider an antivirus software program.

- Back up your system regularly.

- Keep your software and hardware up to date: Whether you're running Apple or Microsoft (or another operating system), your providers will offer regular updates. Making sure you're keeping on top of your updates goes a long way to helping protect your system.

- Be suspicious of all emails: If you're not expecting an email with an attachment or a link, do your due diligence before clicking.

- Limit your file sharing: Remember that Ransomware is a type of Malware which can be hidden behind images, games or videos. Think twice if someone sends you a video (even through social media) as it may contain Malware.
- Watch out for pop-ups on websites – particularly if they ask you to download something.
- Think twice before clicking on any links or downloading any attachments.
- Use strong passwords.
- If you are infected with Ransomware the best advice is not to pay. There is no guarantee they will release your system. Instead restore your system through a backup.
- Educate yourself and your team around cybersecurity.
- Consider whether you need cybersecurity insurance.

## Website hacking

According to the University of Maryland, hackers attack every 39 seconds, on average 2244 times per day. What's even more concerning is that according to IBM, in 2019 it took an average 206 days to identify an attack.

Small business owners are prime targets for hackers purely because their security tends to be lacking compared to larger companies. Effectively we're sitting ducks for those who want to make some quick cash while wreaking havoc on our business.

The easiest way a small business owner will be hacked is through their website. Globally around 35% of all websites are created in WordPress and according to Acunetix's report 'Web Application Vulnerability 2019', 46% of web applications have critical vulnerabilities. Once in, a hacker can (at best) disable your website and (at worst) access sensitive information relating to your business and your clients.

So, how do we protect our websites?

- Make sure you have a security plugin installed (particularly relevant for WordPress users).
- Install an SSL certificate: SSL stands for Secure Sockets Layer and in simple terms it keeps the data between your website and your

clients safe. When you install an SSL certificate you'll see your website address will move from HTTP://www... to HTTPS://www...

- Keep your website updated: Any time there are updates, do them.
- Use a secure password and login details.
- Don't hand out your login details: If you need someone else to access your website set them up with their own login and password.
- Make sure you have a website backup... and it's updated regularly.
- Limit login attempts.
- Have Google Analytics and Search Console set up: If you start seeing your site rank for strange keywords (like buy cheap online) it's a good indication that you've been compromised.
- Auto logout inactive users.
- Consider putting a website manager on your team: You can contract someone to keep your site up to date and backed up.

## Brute force attacks

This is using a piece of software that will continue to generate passwords through trial and error, becoming increasingly forceful in an attempt to gain access to your system.

A brute force attack can pay off for a hack through the insertion of adware in which they will be paid 'commission', or to reroute your website to a paid ad traffic site, or by infecting all of your visitors or client data with additional malware to continue to spread a virus, or even to steal data.

So, how do we protect against brute force attacks?

- Install 'Captcha' on your website. You know when you have to 'click on all the lamp posts'? That's captcha software. It's one way to help ensure someone accessing your data is human, not a robot.
- Use two-factor authentication wherever possible.
- Limit login attempts.
- Look into encryption software.
- Use strong passwords and login credentials. And NEVER hand them out to anyone.

## Internet of Things (IOT)

As more of us look to create 'smart homes' through TVs, smart speakers, lights, fridges and all manner of other devices, we need to be aware that our adoption of such technology in our homes is a potential open back door for hackers and the like to access our lives. Coupling these emerging trends with the need 2020 created for a lot of us to work from home for the first time, we're recognising the weak spot our homes are in terms of cybersecurity.

According to Security Boulevard, enterprise and automotive are on track in 2020 to have 5.8 billion devices connected to the internet and 57% of our IOT devices are vulnerable to medium or high security attacks. As 'security brief.com.au' pointed out, 98% of all IOT traffic is unencrypted, which means your personal and confidential data is being exposed to your network.

So, how do we protect our IOT?

The technology used in our devices is changing and updating regularly. It is imperative that we take responsibility for keeping up to date with everything pertaining to our devices. Apart from being mindful, we can implement the following as well:

- Turn off your devices when not in use. If there is no power the device cannot be hacked or hijacked.
- Use two-factor authentication and maintain strong passwords on all devices.
- Consider setting up a separate WIFI network to keep distance with your devices.
- Change the default password on your device.
- Read and understand what your device can do – switch on any security features your device may offer.

## Social media

While social media can do wonders for our profile and marketing, we also need to be mindful of the security risk it could be creating in our personal and business lives.

One of the biggest ways I see people exposing themselves to cyber threats is with the amount of personal information they're willing to share.

Things like your:

- date of birth (even day or month)
- mother's maiden name
- previous places of employment
- suburbs you live (or have lived)
- pets' and children's names
- schools you've attended
- photos of family members

These breadcrumbs are often enough for identity theft to occur or attacks on computer networks (especially for those still relying on some combination of the above for passwords).

How often do you see those 'harmless' games from your friends asking you to share personal information in the guise of 'getting to know you better'? I'm not suggesting that your friends are doing anything illegal with your information, but be aware these are the perfect roads for identity theft.

Malware is also very common in social media links. Clicking on a URL from a friend can often lead to immeasurable damage to your files or your network.

So, how do we protect our social media?

- Ensure you're operating on each of the platforms you have an account for. Unused or idle accounts are prime playgrounds for hackers.
- Switch on two-factor authentications.
- Use strong passwords.
- Ensure you do not hand out administrator rights to anyone.
- Keep a register of all team members with access to your social media accounts and disconnect them as soon as they are no longer required.
- Beware clicking on links, videos, games. Including in messages: these often contain malware.
- Do not share personal information on social media.

- Be mindful about posting photos or updates while away.
- Do not play any of the games, polls or quizzes (no matter how many of your friends are playing).

## Staff

Understanding our team members are accessing various platforms and systems on any given day means our staff are one of the weakest cyber security links our businesses face.

Knowing whether your team are sharing your work devices with family members when they are home, knowing how, when and why they are utilising your equipment as well as being aware of how they are interacting with the data of your business and your clients is critical to understanding your exposure.

There are many other risks associated with operating businesses in today's environment, and, as technology morphs and changes, there will be new ones to become aware of. The thing to remember is that with awareness of your risks comes the opportunities to plug some of the gaps and shore up your security as much as possible.

So, how do we protect our staff?

Education. Every single one of your team members needs to be made aware of the risks cybersecurity issues are to your business and the impact it would have if your data was breached. Keep cybersecurity top of everyone's mind, and ensure your team are being updated with your business requirements. Some best practice cybersecurity practices to put in place for any business include:

- Protect your data:
  - Be aware of what is being shared online and how this data could be used.
  - Don't share IP outside the office.
  - Have a password management system (like LastPass) that every employee uses.
  - Don't share login credentials across teams.
  - Make sure not to leave client data displayed on screen or laying around.

- – Make sure your computer screen is switched off at lunch.
- – Have a sleep function on all computers for idle mode.
- Have a zero-trust email policy:
  - – Unless your team is expecting an email from a client with a link or attachment, don't open it without checking first.
  - – Don't open, download or click on any attachments from unknown sources.
  - – Don't click on any attachments or watch videos embedded in social media messages on work computers.
- Make sure you have a secure WIFI connection set up:
  - – If your staff will be working from home, show them how to achieve a secure link from their homes.
- Consider a firewall for your business... and for employees who work from home.
- Run antivirus software and keep it up to date.
- Back up everything, often.
- Consider contracting an IT person to maintain and advise on cybersecurity.
- Embrace education around cybersecurity.

## Poor password management

Many of us put effort and consideration into what security and accessibility will look like for our team members while in the workplace, but what happens when we look at home office setups.

Entrust Datacard recently completed a survey which showed approximately 42% of employees still write passwords on paper, 34% capture them on their smartphone and 27% capture their passwords on their computer.

The frightening thing for me reading these survey results is that almost 20% use the same password across multiple systems. Essentially this means if one system is compromised, the hacker potentially has access to many other systems as well.

Poor password hygiene is (in my opinion) the greatest threat to your business and personal data.

So, how do we protect our passwords?

- If you fear you won't remember your password (and you're not using a password management software) buy a small notebook and keep everything on paper. While there are risks with writing information down it's a slimmer chance someone will break into your home looking for your password notebook.
- Don't hand your passwords out... to anyone.
- Consider using a password management system.
- Avoid using common words or phrases like:
  - mypassword
  - 123456
  - Qwerty
  - pasword
  - your date of birth
  - your kids' names
  - your pets' names
- Use longer passwords: Minimum of 8 characters, preferably 12.
- Don't recycle your passwords.
- Don't use the same password across multiple platforms.
- Use two-factor authentication.

# 7. USEFUL SECURITY THINGS TO KNOW

I understand that this section can feel like it's heavy going, but given the world we operate in it's important to understand the risks and how to mitigate them.

While I shared a few ways you can protect yourself against some of the risks, these are by no means exhaustive. With the changing landscape of cybersecurity new software and technologies will be constantly evolving to help you stay ahead of the game.

In saying that there are a few other tips, tricks and ... errrr ... pardon the pun, hacks that you might like to consider for your business and even your personal life.

## Trend Micro Home Network Security

I first heard about this 'little black box' mid 2020, although apparently, it's been around since about 2017 (see, I don't know everything), and we've had it running at our place pretty much since I heard about it. The idea is the box sits between your gateway and your router and screens all of your internet traffic.

Now, my opinion is that every single house should have one of these... especially if you're running any kind of IOT devices.

Basically, it sits on your network monitoring the traffic. That means it blocks shopping bots that try to gain access, or if there's an attack on your smart TV, or maybe your unsecured IOT device ... you definitely want that. The other neat thing it does is allow you to name or group devices and monitor the traffic, you can even put time limits on devices. So, think about how many times you've asked the kids to put their phones, tablets or laptops away... this essentially shuts down their ability to access the net after a certain time of day (or their allotted time). It'll even give you a data download report separately so you can figure out who it is in the house that's hogging the data.

It's good to point out though that this magic little box is not an antivirus or anti malware protector; you'll still need to consider whether you need that or not for your own devices (tip: you probably do). It's also worth mentioning that the Trend Micro Home Network Security is not the only option available in the marketplace, it's just the one we opted for in our home.

You can pick it up from most major retailers and it is pretty straightforward getting it working. You will need to subscribe to the Trend system, there's lots of options in terms of price point, so choose the one that best suits you (we went straight for two years). We had a few glitches to begin with trying to get it to see through our Orbi mesh WIFI system (I'll talk about the Orbi in another section), but it's worth the fiddling for the peace of mind and protection for your home network.

## Password managers

I've mentioned these a few times above, but password managers really are an excellent way to secure your login credentials and keep your business safe. There are a number of solutions around that all work in similar ways but a couple to start you off are:

### Apple keychain

If you're an Apple user, they have a built-in password manager called 'keychain'. The app will sync across all your apple devices and generate random long-form passwords on your behalf. Another nice feature is it will offer the ability to sign in with an Apple-generated email which is synced back to your designated email address. This means if the site you are logging into is hacked your 'real' address details will not be compromised.

### LastPass

Possibly the most popular password manager I've come across, and is the preferred system of most of my clients.

LastPass will not only hold and secure all your passwords, it can be installed business wide, meaning each of your teams can access and use the facility as well. As the owner you hold admin rights and are able to lock out or remove a team member through one portal making it easier to cancel registrations when team members move on.

Another nice feature of LastPass is the ability to generate a temporary or guest password. This can be super helpful when you're needing a contractor to login and complete some work on a platform. Your contractor will only have access to the platform or system for as long as you've deemed necessary.

## Two-factor authentication (TFA or 2FA)

### Egon in the room

You'll see TFA set up across a number of platforms now (Facebook and Google are just two examples), giving you an additional layer of security when accessing a particular platform.

Often when we set up TFA we default to using our mobile as the number to 'text a code to'.

This can leave you vulnerable. If a hacker is already in your account, they can change the text to a mobile number before you've had a chance to do anything about it.

Instead, when setting up your TFA instead choose the code generator option. Google, Facebook and Microsoft all have code generators available to download on the App store. They are just as easy to connect to the app as your mobile number but provide an additional layer of protection.

## Find my iPhone/Mac

If you're an Apple user, you may not be aware that you have inbuilt support if your device is lost or stolen.

It's an app provided by Apple which allows remote location tracking. While 'Find My' won't prevent you from being phished or downloading Ransomware, it will assist if you happen to lose, misplace or have your device stolen.

I can't tell you how many times I've sent chimes out trying to find my phone before I run out the door... It's a super handy little app, and I recommend everyone with any Apple devices have it enabled.

To see if you have 'Find my...' enabled on your laptop go to your Apple Log in.

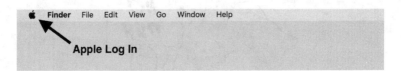

Click on 'Systems Preferences'.

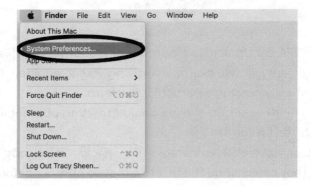

Click on Apple ID.

Click on 'iCloud'.

Click on 'Options' next to 'Find My Mac'.

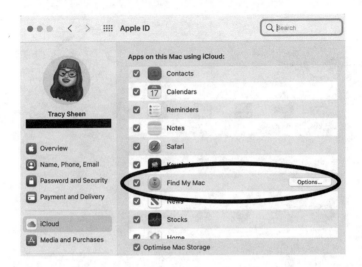

Toggle the 'on' switch for both 'Find my Mac' and 'Offline finding'. Then click 'Done'.

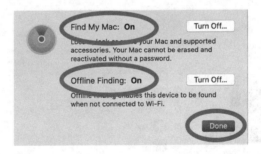

You can mimic the same process through your iPhone by going to 'Settings'.

Click on 'Apple ID'.

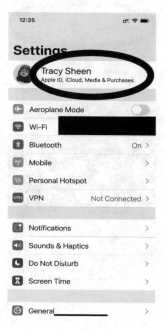

Choose 'Find My'.

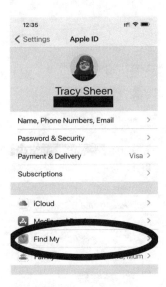

Make sure 'Find my iPhone' is turned to 'On' and (if you choose) you can then add any family who you would like to be able to find your device if needed.

The other neat thing the 'Find My' app does is allow you to share location data with people. Peter and I leave it on between each other, and I have also enabled it on my elderly parents' iPhones.

I've seen it used successfully for families who want to be able to see where the kids are and also with employers who wish to track their employees' whereabouts. I even used it with my niece a few years ago when she was in Brisbane for a music festival. She had no idea where she was and there was no public transport. She called, I got her to switch on tracking and share her location with me. From there I was able to head over and pick her up without any stress to either of us.

For what it's worth, I do believe if you plan on activating it for your employees, they should at least be aware that you have the intention of using this feature.

As with a lot of these type of apps it can be manipulated for nefarious purposes and, sadly, cyber stalking has become a real concern. Many of the family violence centres educate their clients around knowing (and disabling) these types of tracking apps. If you or someone you know is in a precarious situation or feel unsafe, please reach out to one of the many support services for assistance:

· www.dss.gov.au/our-responsibilities/women/programs-services

· www.dvrcv.org.au/help-advice/cyber-stalking-and-harassment

· www.esafety.gov.au/key-issues/domestic-family-violence/
technology-facilitated-abuse/cyberstalking.

## Tiles and GPS trackers

Do you remember in the 80s there were the keyrings that you could whistle at and they would whistle back? I got my Dad one for Father's Day because he was forever losing his keys.

If you're the type of person who puts your keys or wallet or glasses or handbag down and then five minutes later can't seem to find them (no judgement), the whistling keyring has taken huge steps forward in helping you find or track your stuff. Whether they're hiding behind the back of the lounge or you left them at a coffee shop, we now have options with GPS trackers to indicate where our things are.

There is a rumour that Apple is ready to launch their own version of a GPS tracker (which is supposedly called 'Air Tags'). At the time of writing they had not made this public knowledge, but I have a very strong suspicion Apple will have something to market in 2021.

There are a few brands available for consideration, and you'll need to decide which one best suits your requirements. But a couple you can start researching:

## Tiles

Probably the best known GPS tracker on the market. These 'Tiles' come in stickers through to larger tiles you can place on phones, suitcases, laptops... whatever you have that you'd like to be able to track.

The Tile is Bluetooth enabled, and comes with an app – you press 'find' when you want to find something, and the tile will 'ring'. If the Tile is away from you it will give you the last time and place it was updated.

One of the really nice things about the Tile is you can anonymously call on the Tile community to assist you in finding your lost item.

Fair warning though... I've not seen great reviews about the Tiles of late, so please do your own research before you decide on the best solution to suit your purposes.

## BlaqWolf

Much like the Tiles, BlaqWolf can be used on multiple items... including your favourite pets.

I like that these folks are an Australian company and offer a tracking solution for pets. They also offer some different services to Tiles like a lockdown home perimeter and a replaceable battery (which Tile do not have).

Again, it comes down to what you're looking at using the tracker for, but definitely one worth checking out.

# 8. VIRTUAL PRIVATE NETWORKS (VPNS)

A VPN creates a private network for you to operate on when you're connecting to public networks. Effectively it masks your IP address, making your computer and any other devices using the VPN virtually undetectable. Most importantly, it encrypts your data between your computer and the VPN host. That means if you do happen to join a fake WIFI network, your computer can't be seen.

If you are someone who travels a lot and have traditionally relied on hotel or public WIFI networks, then the addition of a VPN is well worth considering.

The types of information a VPN can hide for you include:

- **Your browsing history:** If you like the idea of being able to browse undercover a VPN is a great solution.

- **Your IP address and location:** If you like to keep your search history private and avoid your data being collected and used for ad targeting then a VPN could be a good option.

- **Your devices:** By hiding your address you're adding an additional level of security to your devices from potential hacks.

- **Your streaming location:** Ever wondered how some people access Netflix or streaming services from the USA? A VPN is your answer.

If you think a VPN could be a good solution for you, here's what you need to know. The market is now flooded with VPN options, so here's a few things to keep in mind when comparing your options.

- **Can you set the VPNs on a variety of devices?** When I chose mine, I needed it to be able to work across two laptops, an iPad and two iPhones. Think about how you'll need to use the VPN and what devices you'll want to connect.

- **What are their privacy settings?** Most people are looking at a VPN to increase their privacy and security. Make sure you're looking at a VPN that offers 'no log' policy, meaning they will never log or collect your information of sites visited, etc.

- **Do they have data limits?** Depending on how you use your devices, data could be the deciding factor for you. Make sure your VPN offers unmetered data to the levels you require.

# 9. DEVELOP YOUR OWN CYBERSECURITY POLICY

If you take anything away from this section take this: make the time to develop your own cybersecurity policy for your business.

There are some great online resources to help you create something bespoke for your business. As a starting point, here's some things to consider:

- What are the tech assets you need to protect?
  - List your laptops, tablets, phones, smart speakers as well as any other devices or equipment that need consideration. Don't forget your IOT devices at home or the office.

- Identify the potential threats to your devices and your business:
  - Things like phishing, malware, etc. but also anything that may be specific to your business.

- Identify what information is allowed for your team to share online and what IP needs to stay in-house.

- What is the acceptable use of business supplied devices?
  - Can team members use the devices for personal use?
  - Do they need a VPN or firewall at home if they will be operating remotely?
  - Are there any sites or applications that should not be run?

- How do you want the business to handle and store sensitive information?
  - client details
  - supplier information

- – price lists
- – passwords

- Set your requirements around passwords:
  - – Will you use a password management system? If so, which one?
  - – What's your password protocol?
  - – How often do you update passwords?
  - – How are they stored?
  - – What happens when a team member leaves?

- Explain the importance of unique passwords for each site and application.

- What are your email security requirements?
  - – zero-trust policy
  - – how to block spam and report suspicious emails
  - – when should team members be sharing work emails?
  - – opening or clicking on links
  - – downloading email attachments.

- How do you handle data?
  - – How to identify sensitive data?
  - – When can your team share information or data?
  - – Where and how do you store any physical files/paperwork?
  - – Understanding client privacy.
  - – Destroying data securely.
  - – Respecting client opt in/out of emails and any GDPR protocols.

- Social media and internet access:
  - – What sites are appropriate for viewing/accessing during work hours?
  - – What information should be shared online?
  - – What sites should team members use their work email to log in with?

- Dealing with your technology:
  - – How do you store devices when they aren't in use?
  - – Setting sleep times on desktops/laptops.
  - – Making sure screens are off when people aren't at their desks.

  - Reporting theft.
  - Running updates/security patches – who is responsible and when is this done?
  - Maintaining antivirus software.
  - Scanning USBs and other portable devices for viruses.
- If a cybersecurity incident occurs:
  - How do the team report any incidents?
  - Do these need to be reported/documented to industry standards?
  - What actions need to be taken internally?
  - How to notify clients if a breach occurs?
  - Roles and responsibilities in event of an attack?

Hopefully by becoming aware of the state of play with cybersecurity you're ready to identify and enact your own plan to protect yourself, your business and your personal data.

It is one area that I highly encourage you to gain some expert assistance in. Find a respected IT professional to assist you in putting a plan together and maybe chat with your insurance broker about cyber insurance and whether or not you need it.

While you may never be able to prevent a cyber attack, you can be prepared and ready if it occurs.

* * *

Well done. You made it ...

I totally get it if you need a lie down after making it this far. But I also hope that you realise just how vital it is to your business, your clients and your home that you get this right. It's not difficult to secure yourself, so really, I don't see there are any excuses.

Before we move on I'd like you to make a few notes around the things you've identified that you need to research or invest in for your business or home. If you don't feel qualified to make the decisions, reach out to a cybersecurity expert – it'll be well worth your time.

Now, go hug a puppy or assume the foetal position for five minutes of rocking. Then get yourself a coffee (or a wine, I won't judge). There's much more to go ...

# SECTION THREE

# ORGANISING YOUR LIFE

# Egon in the room

**THIS SECTION HAS** quite a lot of detail in it, I'm talking screen-shots and 'do this if you want to feel like you have more control over your life' kind of detail. It's also worth considering that depending on when you're reading this, the screenshots may look a little different. That's the thing with talking about technology – *blink* and everything has changed. Even if everything looks different, I want you to think about the concepts we're about to cover and how you could apply them to your business, and your personal life. The theory is solid, the execution may just need tweaking.

Everything I talk about is shown as though you'll be setting things up from a desktop or laptop. Now, you can absolutely implement these steps via your phone or tablet... you'll just need to do a little digging yourself to figure it out. Cause seriously, I had to draw the line somewhere. If I screenshotted every option from every device this book would be heavier than *Agra* (which as a side note, is the heaviest book ever produced, weighing in at a whopping 2000kg) and let's face it... no one wants that.

Thanks for understanding... Now, let's get you organised.

# 10. WHAT'S OUT THERE ...

If there's one area that technology can have the quickest (and potentially the biggest) impact on your life, it's around organisation.

I'm not just talking about knowing where your sales team is or what's going on with marketing. I'm talking about right down to the very fundamental level of who's picking up the groceries and what kids need to be at what after-school activity on what day at what time.

I'm guessing many of you grew up with a 'chore chart' and family calendar displayed somewhere prominently (usually the kitchen) in your house. When one of the kids completed a chore, they'd tick the box until their progress showed it was time for 'payday'. There'd be a shopping list where everyone in the household could add their weekly requirements and the calendar would be the ruler of everyone holding the keys to every movement of every family member on any given day.

I'm also guessing every single member of your household (including your kids) also now has access to some form(s) of technology. Whether it's a smartphone, a tablet or a laptop, there will be some kind of device floating around for each member.

Throughout this section, we're going to take a look at the various platforms, apps, and websites that can bring your family life (as well as your working life) into sync. While allowing family members access to add or delete information.

Let me give you an example. In my home, it's just Peter (my hubby) and me. You're probably wondering how hard it could possibly be to track the movements and requirements of two people... am I right? Well, apart from the two of us (oh, and two very demanding 'fur kids' Obi and Watson) we also run two businesses with interstate staff and clients, remote teams, and have responsibilities for both sets of elderly parents, both of whom are living remotely from where we're based.

In any given week there is shopping to do for family, doctors' appointments to monitor, treatments to arrange as well as client meetings, travel and personal appointments to fit in. Add into that we're currently renovating a house, so we've got tradies to schedule and various other people popping by to quote or work.

It's a hectic schedule by any measure.

Thankfully both Pete and I have embraced technology, and between us, we're able to schedule, maintain, and arrange our own lives (as well as each other's) with a couple of very simple apps. Wherever and whenever, each of us can see what's happening right now, all from our phone, tablet, or laptop. And (for the most part) we don't need to be connected to the internet to access the information. Want to know how we keep it all together and rarely drop a ball? (No, I'm not going to say we never drop a ball... we're human too.) Read on. Some of the tips are super easy to introduce, while others will take a little setting up and dedication to use them, but all of them will work for you if you decide they will.

There are so many different tools you can implement to assist you with the day-to-day organisation of your life. A lot of what you choose to use will be based on the information you uncovered during the introduction section when we discussed what operating system (Apple or Android/Windows) you already have in place.

Everything I'm about to share with you is either cloud-based (meaning it will work across any platform) or will have its own variation inside the program you're using.

What I'm guiding you through here is what is available; you may still need to do a little legwork on the specific operation for your own system.

## You need to use a calendar

I know, not earth shattering, and as I mentioned above, chances are you've got a calendar hanging in the kitchen at home – but I'm talking about 'using' the calendar that comes with your device.

Whether it's a Google calendar, Apple iCal or Microsoft calendar, each of them has the ability to do what I'm about to explain.

Let me guide you through what I suggest you do and why.

The first is to sit quietly and think about the main areas of your life. Specifically, the areas you'd like to be able to easily track. Things like personal activities, family activities, work functions, travel, etc. The important thing is to initially identify what these areas need to be and to make a list.

For example, inside my Google calendar (which by the way you can sync to your Apple iCal) I have the following calendars created. Each of these is an area I like to track. I want to know how much time I'm spending within each section on a weekly or monthly basis as it gives me a very quick visual representation on where my business and my personal life may be out of whack:

- **Personal:** For anything to do with stuff I need to do for me. My hair and nail appointments go in here, so do any of my medical appointments or time out I need just for 'me'.
- **Family:** This one is anything to do with Peter and me or our family. I spend a lot of time taking my folks to medical appointments, some of them are recurring, everything related to this is captured here. It also catches up time with the kids, grandkids, friends, and 'date nights'.

- **Travel:** This one wasn't so heavily used during COVID but for me, it's important to know just how much time is being spent in transit. If I'm visiting clients in Sydney, I need to block out two hours of travel to the airport, an hour to wait before the flight, an hour in the air, and an hour to get to the hotel. You can see how quickly the time adds up. By blocking out travel time I can look back and see if there's an opportunity to complete any admin or other activities during that downtime.

- **Office and admin:** If I don't specifically block out time to do administrative tasks, I'll find myself responding to emails at 10 pm or on a Sunday. I use the office and admin calendar to ensure I'm allocating a proportion of time each day and each week to staying up to date with emails, quotes, correspondence, etc.

- **Client time:** Whether it's a phone call, Zoom meeting or in person, if the task is related to client work I make sure to block it in this calendar.

- **Networking events:** I only set this calendar up around 18 months ago, and it's been an eye-opener. Every business breakfast, lunch, or networking event I attend is allocated to this calendar.

- **Learning and development:** This is another relatively new addition to my calendar lists. I decided to add it as I spend a lot of time reading and learning. I was interested to know just how much time I allocate to this task each week, so now every time I'm doing some study or reading a book, I'll block the time to my L&D calendar.

## Next step... colour coding

Once you have these listed, I suggest you put a colour to them. The reason for this is it's a super-quick visual representation of what your day, your week, or your month looks like. It allows you to see at a glance what's eating your time and gives you a quick way to balance the scales if you need to block a little more 'me time' in there.

### Step three... Set them up on your device

I find it much easier to set them up in my device once I know what it is I want to track and why. The setup guides below are for setting your calendars up on a laptop/desktop.

## Setting your calendar up on your desktop/laptop

### Apple iCal set up

Here's what you need to do to set your calendars up if you use Apple iCal (this set up is only for those using Apple iCal. If you'd like to connect your Google or Microsoft calendar, go to the section on Google calendars or Microsoft calendars, below).

1. Open your calendar app on your desktop or laptop.

2. In your drop-down menu under 'File' go to 'New Calendar'.

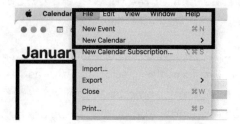

3. If you are connected to iCloud, select 'iCloud', otherwise choose 'On My Mac'.

4. Your new calendar will appear on the left-hand side (see the image below, it is showing as 'untitled'). Type the name of your new calendar.

5. Choose the colour you'd like for the calendar. To do this 'right click' on the calendar. You'll see the colour options displayed; you can also choose from a custom colour.

## Connecting your Google Calendar or Microsoft to iCal from the desktop/laptop

Use this step if you would like to sync your Google or Microsoft calendars with your Apple iCal. I've found this super helpful as I use Google for my business but rely on my Apple devices all day. I don't want to have a separate Google calendar app on my laptop or phone (I'm way too likely to add stuff in the wrong spot). So, connecting the two means I only have to add or look at my Apple calendar to see what's going on everywhere.

You'll 'add' your new calendars via Google or Microsoft, but they'll need to be connected to your Apple iCal if you want them showing on your Apple device.

To connect your Google calendar to your Apple iCal:

1. Open your Apple iCal. Go to the drop-down menu 'Calendar' and 'Add Account'.

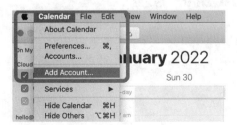

2.  Select your account provider and 'continue'.

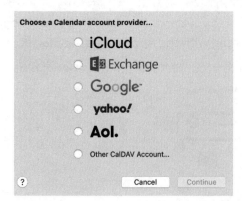

3.  You'll need to enter the email address and password for the Google account you want to connect.

4.  You'll see a screen asking which content you'd like to connect. There is a stack of stuff that will sync with your Apple devices (notes, contacts, etc). If you'd like that content to sync at the same time, tick everything you're interested in. Make sure you have ticked 'calendars' though.

5.  Apple will now start importing all the calendar appointments and events stored in your Google calendar. This could take a while so don't stress if you're not seeing stuff immediately.

## Adding new calendars in Google via your desktop/laptop

If you live in the Google universe you can add calendar to your Google account just as easily as you can with the Apple steps outlined above.

1. Go to your Google G-Suite account. Click on the series of nine dots and select 'calendar'.

2. Scroll down the left-hand side until you see 'other calendars'. Click on the '+' button.

3. Select 'Create new calendar'.

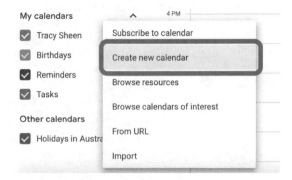

4. Complete the details as you would like them to appear and hit 'Create Calendar'. Remember to check your 'time zone' and make sure it's correct for your area.

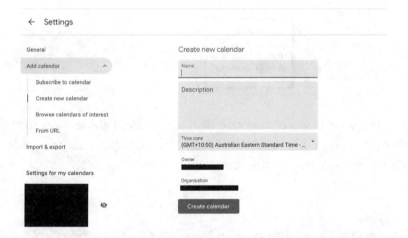

5. At this point, Google will tell you it's creating the calendar. It will then give you the option to 'configure'. This is where you will go if you would like to add other people to be able to view or add things to your calendar or to make it public. (More covered on this in another section... for now though, just know this bit could be important to you shortly.)

6. Once the calendar is set up, exit out of settings and back into the calendar. Scroll down the left-hand side until you see your

new calendar. Click on the series of dots to the side and choose the colour you would like to represent the calendar.

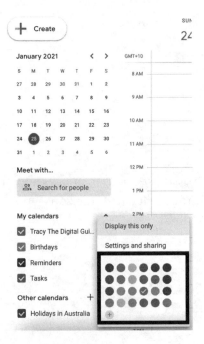

To sync your Google calendar with an Android device. Go to the 'Google Play' store and download the 'Google Calendar App'. When you open the app, everything should sync across for you automatically.

## Setting up new calendars in Microsoft Outlook using desktop/laptop

1.  Open your calendar app and go to the 'Folder' tab. Under the 'New Group'. Click on 'New Folder'.

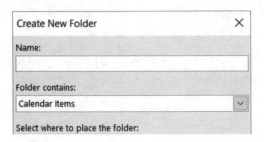

2. In the 'Name' box type the name of your new calendar.

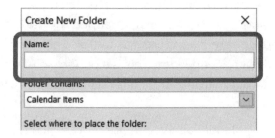

3. In the box saying, 'Select where to place the folder' choose 'Calendar'. Then click OK.

4. To select your colour choice for the calendar, go to the 'View' tab and select your colour.

A note about Microsoft Outlook calendar and Android devices. As of the time of writing, sadly it seems Microsoft and Android don't play very well together. You can set up a one-way sync, but this issue seems to be around editing or adding appointments on your phone. If you own an Android device and you're trying to sync it with Microsoft Outlook calendar keep an eye on the Microsoft support page. (www. support.office.com/en-us/article/can-t-sync-calendar-and-contacts-with-my-phone-or-tablet-8479d764-b9f5-4fff-ba88-edd7c265df9f)

Currently their best solution appears to be downloading a separate calendar app.

## Inviting other people to view your calendar

Once your calendar is set up on your device and syncing across to your smartphone, the next thing you'll want to consider is who has access to your calendar. There are a couple of different options to consider here.

· **Publishing your calendar:** This is typically used when people want to share their schedule with a broader audience (think of any big international band that is touring and wants the media to follow and schedule interviews). Publishing your calendar does not allow the viewer to add or edit events. It's rare I see small business owners or family members publishing a calendar.

• **Sharing your calendar:** This is what I tend to recommend to clients most often. A shared calendar puts everyone on the same page, not just allowing them to see what is happening inside the calendar but (if correct permissions are granted) also allowing them to add or edit events as needed. This is a perfect solution for tracking all the family activities from after school to medical and everything in between.

• Depending on which calendar app you're using, you will have options on the level of access you grant people. (Note: the names of what the calendar applications call these access levels may also vary.) Typically it's broken down into something like this:

  – **View only:** People can see but they can't make amendments.

  – **Editor:** They can view and edit but may not be able to create.

  – **All access:** View, edit, create, and delete events. Think of it as an access all areas pass at a concert.

## How to share your calendar in iCal from a desktop/laptop

In order to share your calendar with someone through iCal you'll need to do the following:

1. Log into your iCloud account (www.icloud.com) and select your 'calendar' application.

2. Select the calendar you want to share from the left-hand side of the screen.

3. Click on the 'symbol' beside your calendar of choice.

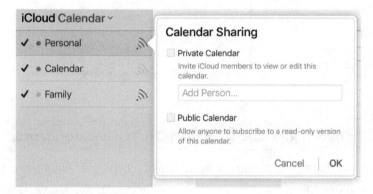

4. If the person you would like to invite also has an iCloud address use the 'Private Calendar' option and enter their apple email address.

5. If the person you would like to invite does not have an Apple email, use the 'Public Calendar' option. This will generate a 'view only' link you can email or share.

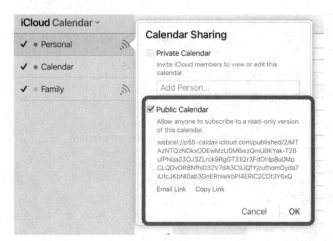

## How to share your Google calendar from a desktop/laptop

In order to share your Google calendar with someone you'll need to do the following.

1. Log into your Google account and select the Calendar application (www.google.com).

2.  Click on the 'Settings' cog 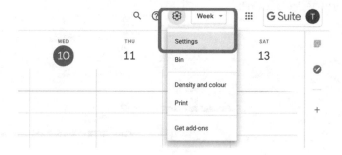 and then click 'Settings'.

3.  From the left-hand side of the screen select the calendar you want to share.

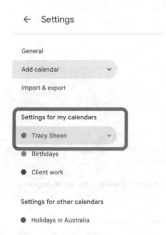

4.  Go to 'integrate calendar'.

5. If you'd like to make the calendar public, use the URL that's shown in the Public URL.

6. If you'd like to share the calendar with someone to use in another calendar application use the 'Public Address in iCal format'.

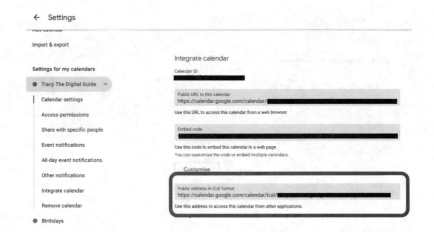

## How to share your calendar in Office 365 from a desktop/laptop

In order to share your calendar with someone through Office 365 you'll need to do the following:

1.  Log in to Office 365.

2.  Click on the Calendar app.

3.  Open the Calendar Settings menu by clicking the cog icon ⚙ (bar at top, on the right).

4.  Click 'Options' (bottom of the menu).

5.  Click on the 'Calendar publishing' option (found under Calendar > Shared Calendars).

6.  Select the calendar you want to use from the drop-down menu.

7.  Go to the section called, 'Shows availability, titles and locations'.

8.  Copy the ICS link.

9.  This is the link you need to paste into the ICS compatible application that you want to share your calendar with.

## Meeting scheduling tools

How many times have you tried to schedule an appointment with a client and the conversation goes something like this...?

> *How are you looking for 2pm Tuesday?*
> *No, sorry I've got a call at 2... What about 3?*
> *No, can't do 3. How about Wednesday at 10 or 1:30?*
> *No, I'm out Wednesday.... How's your Friday looking?*

Sound familiar? Not only is it wasted productivity time but it can be frustrating for everyone involved.

Since I've discovered online scheduling applications those conversations are a thing of the past. There are plenty of options available if you do a little searching, and they basically all do the same thing. If an online meeting scheduler is something that floats your boat, here's a few things I like to look out for:

·   Can the scheduler convert time zones? This one is really handy if you have clients interstate or overseas. Nothing worse than trying to figure out what 10 am Brisbane time is if your client is in Perth, or worse still, overseas.

- Can the scheduler offer different meeting length options? Sometimes you might just want a 15-minute check in call, while other times you need a good hour to talk. Look out for a scheduling tool that will offer you flexibility in meeting length.

- Can the scheduler accept payments? This may not be important for you, but if you were running say a coaching business and clients needed to pay as they scheduled, life is a whole lot easier if your scheduler will integrate with your payment gateway.

- Can the scheduler allow rescheduling and cancellations? Let's face it, sometimes things come up and either party will need to reschedule or cancel. Look for an app that will allow you to do that inside the application, not email you separately.

- Can the scheduler support multiple users? Think about who else in your team would benefit from this tool and look for something that will suit the business as a whole.

- Can the scheduler integrate with other tools you use frequently? I spend a lot of my time on Zoom; I want something that's going to supply a Zoom link as soon as someone books a meeting with me. What other apps do you use regularly that you'd like your scheduler to work with?

- Can the scheduler integrate with your website? This is an absolute must for me, and it should be for everyone. Trust me, make your life a whole lot easier and put a meeting scheduling link on your website.

- Can the scheduler be branded with your business colours, fonts, logo, etc.?

- Can the scheduler book with approval? Sometimes it's handy to confirm a booking time rather than just have it land in your calendar. Being able to approve a meeting time is a handy little asset in your scheduler.

- Can the scheduler offer a range of times? Much like the point above I like to ask clients to choose two or three times that suit when they're booking with me. That way I can find the slot that's going to work best with my day.

There's a bunch of other stuff that you might need to consider for your own circumstances, but if you begin your search with the above criteria, you'll be on to a very handy little organisational tool indeed.

Here's a list of some of the scheduling tools I've used in the past. I don't get paid for recommending, they're just ones I've been exposed to over the years and could be a good place for you to start your search.

· HubSpot Meetings free tool
· Schedule Once
· Acuity
· Calendly
· Appointlet

How you use them will depend on the app you settle on, and there is a little set-up time required. Once it's up and running though, you'll be so glad you invested the time and effort.

## Training your clients and others how to use your invite link

Once you've settled on your meeting invite software, and you've taken the time to set everything up, the next thing you'll need to do is hold fast in asking clients (and everyone else for that matter) to use it.

It's natural for you and your contacts to want to fall back to familiar patterns; after all, they've been scheduling meetings with you over the phone or via email for years, why should anything change?

But if you want to see the uptick in your productivity, you'll need to hold your ground. My advice when it comes to this is simple.

Send a very short email out to your entire contact base to let them know you're adopting a new piece of software to help you manage your calendar. And, you'll need their help using it if it's going to be successful.

You can screenshot or create a quick video showing everyone just how easy the process is to book a meeting with you and asking them to utilise the program the next time they want to catch up.

Let them know your meeting invite link will be in the footer of all your emails from now on, so they don't need to remember links, etc. They'll simply need to click on the link at the bottom of the email whenever they want to talk with you and go through the process of booking a meeting that way.

Explain the 'win' is as much for them as it is for you; they can find the best day and time that suits them without ever having to play the 'how about this time' game with you on the phone or via email again.

Once you've sent the email, be prepared to stand firm. If someone calls or emails needing a time to talk, simply reply with your meeting link and gently remind them this way is far easier for everyone.

Like anything new, it'll take some getting used to for everyone; the results though will be worth it.

Here's an example of an email you could send when you're adopting new meeting software ...

Hi [insert first name]

I hope you're keeping well and you're having a wonderful week.

I wanted to drop you a quick note to let you know I'm adopting a new piece of software into my business that I believe is going to save us both time and effort when it comes to scheduling meetings.

It's called [insert the name of your meeting software]. Essentially it will allow you to choose a day and time for any meetings moving forward without us having to juggle schedules over the phone.

It's super simple to use, I've included a quick walk through video here for you [insert video link] OR below you'll see some screenshots that will walk you through the process.

1. Simply click on this link when you want to book a meeting with me.

2. Choose the length of meeting you'd prefer (15 or 30 minutes).

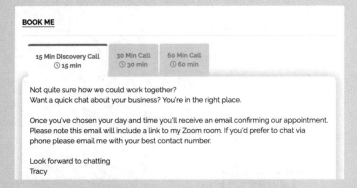

3. Choose the day and time that suits you.

4. Pop your contact details in as requested.

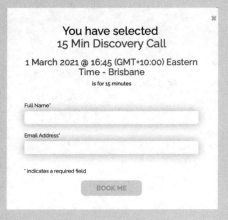

5.  Click the 'book me' button when finished.

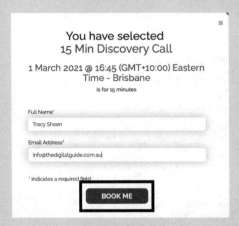

6.  A confirmation of your booking will show on the screen.

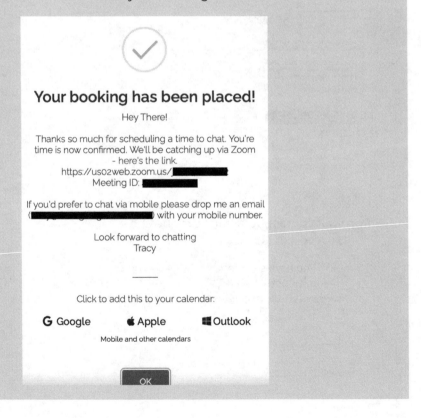

7. You'll receive an email confirming our appointment with a calendar link.

The whole process, I think, is really straightforward and will save everyone time and angst trying to find a time that suits them.

From today you'll notice the meeting link will be included in the footer of all my emails. If you could assist me in making the transition smoother by utilising this link for any future meeting or catch ups I'd be most appreciative.

Of course, if the system causes you any concern, just let me know.

[Sign off]

## Zoom or Skype? FaceTime or Google Meets?

A large part of getting organised in your business and your life is being willing to embrace different ways of communicating with your clients, your suppliers, even your family.

If COVID has taught us anything in business it's that the ability to continue to work virtually was not only possible, but a number of our clients and staff actually preferred it. No more lost time commuting between meetings, rather a smooth day of leaping from one meeting to another using one of the many virtual platforms available.

The platform that seemed to get the most noise during the COVID crisis was without a doubt Zoom. It wasn't without its glitches as many of us adopted this new way of doing business, but, it certainly was the most flexible in assisting us to easily stay connected.

Many people messaged me during this time asking questions about Skype (now known as Microsoft Teams) and Google Meet (formerly known as Google Hangouts). Essentially all the questions were around security and why one platform was better than another.

So, in this section I want to touch a little on each of the major platforms, share a little of their strengths and weaknesses and give you enough information for you to go forth and find the best solution to use in your business moving forward.

## Zoom

As I just mentioned, Zoom certainly got the most press during COVID. The platform itself has been around since 2011. It was created as a video communication platform. You could meet with another person in a virtual space while maintaining as much similarity as a face-to-face meeting as possible.

As a free platform you can schedule one-to-one conversations with people with no time limit, or you can schedule a group call with up to 100 participants for a 40-minute timeframe. You aren't limited by the number of meetings you can schedule each month, and, for the most part, the quality of the calls on Zoom is excellent (this of course depends on participants' internet speeds at their end).

With Zoom you or your participants can share their desktop screen (handy for walking through demonstrations or fault finding) and you can record the conversation, perfect for training calls.

A number of businesses, myself included, have been using a paid version of Zoom for years to allow additional functionality. Once you find yourself with a paid account, you no longer have time restrictions on group calls (well, as long as your meetings are less than 24 hours, that is). With the paid version you're able to 'live stream' to your Facebook or YouTube account (super handy if you wanted to interview someone as an example), and you can begin to get some reporting functionality, like meeting registrations. You can also opt for the webinar functionality if that's something of interest to your business. There were some concerns during COVID around Zoom's security. These gaps have (mostly) been plugged now and, overall, it's the perfect video conferencing tool to use with people who aren't terribly tech savvy as there is nothing to install or do prior to connecting.

I rate Zoom as the top video conferencing performer for small business owners.

## Skype (Microsoft Teams)

Skype was one of the really early players in the video conferencing market, coming out in 2003. Owned by Microsoft, Skype is the preferred means of communication for Government and large corporate organisations, primarily because they are already operating within the Microsoft operating system and because of the inbuilt security features Skype offers.

Skype offers everything that Zoom does, and is perfect if you live in the Microsoft universe.

If you're looking for webinar-style features, you'll need to pay for 'Skype for Business'; once there you can accommodate up to 250 participants.

My main issue with Skype is that it can be a little 'glitchy'. The call quality overall tends not to be as good as what you'll get with Zoom, in part I believe this is due to the additional security Skype has built into the platform. It also tends to be a little more convoluted to get into the platform and connect with people. While Skype say they have removed the need for participants to have installed the app prior to using it, I've had a number of small businesspeople find Skype difficult to use and navigate.

## FaceTime

If you live in the Apple universe (like I do) you may already be familiar with FaceTime. It's the inbuilt app on your Apple devices that allows you to easily call another Apple device via phone or video.

You can chat one to one or do a group chat with up to 33 people.

I love FaceTime for my personal life, connecting with family and friends, but it's not a business application that you'll find yourself using.

## Google Meets (formerly Google Hangouts)

If you subscribe to the Google universe, chances are you already have access to Google Meets... maybe you just haven't come across it before.

It's a great platform for collaboration inside the Google sphere; that is, if your team works in G Suite using Google Docs, Google Sheets, etc. Google Meets is a handy platform to consider bringing your team together on.

Anyone with a Google account can host up to 100 participants for an hour, quickly and easily... perfect for collaborating or team catch-ups.

Like Skype and Zoom, if you're a paying Google client you'll gain some additional features with your various plans, but essentially, it's the same service as the others we've covered. It's worth noting though that like Skype you cannot host a webinar inside Google Meets.

The best usage for this platform for me remains for those clients already operating inside the Google G Suite universe.

\* \* \*

While I've covered the most popular current video conferencing platforms, it's worth mentioning there are a bunch of other options available in the marketplace, particularly if you're interested in hosting and delivering your own webinars at any point ... we'll talk more about webinars later in the book.

WhatsApp and Facebook offer their own video chat features, but these so far for me remain options for our personal connections, not for a business setting.

# 11. SOCIAL MEDIA

Ok, hear me out. I know at first glance you're probably making that (cue '80s TV pop reference) 'What you talkin' 'bout Willis' face, wondering how social media is going to organise your life... but, I've used events in Facebook for a bunch of reasons and found it a great way to connect and keep everyone on the same page. And, during COVID I know we all found a little solidarity in being able to stay connected with friends and family easily through the social network.

We have one message thread constantly going with the four adult kids. They'll share photos of the Grandchild (Theo, and yes, he's gorgeous), work updates and a smattering of random funny memes, etc.

- There's a message thread with my niece and nephew. We all live in different states and they have their own kids now, so it's an easy way for us all to keep in contact.

- I have a message thread with a group of Formula One friends. We basically watch the race together and chat it through in real time on the thread. In between races we'll send updates on stories and share completely random 'in-house' stuff.

You get the idea... Now, I'm not investing hours into these threads every day and sometimes a week or so will go by without anyone posting, but, we all know it's there and somehow that all helps us feel connected.

Don't discount your socials... just make sure you manage them and remember sometimes, you need to meet the people you're trying to organise where they are, and that may just be in cyberspace.

# 12. SOME OF MY FAVOURITE PRODUCTIVITY APPS

Have you checked out the productivity section in your app store lately? That's a rabbit hole you're not coming back from in a hurry.

Fortunately, I'm always on the lookout for new apps to try and I've put together a bit of a list to get you started.

## What 3 Words

Have you ever needed to find a place but it's down some weird kind of alley or side street that doesn't really show in Google Maps and is super hard to give someone directions on? Or maybe you live in a granny flat out the back of a main house with your own entrance but somehow the delivery guy just keeps missing the sign and dropping your parcels at the wrong place?

Enter 'What 3 Words'. Chris Sheldrick (the creator) works in the music industry and was constantly fielding calls from people who couldn't find the stage door or couldn't quite find the loading dock for the venue.

So, Chris reached out to his school friend mathematician, Mohan Ganesalingam, and together they developed What 3 Words.

The premise is this. They've gridded the entire planet into 3m squares and assigned each square with a unique combination of three words.

For example, where I'm writing this section the three unique words are 'Freshen. Fetches. Scorch.'

If I wanted you to meet me there, you'd simply enter the words into the app and it would bring you to my table.

Think of the usage for this in a business context... Never have your delivery drivers, service techs or sales guys get lost again. And yes, the first thing everyone does is find out what their home address is.

Download 'What 3 words' and give it a go.

And, make sure you drop me a message on one of my socials and let me know where I was when I was writing this section of the book.

## WTForecast

We all love our weather apps, but this one just amuses me. Not only does it give you the forecast for wherever you are, but it serves it with a side dish of sass.

There's an inbuilt profanity filter so you can choose between no swearing, PG, some or R rated. Word of warning: some of the comments can be quite, well ... just download it and you'll see what I mean.

## Google Maps

Everyone needs a good day-to-day navigation map in their phone and Google Maps is probably the best. It relies on users being logged in to Google (so yes, it's pulling your data and pinning where you are the entire time. Probably not a problem unless you're Jason Bourne) but the flip side of all that data is the accuracy you'll get with traffic congestion, road closures, etc.

Definitely one worth having on your phone. Just don't believe what they say if you're following the walking instructions and you read 'mostly flat' – I'm sure it had me scale Everest one day to get where I was going.

## Trello

Possibly my favourite app ever. I planned this entire book in Trello, and even planned my wedding using Trello. I've seen friends use it to manage their house and keep the kids organised and I've seen clients use it to project manage client work from first contact to project completion.

Using the Kanban boards (which is basically a bunch of cloud-based sticky notes you put into order under columns) you can create cards and move them around as need be.

Books have been written on how to use Trello effectively and there are loads of YouTube tutorials, etc. if you want to give it a go. Personally, I found it really easy to get the hang of just by following the inbuilt tutorials.

There are plenty of apps like Trello if you don't bond with it, the other most popular one is Asana.

Pick one, download it and give it a go.

## HubSpot CRM

The single biggest difference in productivity my business saw was implementing a CRM system.

Yes, there are plenty of CRM systems on the market, and we'll talk a little more about different ones at other stages of the book, but for now, let me explain how it made me more productive.

Wherever I am I can simply open the app and log a call to a client, send an email, set myself a to-do or reminder, assign a task to a team member, even snap a photo of a business card at a networking event and load it straight to the system. I can even send a meeting link as we discussed earlier.

Removing the double handling of simple day-to-day tasks in my business has saved me considerable time each and every day.

So, it may not be HubSpot you choose to go with, but seriously, consider a CRM for your business. You'll be smug with just how organised you can become.

## Siri or Alexa or Google

I don't try to hide the fact I'm all in with the Apple universe, but when it comes to leaning into your virtual assistants it doesn't really matter if it's Siri, Google or Alexa. Spend the time to train them on your voice and you'll be able to outsource some of the more mundane tasks to them.

I get Siri to take notes, set reminders, remind me to get milk when I reach the shops, call people, play podcasts and send messages.

The bonus is if you do use Siri, you'll get to find out just what sort of personality it has, as the Apple team made sure to include a few random funny things (side note: ask Siri if it has any pets, or for its best pickup lines).

Oh, and sometimes Siri can be … ummm … 'unhelpful', and by that, I mean get things completely wrong and leave you wondering why you even bothered. Fortunately, this is happening less and less frequently as the AI continues to improve.

\* \* \*

How are you feeling? Hopefully a little more in control of things?

This is one big area where if you spend the time setting it up and becoming familiar with the basics, you'll wonder why you never digitised this part of your life before.

So, what are you going to try? Make sure you make some notes and make some time in your diary next week to start implementing... Maybe you could even try asking Siri to set a reminder for you to work on it for next week.

Meanwhile it's time to get up and stretch, maybe make a cuppa or go watch an episode of your latest Netflix binge. You'll need to get your strength back before we move into the next section.

# SECTION FOUR

## MONEY

**YOU MIGHT BE TEMPTED** at first glance to skip over this section, thinking you've got your internet banking sorted and you're all signed up to your accounting package... what else could there possibly be to know?

To be honest, I somewhat agree. While I will cover things like small business accounting programs (for those of you who haven't found your accounting mojo) this section will mostly focus on some cool tips, software platforms and apps that I've found along the way to just make life a little bit easier.

It won't be as long as some of the other sections as I also recognise you don't want to be taking money advice from me (no, seriously, you really don't want to be taking money advice from me) ... But I still do have the odd trick or two up my sleeve that will be worth your while casting an eye over.

Everything we're about to look at is what's considered to be a Software As A Service (SAAS) platform. This means they will all have ongoing monthly subscriptions to consider.

So, let's kick off with some cool apps I've found (some I use, some my clients use).

# 13. ACCEPTING PAYMENTS

There are a number of options available if you're looking to accept payments online. A little research into what you actually need to achieve will yield pages of results. But if you're looking for the top two I consistently hear about read on.

## Square

*www.squareup.com*

Square has a super easy compact virtual terminal that makes it easy for small businesses to capture payments on the run. Simple to set up and easy for your clients to use, Square offers no set-up fees, no hardware fees and no minimum monthly fees. You just pay when you accept a payment from a client.

Square also works with contactless payment (Apple Pay and Google Pay) as well as online transactions.

You can purchase the compact point of sale (POS) terminal from a number of retail outlets across the country.

Worth giving a go, just be mindful if you accept international transactions there are a few more hoops to jump through to get connected.

## PayPal Here

*www.paypal.com/au/webapps/mpp/home*

If you want an alternative to Square but you're still looking for something with a Point of Sale (POS) option, then PayPal Here is worth considering.

Just like Square, PayPal Here has no monthly fees and no long-term commitments, with your funds being available immediately.

The downside is their transaction fees are high (particularly for overseas transactions) and they do not accept EFTPOS (big downside in my opinion).

# 14. PAYMENT GATEWAYS

We talked briefly about Square and PayPal Here without really looking at why you'd consider connecting a payment gateway.

Payment Processing Solutions, another term for payment gateways, are all about providing a way for your clients to do business with your business easily online.

If you're running an E-Commerce business there's a very good chance you're already using a payment gateway in your business (like Stripe, Square or PayPal). If your business is not set up for E-Commerce though you may not have considered having the ability to take a credit card payment from a client.

We'll talk more about the customer experience later in the book but essentially the reason for connecting a payment processing solution is about providing options for your clients and making it as easy as you can for them to do business with you.

Ultimately you want to remove as many obstacles as you can from someone giving you money.

Most of the payment gateways do not have set-up fees or minimum monthly transaction levels, they simply work on a fee per transaction basis. So, you're not paying anything extra for having the facility available.

If this is something you think is worth considering there are a couple of things to think through before choosing a provider.

### Set-up fees and costs

While some of the companies I've mentioned do not charge set-up fees, if you're considering partnering with your existing bank to offer the solution it's worth asking what their fees and costs are. Compare them with the others before making your final decision.

### Contract terms

Again, some of the newer players to the market (by newer, I mean not the traditional banking institutions) don't run on contract periods, but often the banks will. This is another thing to check before you make your decision.

# 15. POINT OF SALE (POS) AND EQUIPMENT

If you run a bricks-and-mortar operation (or you're a market vendor) you'll need to find a provider that has a POS system you can use.

This could be anything from a credit card reader to a POS system on a mobile or tablet reader for collecting on-the-go transactions.

Check in with the companies you're considering and find out if there is a fee (outright or rental) on the device itself... Left unchecked these can get quite expensive.

If you're going to offer online or in-person payment solutions, then it's worth considering the types of payment options you'll offer.

It's a rare person who carries cash these days (which got rarer during the pandemic) and most of us now prefer to 'tap and go' with our payments. This may be a debit or a credit card option. The other thing to consider is whether your provider can offer solutions for Apple and Google Pay also.

I know I pay everything through my Apple Watch and am almost caught out now if I go somewhere that does not have the option for accepting payment through my watch or phone. These payment methods will only become more ubiquitous as we move through the years, so it's worth looking for a holistic solution from the start.

### Customer support

Depending on your hours of operation you're going to want to know your payment processing company's options when it comes to customer support. It's always handy to know you've got someone on the end of the phone when you process a client's payment and things suddenly stop working.

There are dozens if not hundreds of payment processing gateway companies to choose from, and that's without considering partnering with your traditional bank. A simple Google search will provide you with plenty of options – to get you started though, here's a few you can check out.

## Secure Pay

*www.securepay.com.au*

These folks have been around since 1999 and are an option for businesses who have an existing merchant account with a bank and want to work with it.

- No set-up fees.
- No monthly or annual fees.
- Transaction fees are applied to all transactions, including refunds, pre-authorisation and card-issuer declined payments.
- Can transact domestic and international payments.
- Offers Australian bank support.
- Virtual terminals.
- Does not have a POS solution.
- There are a number of hidden fees to watch out for.

## Square

*www.squareup.com/au/en*

Possibly the most popular payment gateway operator I see within my small business community. They support a number of platforms, including:

- Shopify (via a third-party app)
- Vend
- WooCommerce
- Xero

There are a lot of 'pros' to Square, including:

- Virtual terminal.
- Various cards, including:
  - Visa
  - Mastercard
  - Discover
  - American Express
  - Apple Pay, Android Pay, and eWallet payments.
- Good for low-volume merchants.
- Ability to store a card on file.
- Full reporting tools.
- End-to-end encryption for transactions.
- Next-business-day deposits.
- No fees for refunds.
- Opt for a small fee for instant funds transfer.
- For bricks-and-mortar stores they have an iPad app available.

The big cons I've seen levelled at Square include:

- Poor customer support (although they aren't on their own for this).
- Disputes tend to go against the merchant in most of the cases.
- Lack of subscription tools.

## Stripe

*www.stripe.com/au*

This is the other 'big' player against Square for the Australian market. Just like Square they support a number of platforms (some via third-party integrations) including:

- SquareSpace
- Woo Commerce
- WordPress
- Shopify
- Xero
- QuickBooks
- MYOB

The pros to Stripe include:

- Transparent, flat-rate pricing.
- Accepts various cards, including:
  - Credit cards
  - Debit cards
  - International cards
  - Wire transfers
  - Bitcoin
- Global scalability and reach (ideal if you think you'll take on international clients).
- No monthly contracts.
- Customisable checkout solution to suit your business.
- Multiple support channels, some available 24/7.

The cons include:

- Slow email response times and other customer support issues.
- Disputes mostly land with the customer and cost the business money.
- Not an easy set-up for those with limited technical understanding.

* * *

When it comes to choosing your payment processing partner, do some research. Tick off the questions we identified earlier and make sure to implement everything you can with the platform. Remember, the end game is to make your customer's life easier and remove any obstacle to doing business with you.

# 16. ACCOUNTING PLATFORMS

There are plenty of advocates for each of the major accounting platforms, so it comes down to understanding exactly what your business requires (perhaps a chat with your accountant) and then looking at a trial option before going 'all in'.

It's not an easy task to transition from one accounting platform to another. So, this is one time you want to slow down and consider all the options before diving in.

My biggest advice for selecting your accounting program: choose the one that you understand the language for and make sure your accountant works inside the program too... I'd even go so far as to say, pay your accountant to set it up for you in the beginning. Getting your chart of accounts right from the start is super important and you really don't want to be trying to fix mistakes in your system years down the track (trust me... I've gone through it and it's absolutely no fun).

## Xero

*www.xero.com/au*

I switched to Xero around ten years ago and haven't looked back. While I might be exceptionally good at what I do, I hate having to spend time in my accounting program getting things right and organising where things should live.

Xero uses plain English throughout their platform, making it easier for non-accountancy type people (like me) to understand where we need to go and what we need to do. It integrates with a bunch of other sites (like Receipt Bank) and makes life much simpler.

Of course, it does all the stuff your accountant wants from you like BAS and payroll. You can even set up reporting metrics on your dashboard, so you have a quick view of exactly what cash on hand you have vs what's outstanding and what's been invoiced.

## Intuit QuickBooks

*quickbooks.intuit.com/au*

Similar to Xero in that this is a full-service accounting package. Connect your bank accounts, run your BAS statements, control your inventory and stock management, and run your payroll.

The edge I see QuickBooks has over Xero is if your business requires you to hold stock. The system does have a better inventory management system, and they've recently added a cash flow management system. Super handy to help you get a handle on what money you really have and where it's coming from.

I moved away from QuickBooks to Xero around ten years ago as I just couldn't get my head around the language QuickBooks used. I've got a number of friends who use QuickBooks though and swear by how good it is... They do seem to have exceptional customer service, which is always a big tick in my books.

## MYOB

*www.myob.com/au/*

Short for Mind Your Own Business, MYOB is another in the list of accounting-based software platforms. MYOB went through some major changes a few years ago as it was slow to move to a cloud-based system – as a result they lost a fair amount of ground to QuickBooks and Xero, especially for small business owners.

They've hit back hard over the last couple of years, putting teams of people on the ground to ensure their customer support levels are high.

## Wave... Mint and InDinnero

If you don't feel like you need all the bells and whistles that Xero, MYOB or QuickBooks offer but you'd like some kind of support with an accounting program then consider reviewing Wave, Mint or InDinerro.

They aren't as fully featured as the big three, nor do they come with the price tags though. Well worth considering if you're testing a minimum viable product (MVP) before launching or you're running a hobby business.

## Thrive

*www.plusthrive.com*

Due for launch some time in 2021 there is still a lot of unknowns about Thrive as a solution. We know it is partnering with Westpac to deliver its banking solutions and it has been created in Melbourne with a pure focus on Australian small businesses.

Thrive's pitch on their homepage is 'We save small businesses time and money by automating banking and accounting admin.' I've included it here as I think it could be an interesting one to watch come to market.

# 17. OTHER THINGS TO CONSIDER...

Remember most of the phishing and scams around these days come down to wanting to access details and ultimately money. (Now's the time to flip back to the security section if you flicked past it and read some of the tips to protect yourself and your clients against these kinds of attacks).

Before we wind out this section it's worthwhile mentioning a few things to remember:

- Don't Google your bank's online address. It's very easy for scammers to create fake links. Instead save your genuine bank login address as a URL that you can go to directly whenever it's needed.
- Don't do your banking or accounts on a public WIFI.
- Don't click any links that come in an email from (what looks like) your bank or your accounting platforms.
- Don't write your customers' credit card details on paper. Use your payment gateway and store the card as it has end-to-end encryption.
- Don't send bank details via messenger apps (like Facebook); these are not encrypted (yet) and are open for hackers to steal.

I have a zero-trust policy when it comes to trusting emails with links (especially when it comes to looking like a financial institution). If in doubt, call your bank to check the validity of what you've received.

Lastly, remember, your clients are trusting you with the card details. Put every measure you can in place to ensure the security of their data and their financial details. This isn't an area you want to skimp on.

## Expense claims

If you're running a team of people and looking for a way you can track the expenses you could use your accounting platform. Some clients are looking for a standalone program though. If that's you, this is the one program I constantly hear good reviews on.

### Expensify

*use.expensify.com*

Is your team wasting time trying to submit an expense claim but never quite giving you the right information? Expensify could solve those problems for you.

Simply scan the receipt and Expensify will automatically submit an expense claim. To make things easier for your admin team they can auto approve expenses with just a couple of clicks or set up a series of automations and approval workflows to automatically approve certain expense claims immediately.

Integrations available with QuickBooks and Xero as well as many others.

## Payroll

Obviously this is only relevant to those running a team of people. Most of my clients tend to integrate their payroll into their accounting platform, however if you're looking for something that stands on it's own then I hear good things about Gusto.

### Gusto

*www.gusto.com*

If your business is new to payroll this could be worth checking out. The platform allows you to create and store onboarding procedures for new team members as well as sending your letters of offer and all contracts.

Once the team is set up you can lean on their commonly used payroll tools to get things humming. While I've not used this platform myself, it gets exceptional ratings from some distinguished reviewers and appears by all accounts to be easy to set up for folks unfamiliar with the world of employees, payroll and obligations.

## Receipt Tracking

Tracking and logging receipts seems to be a task that brings many a business owner unstuck. From shoe boxes laden with fading receipts to heaving envelopes, we need a better way to monitor receipts in our business. Most accounting platforms will have a place you can upload and enter receipts; if you're looking for something independent that's quick and easy to access here's a couple of options to consider.

### Squirrel Street (formerly Shoeboxed)

*www.squirrelstreet.com*

An online invoice and receipt management system. The big difference I see with Squirrel Street is that someone is entering and validating your receipts for you. They then categorise your receipts for you, making them easier to find and retrieve if needed. Next you provide your bookkeeper or accountant with access to your Squirrel Street account and they can access all the data as needed. If you prefer you can directly upload the information to your accounting software platform of choice.

While Squirrel Street gets great reviews and is ATO compliant, I have to admit to being a little nervous about sending my hard copy receipts off in the first place; seems there's a gap in the process there that should an envelope go missing, you're left in the lurch without a backup.

**Receipt Bank**

*www.receipt-bank.com/au*

This is the one the majority of my small business buddies use, and it seems to be the one most recommended by accountants.

While a similar concept to some of the others mentioned above, Receipt Bank allows you to capture, record and store all of your receipts, invoices and accounts in the one location while connecting your accounting program of choice. Receipt Bank automates the process of logging all of your receipts, invoices and accounts while connecting them to your accounting platform.

## Money-focused data

By the time you make it all the way through this book you'll figure out that one of the things I get most excited about watching small business owners digitise their business is them embracing the power of understanding the data technology offers them.

**To me data is knowledge and knowledge is power.**

This is true in your marketing, in your sales, in your productivity and in your money.

Whichever accounting package you have elected to use (or select if you're not quite there yet) you'll see a section referring to either your dashboard or reports.

This is the section I'd love you to spend some time to set up. Either walk through the help section within your accounting platform or ask your accountant to help you set it up.

Having an easy-to-read dashboard will keep you completely aware of how your business is tracking, and allow you to begin thinking of areas where you can either cut the expenses or increase your sales.

Now before I share my advice on the reports to set up, let me remind you, I have 30 years' experience in sales and marketing... and finance. While I've been a business owner for more than ten years (and I've made my fair share of mistakes in that time), I'm not the person you want to be seeking accounting or cash flow advice from. So... organise a time to chat with your accountant to make sure you completely understand your numbers and what reports they think you should have set up.

In saying that, these are the ones I always want at my fingertips when I log in to my account.

### Accounts receivable (AR) aging

This tells me at a glance who owes me money and how overdue it is. My accountant once said to me if you have too many people sitting here you either have no process telling people how to work with you or you're working with the wrong people.

### Cash flow report

I want to see what I have in the bank today, what I have to pay out and who owes me money that's outstanding. This (at times) can be a confronting report to look at, but if you're in business for yourself, you need to know it.

### Accounts payable

This tells me who I owe what to and when. A simple report but super important.

### Revenue by customer

This report tells me which of my clients is worth the most in terms of revenue and what they're spending month to month. Knowing this, I can see at a glance if the majority of my money is coming from one or two clients or more. Knowing this allows me to ensure I'm not going to bottom out if the work suddenly stops.

### Profit and loss (P&L)

A traditional report that lets you know how the business is tracking over a period of time. While this is a super important report it's not one I'll check every day. Definitely one worth spending time with your accountant to understand what all the numbers mean though.

### Balance sheet

Like the profit and loss report this isn't something I'd refer to every day; it is one that you need to understand. It essentially gives you a snapshot of what your business has and what your business owes at any one time. Another one that's important to sit down with your accountant and make sure you completely understand.

## Money and accounting tips, tricks and hacks

Ok, maybe less of the hacks and more of the tips and tricks I've picked up around the technology along the way.

### Xero

If you're a Xero user, you're going to love some of these.

Email an invoice or bill direct to Xero for coding:

- Log in to your account.
- Click on your account name (top left).
- Select 'Files' in the drop-down menu.
- On the right of that page you will find an email address which is specific to your account.
- Save the email address as a contact so you can add it easily to emails.

Create a quick login to Xero:

- login.xero.com/?username=REPLACE_WITH_YOUR_USERNAME
- All you need to do is login with your password.

View multiple pages within your organisation in Xero:

- To open a link in a new tab on a PC, right-click on a link and select Open a new Tab.
- To open a link in a new tab on a Mac, hold down the Command key and click on the link.

If you need to look at multiple organisations at the same time:

- Open them in different browsers e.g. one in Safari and one in Chrome.
- If you open them in the same browser the information can be accidently cross saved.

You can have multiple people logged in and working in your account at the same time. If they're working on the same item, whoever saves last will have their changes applied.

You can create favourite reports through the advanced settings tab.

If you use G Suite you can approve Xero to access Google Sheets, then share any report you like directly with your Google account.

Xero also has a list of keyboard shortcuts which can be extremely useful. To find these go to:

www.central.xero.com/s/article/Tips-and-shortcuts#Dateentry shortcuts.

### MYOB

MYOB also has a list of keyboard shortcuts you can access inside the program. To check these out go to:

help.myob.com.au/prem19/win/introduction_18.004.htm.

### QuickBooks

Did you know you can set up split-screen monitors in QuickBooks? To do that go here and walk through the instructions to suit if you're an Apple or PC user:

www.quickbooks.intuit.com/learn-support/en-us/display-preferences/use-quickbooks-on-multiple-screens-or-in-multi-monitor-mode/00/186043#.

There are a bunch of other keyboard shortcuts available in QuickBooks; you can check them all out and choose the ones you like here:

www.quickbooks.intuit.com/learn-support/en-uk/configure-products/keyboard-shortcuts-for-quickbooks-online/01/239027#M1300.

\* \* \*

If you have a CRM (Customer Relationship Manager), check whether you can integrate your accounting software with the program. Doing that opens up a world of additional access and possibilities.

If you don't have a CRM, keep reading, we cover them later in the book and hopefully have you committed to implementing and using one real soon.

Ok, heavy lifting done. Time to review what you took away from this section and make a note of the things you need to follow up on.

Once you've done that, go for a walk or call a friend (or your mum) for a chat. Your brain needs a rest.

# SECTION FIVE

# WORKING REMOTELY

# 18. WHAT DOES IT MEAN TO 'WORK REMOTELY'?

I feel like we need to break our lives into 'before COVID' and 'post-COVID'... only a few months ago, if I was chatting with someone about working remotely it would mean they were looking at packing up their car, grabbing their laptop and hitting the road. Looking to find locations they could do a bit of work while they were out seeing the countryside, or the world.

For others, it meant they wanted to be able to get work done while they were in a coffee shop around the corner from home, snatching a few precious moments before their next client, or their next meeting.

Since COVID though we've all experienced in one way or another a new definition of remote working.

For some, it was trying to work from the dining table, while their partner had the spare room and the kids were trying to learn in the lounge room or their bedrooms. For others it meant needing to set their staff up to be able to work from home, finding secure ways to connect to the internet, to collaborate with other team members and to remain connected to the business as a whole.

Whatever your circumstances were, there's no doubt we've all learned that (most) businesses can function without the need of bricks-and-mortar premises... Or at least without the need for premises full time.

The conversations I've had with small business owners throughout the COVID experience, and more so as we're emerging into our post COVID business realities, have all been around the need to be more fluid in the way they do business. Small businesses are mostly looking now to be agile, to be lean with their costs and to better understand how the digital landscape can help them refine, reinvigorate or redesign their business.

Whether you're looking for ways to streamline what your business developed during COVID or you'd like to pack your life into a suitcase and wander the world while keeping your business profitable and connected, this section on working remotely will have tips, tricks and ideas you can easily implement right now to make an immediate difference to your business and personal life.

## Places you can work from when you're on the road

Over the past decade my hubby Peter and I have worked from some pretty weird and wonderful places. As long as we have an internet connection we're good to go; this has meant I've hosted group calls with clients from the front seat of my car in Cann River (in the East Gippsland area of Victoria), a pub in Woolgoolga (mid north coast NSW), libraries in far too many towns to mention, cafes, and even picnic tables overlooking oceans and lookouts up and down the East Coast of Australia.

There are definitely some better places to set yourself up if you plan to work remotely, and some you probably want to avoid unless you find yourself stuck. And to be honest it depends on what type of work you need to get done. If you need to speak with clients, suppliers or team members it's probably best you find yourself a quieter place (like a library) where you can spread out and won't be interrupted... there's nothing worse or more distracting than to have a waitress or patrons wandering past in the background of your video call or stopping to take an order while you're trying to go deep and meaningful with a client. You also need to consider the privacy implications of your discussions if you're operating from a cafe. What data could be seen by people wandering past while you're chatting?

## Libraries

The notion of the old stuffy library where you can't make noise for fear of earning the wrath of the librarian is gone. In fact, libraries are one of my favourite places to host video conference calls when I'm on the road.

With a little prior research, you'll find that most libraries will have little meeting rooms you can book (often for free) that are private, and have power, so it's a double win being able to charge your device while chatting with your client.

The biggest bonus to this is they'll usually have very clean public facilities on hand! Another thing that's often hard to find when you're on the road.

## Cafés and pubs

Depending on the location and the time of day you'll often find a quiet little corner you can ensconce yourself in for an hour or two.

I do believe there is some etiquette to working from a café, a restaurant or a pub, and that is you need to spend some money. These places are often owned and operated by other small businesses, so please be mindful that sitting at a table for 8 hours to get your emails answered and your invoices up to date with nothing more than a cup of coffee will not be looked upon favourably.

I enjoy working from cafés mid-morning and mid-afternoon, there's something about the hum of people chatting about their lives over coffee that is the right mix of 'white noise' for creativity. I'll always make sure I order some kind of drink and usually a cake or sandwich to go with it. I always ask if they mind if I do a little work while sitting, and I keep half an eye open to what's happening around me. If I see them filling up with patrons who want the table, I'll pack up and move on ... or order something else.

## Shopping centre food courts

Much like a cafe, you can always be guaranteed of white noise in a shopping centre food court.

The big bonus a food court has over an independent cafe though is there is no expectation to purchase food or drinks to keep your table. If I have a big day of admin tasks or content creation, I can easily spend a good six to eight hours working from a food court.

Another bonus of the food court is if you're able to get there early enough you'll find a prime position near a power outlet... very handy indeed if you think you're in for the long haul.

Be mindful what you work on in a place as open as a shopping centre food court though; you never really know who's reading things over your shoulder or eavesdropping on conversations.

### Hotel foyers

This one only works if you have larger, 4- or 5-star hotels in the area you'll be staying.

I've found the foyers of these hotels fabulous to work from. They're usually spacious, well appointed, and for the most part busy enough that you won't be bothered by the staff.

Amenities are clean and they usually have their own coffee shop on hand so that you have enough room to move around throughout the day.

Bonus: if you find yourself working into the evening, they usually have great wine and cocktail menus to celebrate a hard day's work.

### Local co-working or hot desk places

This one depends on where you're travelling and doing a little prior research, but the local co-working and hot desk offices are worth getting to know. Especially if you have client-facing work to do (like Zoom calls).

You can be guaranteed of a little privacy, you'll have access to power, and usually clean amenities. The big bonus, you'll be able to leave your stuff strewn across the desk while you nick to the bathroom or to make yourself a cuppa... something you're unlikely to be doing operating from a public space like a food court.

Be prepared to pay to utilise these facilities, anything from $20 for the day through to a couple of hundred, depending on the 'brand' of the co-working facility and the location.

I usually find these places by Googling or contacting the local Chamber of Commerce when I get to town.

### Chambers of commerce and associations

This one is particularly helpful if you know you're going to be in town for a few days or longer.

Many of us are already members of various associations and perhaps our local chambers of commerce. Why not reach out to them and see if they have any reciprocal arrangements with anyone in the area you're travelling?

This one may take a little forward planning, but you can snag some great working spaces just by asking the question of your membership associations.

### Use your network

The other thing I've found extremely helpful when I'm working remotely is to put a call out to my community and let them know where I'm going to be and for how long. I'll let them know what I'm looking for, (e.g.: quiet desk with access to power and clean amenities) and I have to say in doing that I've been surprised at the number of times people have tagged friends in that town to introduce me.

I've often found a 'home' for a day or two for the cost of a good conversation with another business owner and maybe a lunch as a thank you.

### Your accommodation

This one has to be said. If you know you'll need to work while you're 'on the road' then put a little thought into what and where your accommodation will be.

Whenever I travel now, I'll look for an apartment over a hotel room. Not only does it give me a kitchen and laundry room to help lessen travelling costs, but they almost always have a good desk to work at.

The benefit of working from your accommodation is privacy. You know you'll be able to communicate with whomever you want without concerns of someone looking over your shoulder or listening to your conversation.

My only advice on this one is to ask what their internet reception is like before booking. I've made the mistake before of getting (what

I thought) was the perfect room to work in for a few days, only to find I couldn't get any kind of internet reception until I went to the coffee shop downstairs.

* * *

So, you see, with a little forethought and creative thinking, you'll never be stuck for a place to work while you're on the road.

My caveat to all of the above is this: do not under any circumstances utilise the public WIFI in any of these places without first getting yourself a VPN. I talk more about that in the section on 'security'. Let it be enough to say here *don't do it!*

When I find myself working from remote spaces (like any of the above) I tend to tether my phone to my laptop and rely on my own mobile data. The data plans you can get for mobiles now are ridiculously cheap for the amount of data you get... again, I'll share a little more on that shortly.

## Choose your devices

One of the most frequently asked questions I get from folks who want to be able to work well from wherever they find themselves is this: *What device or devices do I need ... and why?*

Let me start by asking you what you would 'normally' use when you're in your office? I have my phone (currently the iPhone 11 pro max) and a laptop. However, Peter struggles to use a laptop as he's become so adept at running his business from his phone and his iPad.

So, as with so many things in life, it comes down to 'what are you most comfortable with?' Don't go buying a bunch of new equipment just because you want to hit the road for a few days, weeks or months. Get the best equipment that you'd use in your everyday life and then make the remote working lifestyle fit in with what you have.

Ask yourself what you'll need to be doing while you're away from your base.

For most of us this will include:

· **Some admin tasks** – answering emails, sending quotes, checking on client deliverables, etc.

· **Some finance tasks** – entering receipts, raising invoices, chasing payments, etc.

· **Maybe some marketing tasks** – newsletters, landing pages, social media updates, maybe some blogging or videos, etc.

· **Checking in with clients** – phone calls, Zoom and email.

· **Checking in with suppliers** – phone calls, Zoom and email.

· **Checking in with your team** – phone calls, Zoom and email.

· **Checking in with your family and friends** – phone calls, Zoom and email.

While you can do all of the above tasks from your smartphone, if you're anything like me (fat fingers) you'll find the process extremely frustrating.

So, first of all, just like when you're based from your office, you'll need a good smartphone, and you'll need either a laptop or a tablet, depending on what you're more comfortable working on usually.

The only thing you'll need to take into consideration is which applications, websites and software platforms you use day to day in your business. And make sure that those platforms will operate to their full functionality on a tablet or laptop. The features available on a smartphone or tablet for a system that you use do not always match what's available on your desktop computer in your office.

We've had firsthand experience with this using G Suite. Using Google Docs or Sheets is super easy on a laptop (you can even have an offline version to work on if you know you'll be out of coverage for a time), but trying to get Google Docs to work as seamlessly on a tablet or a smartphone … well, let's just say, I haven't had the patience to make that happen, yet.

# 19. DON'T FORGET TO PACK...

When I was travelling a lot (you know, back before COVID and 'iso'), I had a special remote working travel kit that would stay packed ready for each trip. The pack had developed over years of short and long trips, spending far too many evenings wishing I'd brought this, that or the other thing. It got to the point after a while where each time I'd think of something, I'd go buy it and put it in my travel bag.

You may not need everything in your travel kit that I need as I'm often travelling to deliver workshops, training or keynotes, but as you read through, I'm sure you'll be able to create your own perfect working remotely travel kit from the list below.

These days I don't have to run through a mental checklist, I just grab my bag and I'm good to go.

To write this section, I've unpacked my travel bag to lay the contents bare so you can create your own kit fit for purpose:

- **A power board** – can't tell you how many times I've checked into a hotel and looked in vain for a spare power point. If you don't want to be unplugging the lamp in the corner to find somewhere to charge your phone, a power board is the first thing to go on your list. I also recommend you look for a power board with a few USB slots in it. It makes charging your devices that much simpler.

- **An external phone battery charger** (or power bank as they're sometimes known) – my favourite accommodation in Ballina,

Northern NSW only has power points beside one side of the bed, frustrating if you like to have your phone on charge beside you to act as an alarm clock. I always make sure to have a 'power bank' with me to charge my phone overnight (and then remember to put the power bank on charge through the day when I'm out).

- **A various assortment of charging leads** – I usually carry two or three different lengths for my phone, my watch charger, and power bank charger. It's good to have an assortment of sizes, depending on which devices (and ages of the devices) you use.

- **An extension cord** – Just like the power board, it's come in handy on more than one occasion to have an extension cord in the bag.

- **Various adaptors to fit my Mac** – this one is more for anyone speaking or presenting who travels. The number of times I've got to a venue to set up only to find their projector (or TV) needs a special type of adaptor... I always carry every type of Mac connector I can find with me; it's saved me on more than one occasion.

- **Google Chromecast** – this one is more for my own amusement of an evening or during downtime. I've discovered that in most places I stay the TV has a HDMI port, meaning I can plug in my Chromecast and keep up to date with my favourite streaming shows while I'm away.

- **First aid kit** – I recommend having a remote working 'first aid kit' which includes things like:
  - Paracetamol
  - Ibuprofen
  - Cold and flu medication
  - Cough syrup
  - Multivitamins
  - Herbal sleep formula
  - Bandaids
  - As well as a backup supply of any regular medications you may require in your daily life.

- **A backup set of glasses and sunglasses** – this one has caught me out before. Now I make sure I have a pair of glasses (usually my last prescription) that stay in my travel case. If for any reason I forget or lose them (like has happened to me), I'm not stranded without good vision.

- **An HDMI cord** – having my own HDMI cord has saved my skin more than once when I've arrived somewhere to find their cord is broken or can't be found. Again, only relevant to some.

- **A spare HDMI cord of a different length** – same as above, just in case yours fails, or isn't long enough.

- **A backup laptop charger** – nothing worse than being away from home and having no way to charge your laptop.

- **My mobile WIFI dongle** – I carry a prepaid mobile WIFI with each of the three carriers (Telstra, Optus and Voda). It's hard to know which area will have the strongest reception and sometimes you'll need to bounce between a few to get your work done.

- **A backup laptop** – I only go to this level of preparation IF I'm off to do a big presentation... I refuse to be caught out by my laptop deciding not to play nicely with others when I have a group of folks waiting for me. If you're not travelling to present though I'd suggest this one is overkill.

- **USB stick with my presentation as a backup and my laser pointer and charger** – again, these ones are more for my fellow presenters, but have saved my skin having my presentation backed up to the cloud and to a USB 'just in case'. You may also consider emailing a copy of your presentation ahead of time to the organiser, just to be sure.

- **Travel printer** – again, only if I know I'm presenting, and I may need to quickly print off additional materials. I'll always have my workbooks, etc. backed up on a USB stick so I can outsource them to an Officeworks or the like, but sometimes you may be travelling where you don't have that luxury. That's where your travel printer can come in real handy.

You may find it interesting to know that I also have a travel bag of makeup and toiletries prepacked. It makes life so much easier to just grab my travel kits anytime I have to pack and not worry about whether I've got shampoo or my toothbrush or makeup for my first meeting. It also makes packing for any trip a whole lot easier; I have a bunch of containers with my various bits in them that I can grab at a moment's notice and throw into a bag and be out the door.

The point is, think about the things related to your business and personal life that are 'mission critical' – what do you absolutely need to continue to run your business? Once you know what that is, you've got your remote working travel kit ready to go!

# 20. NOT ALL MOBILE PROVIDERS (OR DATA PLANS) ARE CREATED EQUAL

If you're planning on doing a bit of travelling, even if your plans are just to be able to work from coffee shops or other 'out of office' locations as needed, then one of the biggest boxes you'll need to tick is having access to reliable data.

Ten years ago, when I started spending more and more of my time as a 'laptop business', the biggest expense I had was maintaining data. These days though data plans are as cheap as chips, but there are still a few things you'll need to consider before you make your decisions around providers.

Where are you planning to travel? If the majority of your travel is within metro or capital city areas, then you'll find 'most' of your major providers will be fine to commit too. However, if having access to data is mission critical, I've found it's worthwhile considering access to more than one provider. While it may seem strange, I've found myself on more than one occasion sitting in the heart of Sydney and Melbourne CBD and unable to access decent data from one of the Big Three providers and needing to transfer to another provider just to be able to connect a Zoom call.

If you're looking to go a little more regional then you'll need to do some research as to who your best option will be. By far currently we find that Telstra still holds ground for regional connectivity, yet in some of the regional mining communities in WA or remote QLD the companies have struck deals with Vodaphone and I find myself only being able to connect and work utilising the Vodaphone network.

My suggestion is if you'll be travelling throughout various regions grab yourself a prepaid sim from a number of different providers with the best data plan at the time and keep all of them topped up. Having the peace of mind of being able to switch sims and activate a different network when needed is far simpler than connecting to public WIFI (which is often horrendously slow and fraught with security and privacy issues – refer to the earlier section on VPNs and Public WIFI for more information on this).

What tasks are you needing to complete?

Different software platforms will require different amounts of data to substantiate and maintain a connection. A 2017 study from Deloitte shared that around 63% of Aussies have no idea how much data they actually use each month. If you plan on becoming savvier around remote working you're going to need to get a better understanding of what data you're using and for what tasks.

Checking and replying to emails, for example, is quite a low data requirement. Hosting or participating in Zoom calls, uploading videos or streaming a Netflix show at the end of the day ... well, that's going to take a bit more of your data allocation.

Having a good understanding of where your time and activities are spent online will give you a good understanding of the level of data you'll need to have access to on a monthly basis.

| Task | Amount of data required per hour* |
|---|---|
| General web browsing (such as reading the news) | Approx. 60Mb per hour |
| Send or receive an email (no attachments) | Approx. 5Mb per email |
| Scrolling Facebook (no video) | Approx. 150Mb per hour |
| Scrolling Facebook (video) | Approx. 160Mb per hour |
| Scrolling Instagram | Approx. 750Mb per hour |
| Uploading an image to social media | Approx. 5Mb per photo |
| Streaming YouTube videos | Approx. 360Mb per hour |

| Task | Amount of data required per hour* |
|------|-----------------------------------|
| Streaming podcasts | Approx. 60Mb per hour |
| Streaming music | Approx. 150Mb per hour |
| One-to-one Zoom calls | Approx. 1Gb per hour |
| Group Zoom calls | Approx. 1.3Gb per hour |
| Watching Netflix in standard definition | Approx. 1Gb per hour |

\* The key to everything listed above is they are averages. The actual amount of data you will use will depend on the quantity and quality of what you're streaming (e.g. lower quality or higher quality video).

Before choosing your data plan, take a look at an 'average' workday and get a sense of what tasks you would be conducting. For example, if I look at a typical day in my calendar last week, I'd see the following:

| Task | Time | Data Used |
|------|------|-----------|
| Zoom calls/webinars | 3 hours | 3Gb |
| Emails | 1 hour | 50Mb |
| General web browsing | 1 hour | 60Mb |
| Social media | 1 hour | 150Mb |
| Working in Google docs | 2 hours | 120Mb |
| Chilling with Netflix | 1.5 hours | 1.5Gb |
| Total approx. data usage each day | | Under 5Gb |

Working on an average of 5Gb per day and relying solely on mobile data, I'd need to look for a minimum of 150Gb per month plan to meet requirements.

## What kind of speeds are the data plans offering?

Not dissimilar to the above point, knowing what tasks you'll likely be completing on a daily basis will give you a good idea of what speeds you'll likely need to have access to, to complete your work without waiting for hours for things to happen.

There's nothing worse than trying to watch something on Netflix (or upload a video) and have the buffering issues kick in. Understanding your requirements will give you a good idea of what speeds you'll need.

## The difference between bits and bytes

Just to make things even more confusing, data is explained in downloads and speed. These are calculated using two different measurements. Data downloads are measured in 'bytes' while speed is measured in 'bits':

- Downloads are measured in bytes: Megabytes (Mb), Gigabytes (Gb), etc. Each increment is 1000x larger than the one before it. So, if you needed to download a file that was 500Mb, you would use 0.5Gb of data.

- When we talk about internet speed we are talking about 'bits' or Megabits per second (MBPS). There are 8 bits (of speed) in a byte (of data). So, if you run a speed check on your modem and you're seeing a connection speed of 100Mbps, it means you could download 12.5Mb of data each second. So, if you find a movie you'd like to watch and it's 1Gb in size, it will take your internet 80 seconds to download the movie.

Do you need a 'mobile broadband' or can you get away with a generous data plan on your mobile phone? If you're planning on travelling a lot or being away for long periods of time, I'd recommend looking at mobile broadband.

Mobile broadband is basically like the WIFI you have at home ... but mobile. You'll get a 'device', which – depending on which provider you decide to go with – will be quite compact and easy to travel with.

I find my mobile broadband super easy to set up and connect to. Once you're through the set-up phase your devices (phones, laptops, etc.) will automatically connect, just as they would to your WIFI at home or at the office.

I use one and leave it connected in my accommodation to act as my WIFI throughout my stay. You'll pay a few hundred dollars for the device in order to get a prepaid account, or you can connect on a plan and get the device included. It will also save you burning through the battery on your mobile phone (using your phone as a hotspot chews through your battery life super quick).

I maintain a large data plan on my mobile phone as well to ensure when I'm working from a cafe for a few hours or want to stream a podcast while I'm driving, I have sufficient data to allow me to do what needs to be done.

The general rule of thumb has been that fixed data (like your home WIFI) has traditionally been cheaper than using a mobile solution or your phone... Things are changing though, and plans change every other week. So, the big takeaway here is stay flexible with your choices and watch out for 'legacy' plans (a legacy plan is an old plan the provider no longer offers). A perfect example of this is we recently gave my Dad an iPhone. He's been on the same $15 per month Optus plan since I set him up in the early '90s. Until now he'd never used his phone for anything other than phone calls. If we'd not been aware of his plan, he would have racked up a $300 data bill in the first couple of days of having his phone just by watching his YouTube clips and checking Facebook!

## Tips to conserve your data

- Set your Netflix or movie streaming channel of choice to only stream in SD (Standard Definition. Some are set to HD High Definition by default).
- Only upload your photos or videos to your cloud service when connected to your WIFI.
- Download your music, podcasts and audiobooks when your phone has access to WIFI.

- Complete any computer or phone software upgrades when connected to your WIFI.
- Keep an eye on your phone's data settings and monitor which apps are using the most data – you may be able to switch some of them off if not needed.
- Turn off video autoplay on your social media platforms.

## Other things to consider when looking at mobile data plans

- Maintain flexibility and where possible look at prepaid plans. My main reasoning for this is simple: if you're on a prepaid plan you can easily manoeuvre wherever the best deals are at the time. If you lock yourself into a contract, well, you're locked in. Flexibility when working remotely is vital.
- If you're travelling or working remotely with a partner, take into consideration whether your data plan will allow you to 'share' or gift data to another account. I've often found it handy over the years to hand off excess data to Peter before he's headed off on a solo trip. If you're working together then you can often tether or hotspot to each other's devices to maximise coverage and data plans.
- If you can't data share, look at whether your plan will allow you to roll data over. (Put simply, rolling your data over means you can 'bank' it to use the following month.) This can be extremely handy if you find yourself at home for a few months (hello COVID) but know you'll be away for a stretch of a few months. Being able to roll your data over can help you out with future planning trips.
- Keep an eye on your data usage. The big three providers in Australia all have great mobile applications where you can see at a glance how you're tracking with your data usage vs the number of days you have remaining before your next bill cycle. Keeping an eye on this has saved me from bill shock (see next point) more times than I can tell you. You may even be able to set up a text message alert for when you are getting close to your data limit.

- Watch out for additional data charges. This one catches more people out than anything else. If you're not monitoring your data, you can find yourself with a nasty 'bill shock' as most companies will charge around $10 per additional Gb of data once you've reached your monthly limit... and they don't give you warning!

# 21. MANAGING STAFF

One of the greatest challenges to working remotely is managing your team. Whether you have a group of people all working back in an office or you're dealing with contractors across the world, keeping everyone facing in the same direction and working together can be difficult.

Fortunately, through the collaboration tools available now, this is becoming less of an obstacle. Here a few things to keep in mind if you're looking to work remotely or have a remote team:

**Make your expectations very clear early on and (gently) remind the team as needed:**

- Often your team will need more guidelines on work/life balance if they work remotely. Remind them not to burn themselves out.

- Continue to have key milestones and KPIs the team are accountable for, and are aware of.

**Communication:**

- Ensure there are opportunities to discuss and collaborate.

- Be prepared to adapt. Shorter, more frequent virtual catch-ups may work better than longer in-person gatherings.

- Consider a platform like 'Slack', 'Microsoft Teams' or 'Google Workplace' where the staff can be chatting or have calls as needed.

- Keep people updated with deadlines, and let them know how things are tracking.

- Check in often and be prepared to make changes based on feedback.

**Get organised:**

- Have all your policies and procedures in place.
- Have everything in a cloud-based platform which is easily accessed by everybody.
- Make sure everyone knows where to go for information.
- Be prepared to be flexible: Does it really matter when your team put their hours in if the work gets done?

**Operations:**

- Decide who needs access to what.

**Logistics:**

- Decide what you need to track.
- Continue to work to a schedule, maybe look to implement a project management system (such as Trello) to track progress.

**Provide the right collaboration tools:**

- Platforms like Google and Microsoft have systems where multiple people can be working on the same document at the same time.
- Having the right tools in place will ensure remote working success.

**Resist the urge to shadow your team:**

- You've chosen your people for their roles for a reason, let them do what you've employed them to do.

**Celebrate the wins:**

- Look for ways you can share the successes and celebrate the wins in a way that includes the entire team.

There are two main systems for consideration in a collaborative environment: Google or Microsoft. (Okay, there are other options, but from a small business perspective it's Google and Microsoft.)

Let's take a look at the two of them side by side...

| Feature | Google G Suite | Microsoft 365 |
|---|:---:|:---:|
| Business email and shared calendars | ✓ | ✓ |
| Online storage and personal space allocation | ✓ | ✓ |
| Productivity apps: spreadsheet, presentations and word processing | ✓ | ✓ |
| In team communication: messaging, online meetings and video conferencing | ✓ | ✓ |
| Security and admin features | ✓ | ✓ |
| Simultaneous editing of documents in the web browser | ✓ | ✓ |

The big differences come into play with the features you require within your own business. For example, if you're familiar with Word and create a lot of documentation in your business then there's no doubt that Word is a fuller featured word processor compared to Google Docs. The same goes for Excel vs Google Sheets.

But... with Microsoft comes the price tag.

While with both platforms you will pay per month per user, the difference between price points between the two systems is significant. From a collaboration standpoint though there's no doubt being able to have a few team members in the one document all working to achieve the best result fosters efficiency, camaraderie and collaboration.

The one thing I will say on choosing your platform. Hasten slowly. My business has been with Google G Suite for around seven years and we're in the middle of doing analysis on whether we actually need the fuller functionality that Microsoft includes. If we do jump (and I have to say, I really don't want to), it's going to be a massive undertaking. So, really do a full needs analysis on what your requirements are before committing to a solution... you don't want to be seven years down the track and thinking about shifting thousands of documents and communications over.

# 22. OTHER COOL GADGETS, APPS AND SOFTWARE THAT ARE AWESOME FOR WORKING REMOTELY

Along the way there's been a bunch of other cool things I've tripped across that have made a huge difference to the way I work when I'm away from my office. Some are apps, some are software and others are bits of tech that I've accumulated. There's no particular order to them, but I thought you might enjoy checking them out.

## Grid It organiser

One of the things that used to drive me nuts when I was travelling heaps was opening my laptop case and finding all of my cords had decided to create some kind of weird cord mosh pit in the 15 minutes (or 15 hours) it took to reach my location. I'm not the most patient of people to begin with, but having to unravel my various chargers just to get myself set up for work was enough to drive me to drink.

First of all, I started wrapping them individually with an elastic band, but this was time-consuming too. Then I discovered the 'Grid it' organiser.

Imagine a flat board with interwoven stretch bands. You pull back a band and slide your charger in – repeat this over and over with each item until you have all your cords set up in a nice, orderly board.

It's the simple things that make me happy, and this makes me smile every time I think about it.

Check them out at Cocoon Innovations – there's a stack of different styles available and dozens of possible uses: www.cocooninnovations. com.

## Morphie powerstation

I always carry my powerstation when I'm travelling; it's a little chunky for the handbag but this thing packs a punch. It's got enough grunt to charge my laptop and my phone at the same time.

Super handy, but not cheap (a couple of hundred dollars). But OH so worth it.

You'll find them at most big retailers.

## Bose Soundlink Micro Bluetooth Speaker

We all need good-quality sound when we're away, not to mention if you're running a workshop or presentation and you want a backup… just in case.

This little speaker is about half the size of an iPhone in height and not much wider – it pack a punch with its sound quality. Battery life is excellent and it's super quick to set up.

Considering it's a Bose it's a pretty good price too.

## Satechi Aluminum Multi-Port USB-C Adapter

These types of adapters are critical to have on hand if you're a presenter of any description. Nothing gives you heart palpitations more than arriving somewhere to find the venue has different connection points to your device.

This multi-port adapter has saved my skin on more than one occasion.

## Foldable Bluetooth keyboard

Not such a biggie for me (I work from a laptop when I'm away) but before Pete (my hubby) moved to the keyboard with his iPad I would find myself occasionally needing to log in and respond to a few quick things from his device and feeling lost without my keyboard.

The foldable Bluetooth keyboards are super easy to connect and work well for what they are. If you'd like a bit more flexibility with your tablet, they're a great option to consider.

## Anker PowerConf Bluetooth Speaker

Now, I haven't actually purchased this one myself but it's on my 'wish list' (Anker, if you're reading this, I'll happily provide my address and offer a review).

It's a portable Bluetooth speaker with six microphones built in, meaning you can take this thing on the road and hold a conference call (or record a group conversation) without stressing about everyone hearing each other.

## GPS Logbook

One of the things I hated about travelling so much was having to maintain a logbook for the ATO. It's time consuming and just boring to do. A number of years ago we came across GPS Logbooks and these days we just wouldn't be without it.

Essentially, it's your logbook connected to GPS. So, it automatically tracks where you've been and gives you the list on Google Maps. You can pop client addresses in (and it remembers them) and the app will log all the details on your behalf.

Best of all its ATO compliant, so you can just load up the data and away you go.

## Remarkable 2

The Remarkable has been around for a couple of years now and suits my personality. I still like to take handwritten notes when I'm in workshops or meeting with clients, but I can never find what I've done with them after I start a new book. I'm also a doodler to help me think when in a learning environment.

The Remarkable provides you the feeling of writing on paper while still being digital. All it does is allow you to take notes... not connect to the internet, not get distracted by Facebook... Just notes.

I've been using mine for a few months now and I'm absolutely loving it. Definitely a device to consider if you're someone who enjoys the art of note taking.

\* \* \*

Well, that's it. The end of another section. How are you feeling about all the information we just went through?

Any changes for you to make with your remote working set-up? What about your staff and clients? Any adjustments you've recognised you could integrate into the business?

Take some time while it's still fresh to jot down a few notes. Maybe research some of my favourite remote working tools and see if anything floats your boat.

When you're done, get up and have a big stretch. Maybe download a podcast and go for a walk. Then, when you're ready, I'll see you back for the next section, and some advanced warning: it's the chunkiest section in the entire book.

# SECTION SIX

# MARKETING

# Egon in the room

**THIS SECTION IS** the l-o-n-g-e-s-t section you'll read in this book. You'll need plenty of breaks where you can stretch (maybe download one of the yoga apps before we even start so you're prepared). There's a very good reason for it though... If you're reading this book, then there's a very good chance you own your own business. And, I'm going to go so far as to say one of your biggest frustrations in your business is how to market yourself.

Websites have been around long enough now that we all (kinda) get that we need to have one (even if there are cobwebs growing over it and the last blog was from sometime in the late 1990s) and we've even come to acknowledge we need some kind of social media... although what that is, what we do with it and how it actually adds value (if at all) is still up for great discussion.

The point is, after 30 years I know there is a lot more 'stuff' to chat about in marketing than any of the other sections. So, grab yourself a water (you'll need to stay hydrated for this) and get comfy. We're about to cover a whole lot of stuff that could turn your world upside down.

Oh, the other thing I need to mention is you'll see a lot of screenshots as examples in this section. Hopefully this will make it easier for you to follow along. I've created everything from an Apple laptop, which means if you're viewing from a mobile or a PC things will look a little different. And that's okay, different is good... we embrace difference. Just be aware that if it doesn't look exactly like it does in the book it doesn't mean you're wrong or I'm wrong.

Oh, and if you come across something that is irrelevant to what you're looking at doing, then you have my permission to skip over it. No point wasting time on things you're never going to do.

Okay ... elephant addressed ... let's get on with it.

# 23. WHERE TECHNOLOGY CAN (POTENTIALLY) HAVE THE BIGGEST IMPACT

Without a doubt marketing is the area in your business where technology can (potentially) have the biggest impact.

When I first started working in the technology area in 1990 it was rare a business was sending emails on a daily basis. There were still a lot of faxes, and we were just becoming comfortable with the idea of having a mobile phone (though they were still the size of house bricks).

As consumers, we would pore through the catalogues that retailers created and would gain most of our marketing information from TV or radio advertisements. We certainly weren't looking at companies' websites or checking out their Google My Business page to see what other consumers had thought about their experience with a company or product.

Yet in three short decades, you are no longer considered a 'real' business if your prospective clients can't easily navigate your website. Never mind the expectation that you'll feature on at least one or two social media platforms and be able to respond to a client enquiry via mobile, email and messenger. If clients can't easily Google you and learn about your services and previous client experiences, you're dead in the water.

The digital tools we now have at our fingertips to understand our clients mean we no longer need to assume anything about them. Smart business owners understand from websites, social media and their CRM exactly how many people are visiting their websites, at what times, from where, what device they're using, how long they're hanging around, where their mouse hovered on the site, what buttons they clicked and where they went after visiting you. The data and analytics is not only easy to set up but critical to the success of your business moving forward.

**Remember, data is knowledge and knowledge is power.**

It's not a stretch to say that we have reached a point with technology that we can accurately predict our return on marketing investment as well as being able to accurately measure how our clients are finding us, how long it will take them to become a client (rather than a prospective client), and how engaged they will be with our brand once they convert to a client. We can also analyse how likely our clients are to recommend us and how long they will remain a client.

The leaps that technology has made in the marketing arena – if nothing else – should be the thing that converts you from being a technophobe to someone willing to engage with and embrace all that the digital world has to offer.

The purpose of this section is to introduce you to some of the tools that are available, why you would use them, and which ones you should be taking the time to investigate and adapt into your business. The expertise in understanding and applying them may require you to engage someone who has decided to specialise in this field, but after reading this you'll be armed with enough knowledge to ask intelligent questions and be able to interpret the data that you'll have access to.

## What is inbound marketing?

Inbound marketing refers to marketing activities you do within your business that cause clients or potential customers to reach out to you.

Traditionally most business owners have thought of marketing as an outward form of communication, not dissimilar to standing in a store spruiking your wares, telling everyone what you sell and how good your 'stuff' is.

If you do that these days, you'll be without a business quicker than Video Ezy. Our clients are now looking for a very different relationship with us, and we need to be prepared to put the time and effort into creating that rapport with them before we even go near a sales conversation.

In 2011 Google released a piece of research called 'The Zero Moment of Truth'. Essentially ZMOT, as it's become known, is that moment we all reach as consumers when we move from thinking about purchasing to actually committing to buying. What the research showed us is that typically consumers are looking at three big numbers in the lead-up to the decision around whether or not they will purchase from you: 7, 11, 4.

Seven hours spent consuming 11 different pieces of content across four different platforms (website, social media, etc.).

What that means for you is quite simple. You need to be prepared to give away your best content in various different styles across various different platforms if you want to work with what marketers would deem your 'ideal clients'.

You can't be concerned about people learning the secret to your sauce. I say, give them the recipe... quite simply, it will make the process for your clients significantly easier and it will save you a lot of time trying to convince the wrong people to work with you.

I've seen it time and time again. A client will say to me, 'I don't want to give away too much'. When we drill into it, it's because they're concerned the client will learn how they do what they do and will no longer need them.

But here's the truth: if people can read your methodology, one of three things will happen:

- They will take the information away and go and do it themselves. If that's the case, they were never your client anyway, so don't worry.

- They will take the information away, attempt to implement it, realise the effort and work that goes into your product or service, have a greater level of respect and come back to you converted. That's a win for any business.

- They will review all the information and realise there's far more to this than they gave credit for and decide you're the best person to implement on their behalf. They don't even attempt to implement the solution themselves! The perfect outcome as the client comes to you presold.

Whatever you're thinking on the topic of inbound marketing, we know that it works. We know that if you stick with creating high-value content and putting it out to market across different platforms in different ways then your prospective clients will see you as a person of authority in your market and begin to develop the trust and relationship with your business that helps make the buying decision easier.

So, what does inbound marketing have to do with technology? Quite simply, by utilising and engaging some smart digital marketing platforms, you can analyse and create content that speaks directly to your target audience, saving you hours of angst over the best piece of content to create or the best location to place it. But more about that as we progress through this section.

For now, I just want you to get your head around the fact that in order to embrace and maximise your success from inbound marketing you need to accept you'll need to spend more time creating and developing content that engages with your audience.

If you'd like to do some further reading on the benefits of inbound marketing I highly recommend reading *Content Inc.* by Joe Pulizzi.

## How to map out your inbound marketing (content) strategy

You may be surprised to know that the technology doesn't even begin to factor into your marketing until you've become super clear on a couple of very major points.

### Why are you doing this?

Why are you in business? God knows anyone who's ever worked for themselves has asked that question more than once. You need a strategy to get you from here to where you want to be. Some people call it a USP (unique selling proposition). I call it the thing that makes you get out of bed every day, when it would be easier to take 4 weeks paid holidays and guaranteed superannuation every year. It won't matter how good your tech is – if you're not clear on that you'll never get where you hope to be.

### Who are your clients?

Every business I've ever worked with (including my own) has products or services that suit a range of people. Typically, what I see is a business owner trying to sell everything to everyone. If this is you, STOP IT. It's akin to teaching a pig to sing. It's wasting your time and annoying your clients. Instead you need to become super clear on each of your target clients and develop personas. Doing this allows you to really take advantage of the power marketing automation (the technology) can offer your business and your clients.

### What products or services do you have to offer for each of your clients?

Being very clear on what you have to offer each of your identified client personas will help you understand 'how' to market to them.

### What is your client's typical pathway to purchase?

Unless you're selling fidget spinners (boy, they really lasted a long time ... not!) your clients typically will go through a decision process before they purchase from you. What is it? How long does it take them? And what are the key points along their journey? Answer each of those questions and you'll know exactly what content you need to be creating.

### What content do you need to create to match their pathway to purchase?

Once you understand the steps your clients take in their decision to purchase from you, you'll have a better understanding of the questions they'll be asking along the way. These questions, coupled with the knowledge of your personas, will help you to identify what types of content you need to create to fill in the gaps.

### Identify your channels

Just because you love Instagram doesn't mean your clients use it. And just because you 'hate' doing video doesn't mean your clients don't want video. Understanding what your clients are looking for from you in terms of content and where they're hanging out means the difference between a successful business and not.

### And then what ...

We get so focused on bringing new clients through the door we often forget about our existing clients. What have you got to offer the folks who have been working with you or buying from you for years? They also tend to be the folks who are far more likely to engage and spend money with you again ... So, develop a plan to keep them working with you.

### Where to start?

Well, first let me remind you that this is a book about digitising your business. There are plenty of people who have written at length on marketing strategy, client personas, etc. My advice is to get that sorted before plugging any kind of technology into your marketing.

If you have a fair idea and you just want to check you're on track then I've developed a couple of templates to run through and make sure you're happy before we continue. You'll find these at my website.

The templates include:

- Why are you doing this?
- How to develop your client personas.
- Developing your content strategy.
- Identifying your channels of communication.

An excellent resource that may assist you to further understand the process of creating your client avatar is *Building a StoryBrand* by Donald Miller. He has an excellent framework you can follow to help you build out the details behind the clients you'd like to attract.

Remember adults are not dissimilar to children in the way we learn and acquire information; we will all have a preferred way of taking new information on board. For some of us, we may enjoy listening to a podcast to learn something new. Others enjoy watching a 'how to' video on YouTube, while others would rather read an article or a book to understand a topic.

It's important to take these different perspectives into account when creating content and ensure that you are building out a suite of different ways that people can access and consume your information.

It's also important to take your own time into consideration. Be realistic. Can you spare one day per week? Half a day? A couple of hours? Maybe just an hour? Whatever it is you need to factor that into your overall plan.

We all have one preferred method of content creation. Some of us find writing quite easy, others would prefer to do a quick video. Whatever it is, that is the final piece of your inbound strategy. I'll talk a little about repurposing your content later in this section but for now, just focus on creating the type of content you enjoy.

# 24. YOUR WEBSITE

The single most important piece of digital real estate your business will ever own is the website. It is also likely one of the ways you've already digitised your business... we often just don't acknowledge a website as the digital asset it is for our business.

You don't own your Facebook page or any other of your social media profiles. In fact, on more occasions than I'd care to remember I've spoken with disheartened business owners who put all their stock in their Facebook page only to have it removed, hacked or taken down.

Every small business needs a website, period. I don't care what business you're in – if you're serious about being a business owner you need to have a website. Think of it as your 'home base'. It's the place you'll direct people to for information. It needs to be tended regularly (like a garden), so make sure when allocating time to things you're making sure you can put some time into keeping your website up to date and filled with valuable information for your ideal clients.

It doesn't need to be fancy; it doesn't need dozens of pages. But it needs to be current and provide useful and helpful information to your potential customers.

Thanks to technology you can build your own business website pretty easily. When I say pretty easily, I mean, you'll need a bit of patience and to allow yourself a few days, but there are plenty of options that provide you with a great website template to start and allow you to drag and drop content into place to make the site look like something you'd be happy to show clients.

If you have a modest budget, you can have someone build you a basic four-page site from around $1000 to $1500. Which will save you the time and learning curve, but you'll still need to write the content and find the images.

If you'd rather build your own site, you can have a look at the following website builders.

## Wix

*www.wix.com*

When you first land on the Wix website you'll notice how simple they make the process look. I'm sure you're smart enough to realise that anything you've never done before is going to have a learning curve, and Wix is no different.

They have hundreds of predesigned templates that you can choose from, and for the most part it is pretty easy to understand. You can change font size and colour, add images or videos and the site will automatically ensure it fits mobile as well as a desktop for you (note: having a mobile-friendly site is super important to Google, they will heavily impact your authority if your site does not display well on a mobile phone).

- **What I like:** It's pretty easy to get the hang of and there are plenty of templates to choose from. There's a lot of flexibility to be able to change the look and feel of your site once you're in the swing of using it. The sites look good and you'll get one built in a relatively short period of time.

- **What I don't like:** It's a little glitchy to connect with Google Analytics (that's important to have and I'll explain more about that in a later chapter) and the load time can be a little slow, which will give you a black mark in Google's eyes.

## Squarespace

*www.squarespace.com*

Not dissimilar to using Wix. The big difference I found with Square-space is it appears to favour more image-rich sites. If you're a photographer, an artist or someone who likes to display a lot of photos, Squarespace may be more suited to your business.

- **What I like:** It has a similar drag-and-drop editor to the Wix sites and there are plenty of templates to choose from. Your clients will think it looks professional and they're easy to navigate.

- **What I don't like:** It doesn't seem to have the same level of flexibility as Wix and I've heard similar issues of site load speed and Google Analytics connection.

## WordPress

*www.wordpress.com*

WordPress is now the most popular website builder globally. They started as a blogging site and grew into the phenomenon they are today. Word Press is far more customisable than either Wix or Squarespace and will give you a lot more long-term flexibility in your business.

- **What I like:** There are always new templates being added to the mix and the number of WordPress experts available to help you build or maintain your site means you'll never be stuck looking for someone who can help you with something.

- **What I don't like:** Being the most popular website platform globally also means they are the most hacked. It seems there are new security patches coming out daily and often one new fix causes three other existing things to fail. I wouldn't be tackling a WordPress site without the aid of a website developer.

## Shopify

*www.shopify.com.au*

If your business requires you to have an online storefront, or you wish you could sell products easily online, Shopify could be the website you've been looking for.

Created as an e-commerce website builder, Shopify helps businesses get their stuff online to sell. Like all of the others listed above, Shopify has a bunch of predesigned templates you can choose from and will make getting your products online considerably easier.

· **What I like:** As opposed to an e-commerce plugin like Woo Commerce that is an afterthought to your WordPress site, Shopify is built as an online shopping platform from the ground up.

· **What I don't like:** This isn't a website I'd be tackling without some expert assistance.

There are many, many more website builders you can choose from, including:

· Joomla
· Kajabi
· HubSpot
· Motifo

I've listed the above options in some detail though as in my experience they seem to be the ones that I'm asked most often about. Like anything in your business, hasten slowly and choose the platform that feels right for you where you are.

## Other things to keep in mind when considering your website

### Make sure you own your domain

A domain is your website address (e.g.: www.tracysheen.com.au). I'm seeing a lot of website companies spring up that are offering to build your website for a nominal fee each month. When you look into it though you're only renting the domain and never actually own it.

Domain names are as cheap as chips to buy now (from around $10 per year), so consider owning your domain name as an investment in the future of your business.

### Where is your site hosted?

Think of your website hosting like paying a landlord for your office rental. Hosting can be quite cheap (from a few dollars per month) through to quite expensive (several hundred dollars per month). Always ask what is included in your hosting package and where the site is actually hosted as this can affect the speed at which your site will load and the security of your site.

### What's the purpose of your website?

Do you want a site that will showcase your credibility and authority to your ideal clients on arrival, or are you looking for a site that will act as a showroom? Having a clear idea of the role you want your website to play will help guide your decisions when choosing the best place to build your site.

### How easy is it for you to update your site?

Whichever platform you choose you'll need to know how to access your site to add a blog, an image or a video. You'll need to be able to update information and change things to suit what is happening in your business at that time. Make sure you choose something you'll feel comfortable accessing and modifying as the need arises.

### Can you easily connect Google Analytics and other tools?

Depending on how far you want to take your digital dependence, you may find you'll need your site to become a little more flexible with its ability to plug other things in. You'll definitely need to have Google Analytics connected from the get-go (I'll talk a little more about Google Analytics shortly), but think about your desire to use a CRM tool or gather client information to add to a newsletter, etc.

## What's the site look like on mobile and tablet?

When we're building our sites and reviewing, we'll most often default to checking them out on our laptop or desktop. It's important though to ensure your site is responsive to both mobile devices and tablets.

I mentioned earlier that Google is punishing sites that are not mobile friendly; while I'll talk about that in another chapter it's an important one to consider upfront.

## What Google is looking for in your website

There is a saying in marketing that 'you are who Google says you are'. When we first look to create our website, or, if you're looking to refresh your website now, there are a few things to keep in mind.

Google is by far the most used search engine on the planet, and they have their own way of ranking your site based on usefulness to your clients. One term you have likely come across over the years is 'SEO' or Search Engine Optimisation.

This is just a fancy way of figuring out how to get Google to favour your site above your competitors.

There are a bunch of things Google are looking for in any site, and these tend to be a somewhat moving target. There is a real skill to helping people organically rank their website, and if this is something that interests you, I suggest you reach out and I'll put you in touch with an SEO person I've worked with whom I trust. There are also a lot of spam emails we all receive promising page one results in 30 days... Please, whatever you do, do not engage the services of one of these companies, there is no surer way to earn the wrath of Google than by attempting to rig the system.

So, what are the things that Google is looking for that we can have some control over?

Well, let me first remind you that Google can update and completely change things at a moment's notice. So, what we know to be true today may not be accurate in six months. Right now, though, we know the biggest thing that ticks their boxes is producing regular and engaging content that helps your customers find answers to their questions.

We do know Google has little 'bots' that come through our sites on a regular basis looking for various things, and one of the things they like is words.

Making your homepage around 2000 words will tick a very big box for Google. The caveat to that is as long as the content is engaging and doesn't read as though you've just stuffed it full of words you believe your clients would search for.

In the past this was known as 'keyword stuffing' and these days it will earn you a very black mark indeed.

The first thing you need is long-form content, regularly updated that is useful and helpful to your audience.

The second thing Google is looking for (in no particular order) is 'dwell time'. That is how long someone is hanging around on your page and your website reading, listening to audio or watching videos. The magic number for Google is around three minutes (though this can change depending on their current algorithm). So, my advice is always to make sure you have enough variety on your website pages that when anyone lands they want to hang around and read, or watch, or listen.

The third thing to keep in mind for your site is the 'load time'.

All this means is if anyone goes to your website, how long does it take for your site to appear from when they hit enter in the search bar? We've all been to sites where it feels like we're waiting forever for the page to appear, and I'm sure you've given up on more than one of those sites, choosing instead an alternative site to visit.

Well, Google hates long load times too. Rule of thumb is to keep your mobile site under five seconds and your laptop/desktop site under three seconds. Anything longer, you're being penalised.

As a side note, the quickest method I find to fix a slow load time is always check the size of your images. If I was a betting person, I'd guarantee you 9 times out of 10 the images on the site are too big.

The fourth thing to check is your 'metadata'.

That's the two lines of words that appear under your website when someone searches for you on Google (see following example).

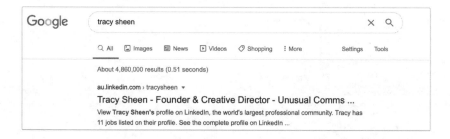

There are two things about metadata that Google dislikes. The first is when the words are the same for every page (or 'duplicate metadata' as Google call it). The other is when we haven't used the 'right' amount of words in our metadata – Google likes between 155 and 160 characters. If you exceed this number, you'll see '...' after your sentence (see following example).

Lastly, one of the other pieces that Google looks for that you can easily fix is keywords and 'LSI' or Latent Search Indexing. These are other words or phrases that people may use to find a product or service that you offer.

Including your keywords in your page title and referring to similar phrases throughout your content show Google the content is relevant to your clients.

Keeping an eye on all of the above when you're creating content or updating your website will ensure you keep in good with Google as you go. There are a bunch of other things that Google will look for, but, my advice is focus on getting their big-ticket items right and then if you're still interested in learning more about SEO, check out websites like Uber Suggest by Neil Patel: www.neilpatel.com/ubersuggest.

It's a free site where you can conduct your own site audit and check for errors or things that require fixing.

As this book goes to print there is much speculation around what Alphabet (the parent company of Google) will do if Australia's proposed 'media code' becomes law. For what it's worth I don't think Google will walk away from the revenue Australia offers, however it's worth remembering when looking at your SEO and optimisation strategy to keep other search engines in mind.

# 25. WEBSITE ANALYTICS AND DATA GATHERING

Okay, now we're starting to get into where technology can help you get some really great data and insights into what people are looking for ... and data and insights on your website.

I can totally geek out on this stuff so just know while I try to keep everything top level here, if I lose you at any point I've got some webinars and things you'll be able to find on my YouTube channel that will help you to further decipher what I'm talking about. I'm a big believer in understanding the basics of how various digital solutions could work for your business so you'll be able to find the best person to assist you with implementation if needed.

## Google Analytics

The most popular analytics tool for your website without a doubt is Google Analytics. It's free to connect, and one that you absolutely want to have in place as early into your website journey as you can.

If you don't already have Google Analytics, the place to start is to sign up for a free account. You can do so by visiting their website: www.marketingplatform.google.com/about/analytics.

Give yourself around 30 minutes when you plan to set it up as there are a few bits of information you'll need to provide.

There are a few reasons you want Google Analytics connected to your website. In no particular order these are:

- It's Google... so you'll get information about your clients that only Google would be able to provide you.

- Know what page(s) people are visiting. See at a glance which of your website pages people are spending time on, and which ones they're avoiding. With information like that you're able to hone your content even further to ensure its engaging with the right people.

- See how long people are spending on each page. If you can see people are hitting a page and leaving immediately, but landing on other pages and hanging around, it gives you a much better idea of what content is connecting and resonating with your audience.

- See what people are 'active' on your website right now. You can see how many people are looking at your website right now as well as what content and pages they're consuming.

- See what devices people are searching your site from. A handy one to know is if you have more people viewing you from a mobile or from a desktop. Information like that allows you to streamline your site to further suit your audience.

- See where people are visiting your site. Is your business only servicing people in Australia, but you're getting a bunch of views from the US? Better to know and be able to adjust your keywords to include areas you service than wonder why no one ever reaches out.

- See what time and day your site is most popular. If you're releasing a blog each week on a Wednesday at 10 am and you see a spike in traffic around 10:30, you'll know you have a group of dedicated blog readers. It can also give you insights into when and on what days you should be sharing your content.

Connect the site when you're ready to run Google Ads and know you're targeting the right people.

If you're interested in learning more about Google Analytics (and, you should be), I can't think of a better place to send you than Google themselves. They have an amazing array of free online learning tools designed to walk you through set-up, understanding and building customisable reports.

You'll find the free Google training at: www.learndigital. withgoogle.com/digitalgarage.

There're over 134 courses, some even with certifications (if that interests you). So, you'll have plenty to hone your skills and start down the Google rabbit hole.

## Hotjar

The other analytics tool I love having connected to websites is 'Hotjar'. This tool gives you a super-quick visual representation of where people are clicking on your site and the journey their mouse makes as it travels around your website.

Super useful information to help you figure out if you're putting buttons to take clients off to further information in the 'right' place on your website and just how people read through your content.

It's free to connect, but you can choose to pay if you'd like a lot more detail. I suggest, start with the free version and get used to just how much cool information it will give you in a really quick time.

You'll find their website at: www.hotjar.com.

# 26. BLOGGING

One of the things Google loves is fresh content, and, if you're planning to build an inbound content strategy then blogging is going to become one of your best mates.

People get caught up in creating and writing blogs; while I'm not going to go into too much detail about how to blog here, I will say the biggest thing I learned when I was copywriting is there is a formula to everything. Figure the formula out and you'll nail the process.

Lucky for you I have a template on 'how to write a blog', which you'll find in the book resources section of my website. Hopefully you'll find it self-explanatory and it will save you hours of anguish.

There are a few really helpful websites that I advise clients to lean on when it comes to their content creation ... you'll be pleased to know I'm about to share them with you.

## Answer the Public

*www.answerthepublic.com*

This magical little site will take your phrase e.g.: digital marketing and share the questions people are asking about it in real time.

The site trawls Google looking for all the relevant questions, and then delivers them to you in a super-handy visualisation wheel. (See opposite as an example search.)

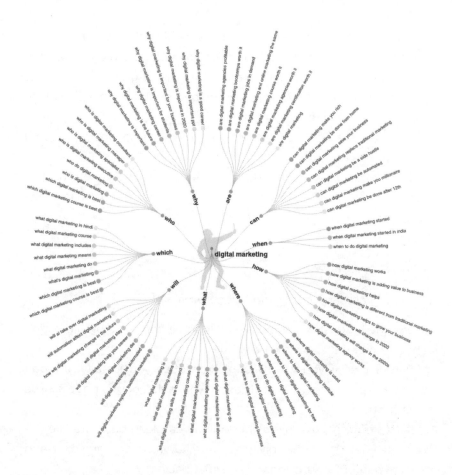

As a personal preference I usually change this wheel to a list format (I find it easier to read) – see a snapshot example below.

Why is this so handy? Well, Google is looking for helpful content. And what could be more helpful than you writing a blog answering a question that is being asked today? It's also a great way to make sure you're aware of everything your potential customers want to know about your product or service.

The site is free to use (though you can also opt for a paid subscription).

**Tip:** Make sure you change the search area to the country you want to be known in. If you only work with people in Australia, make sure the search area is set to Australia.

## Blog Title Generator

*www.seopressor.com/blog-title-generator/*

One of the biggest questions asked when it comes to blog creation is how to come up with a catchy title.

Remember, if you want Google to notice you it's always good practice to put a keyword or phrase in your title... now is not the time to be subtle.

If you're really struggling though you can lean on a site like the blog title generator. Simply pop your keyword or phrase in and et voila many, many options will be spat back at you.

If you're still stuck for content ideas, keep these in mind also:

- Humans love lists:
  - The three things... Five reasons, etc. Try to keep it to an odd number; our brains are happier with an odd number.
- Flick through your favourite magazine or newspaper. You'll often find a headline you can swap out words and repurpose as your own.
- Hacks, tips and tricks:
  - We love to think we can hack the system. 'How to hack your blog creation' always gets attention.
- Why successful people do ...
  - Using a celebrity name to leverage off your title can be useful. e.g.: 'Why Steve Jobs always wore the same clothes and you should too.'
- Experience:
  - Utilising our experience within our industry. e.g.: 'What 30 years in sales and marketing has taught me about small business.'
- Be controversial:
  - Being prepared to take an opposing stand to the current thinking can pique your readers' interest.

## Fat Joe

*www.fatjoe.com/content-writing*

If you are totally onboard with creating blogs and building content but just don't have the time, the energy or the inclination to do it, then Fat Joe could be the answer you're looking for.

Simply complete the brief of what you're looking for, how long you want the article to be and whether you're looking for a basic or pro writer, and the Fat Joe team take care of the rest.

What I like about these guys is they write in UK English, so there's no spelling to correct before you load it to your site. It can take a little finessing to get used to the briefing process, but I have a number of very happy clients who have been using this service for quite a while.

If you like the idea but not the company there are plenty of alternative content creation companies available; simply do a Google search and choose the one that best suits your requirements.

## Fiverr

*www.fiverr.com*

If you have a bit more time on your hands but you'd still like to outsource your content writing, then consider giving Fiverr a go.

You'll definitely have to try out a few different contractors, so my advice is finding two or three who appeal and give them all exactly the same brief.

Compare how long they take to turn your job around, the quality of the work and the cost. You may need to go through this process a few times, but I've struck gold on Fiverr a few times when I've needed to get small projects completed.

\* \* \*

The final tip I have for you around blogging is this. Choose a frequency of how often you'd like a new blog to go live on your site (monthly is a good starting point) and stick to it. Google will love the fresh content hitting your site and your customers will get used to when your content goes live. Nothing kills your content marketing quicker than a lack of consistency.

# 27. SOCIAL MEDIA

A section on digital marketing wouldn't be complete without touching on social media.

There are plenty of other fabulous resources available on the value social media can bring to your business, so I'll focus in on the things I believe are (mostly) missing when we talk social media.

Before we get into each of the individual platforms, I want you to really consider your strategy for using socials. PLEASE do not solely rely on a Facebook or Instagram page for your business. Always, always, ALWAYS have a website. Remember, your website is the only piece of digital real estate you'll ever own, and I've seen far too many folks have their social media pages yanked out from underneath them, leaving them no digital safety net.

So... website first, and use your socials to drive traffic back to your website.

That being said, let's take a look at the various platforms and the information they can give us around our business.

# 28. FACEBOOK

It makes sense to start with Facebook. It remains by far the most utilised platform (this is certainly true in Australia). While I'll always say you need to base your strategy on what you know about each of your target segments (that is, client personas), Facebook is the one exception I feel most people should at least have a presence on.

Whether your business works B2B (Business to Business) or B2C (Business to Consumer) I will almost guarantee you that your target audience will have a personal Facebook account themselves. Meaning you may be able to slip your content under their personal radar while their business hat is not on.

A few things you need to know about Facebook though…

Although Facebook will never actually tell us how their algorithms work, we know (because I read a lot and have worked with enough people) that your organic reach (that is, how many people will see your post without you paying for it) is around 1%. Meaning if you have 100 people who like your page around 1 person will see your post 'organically'.

Now, a couple of things can affect this:

- If you have a core group of customers who are actively engaged in liking and commenting on your posts, then your organic reach will be higher.
- If you can gain 'around' (it's not an exact science) 20 comments on a post within a two-hour period, then your post will be seen by more people.

As a general rule though, expect that around 1% of your page audience will see anything you post day to day.

So, if the numbers are so low, why bother doing it at all?

Well, quite simply our customers and potential customers will generally do some research on you before they choose to work with you (remember the Google study Zero Moment of Truth we discussed earlier) – that means if I'm checking you out to decide whether or not I want to work with you, I'm very likely going to:

· check out your website

· visit your social pages

· read a blog, watch a video or listen to a podcast.

If you don't have fresh content posted on your page then I'm going to assume you're not actually that active and maybe, just maybe you're not the right business for me to work with. At the bare minimum it will put a psychological objection in the mind of your potential buyer.

So, if the aim of posting on Facebook is to get more eyes on our page how do we know the best time to be posting? Or... who is even looking at our page?

## Facebook analytics and insights

That's why you need to know about your analytics. First things first, if you haven't ever looked at your analytics before you'll want to go to www.facebook.com/analytics in your browser. It's going to bring up a page that look like this (see image below).

Bookmark this page. It's without a doubt the most powerful and useful page Facebook will share with you. Let's walk through what you can learn from your insights or analytics.

Before we get started though ... I want you to log into your 'Settings tab'.

Make sure your display is set up for your time zone and currency – this will be super important as we start reviewing our insights.

**Display**

The following settings will be applied for all users of this Facebook Page in Facebook Analytics.

Time-related data in Facebook Analytics will be displayed in the following time zone.

**TIME ZONE**  (GMT+10:00) Australia/Brisbane ▼

Monetary data in Facebook Analytics will be displayed in the following currency.

**CURRENCY**  Australian Dollar (AUD) ▼

Once you've done that, click back to 'Overview' and we can start looking at all the juicy information.

The first thing worth knowing is that you can drill into any of the areas further by simply clicking on the box.

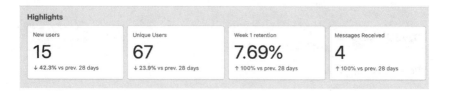

For the moment though, let's look at the pieces of data I believe it's important you get to know, follow and understand.

Now, the way Facebook break down their analytics is into:

- **Highlights:** The top-level picture or snapshot of how things are tracking.
- **Growth metrics:** Is the page gaining traction and reaching more people?
- **Engagement metrics:** What does your audience find engaging and when are they viewing the page?
- **Page metrics:** This covers things like the number of new page likes, post shares, comments, etc.

Let's take a look at the highlights metrics first.

## New users

This tells us how many new people we've had visit our Facebook page over the set period of time (in this instance 28 days).

A handy one to keep an eye on, and ideally you want this to be green (growing). When I see something in the red (like in the image below) it tells me you haven't had time to spend on your Facebook page promoting, sharing and pushing your content out.

## Unique users

### *Week 1 retention*

How many people continue to visit your Facebook page once they have interacted with it over the set period of time (in this instance 28 days)?

## Messages received

The number of private or direct messages (pm or dm) you have received to your Facebook pages over the set period of time (in this instance 28 days).

If you're into getting messages through your Facebook page, then it's one you'll want to make sure is in the 'green' and increasing each time you review. For most folks I work with though it's a bit of an empty metric.

## Growth metrics

### *Active users: last 24 hours*

Shows you the number of people who visited your Facebook page in the previous 24 hours. The larger dot you see on the right-hand side is the data for the current hour.

It's not one to spend a lot of time analysing.

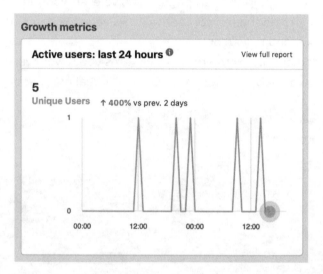

## User activity

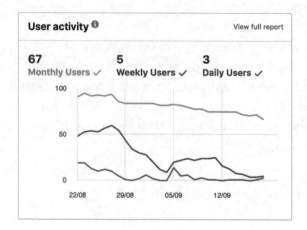

## Engagement metrics

### *Active users: by hour*

This is probably the handiest one you'll view in your Facebook analytics. And it's the reason you want to make sure your time zone is set up correctly to begin with.

Users by hour gives you a really good view of the days and times people are popping by your page. If you've ever wondered the best time or day to be sharing content to your Facebook page – this is the report you need to lean on.

The darker the box the more viewers. As you hover over each box on your own analytics page, you'll see the actual number of people.

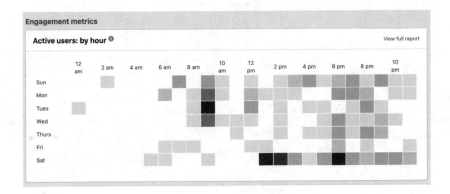

### *User retention*

This little graph will let you know how well your page holds the interest of those people who visit.

When you're first starting out, this isn't one I put too much stock in. It's enough to know you're getting people visiting your page. You'll get far more insight into your audiences likes and dislikes following some of the other insights we've discussed. Just know what it does, and if the numbers are tracking upwards keep doing what you're doing.

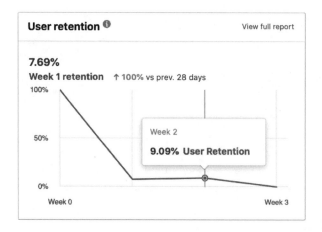

### Posts with the most reactions

This is definitely one to keep an eye on. Watching what your audience is interacting with tells you what content to do more of, and where to put your focus.

| Posts with the most reactions ❶ | View full report |
|---|---|
| **Post (Pages)** | **Unique users ▾** |
| All other | 41 |
| 3500 words today... not a bad effort Staring ... | 21 |
| Book update... Things are getting real as I si... | 13 |
| Unknown | 12 |

## Page metrics

### Post reactions

I wouldn't even bother with this report unless you're interested in running Facebook ads, then you'll want to keep an eye on it.

Essentially, it's telling you the different sources that people track through to find your page (Facebook pixel, page, etc.).

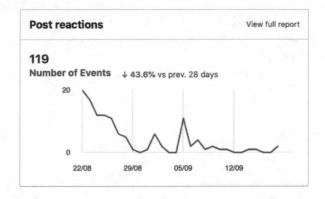

### Post shares

The holy grail of content creation is getting someone on your Facebook page to share one of your posts. This report will tell you if and when it's happened. Ideally you want to see this report in the green and growing.

Remember, if someone has shared your content it's because they've found it engaging. Do more of that.

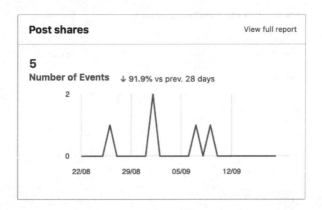

### Post comments

The next best thing we can hope for on our Facebook page is comments on posts. This report will give you the insight into which of your posts enticed your audience to leave a comment.

When you look at this graph, you're looking for the days that people commented so you can create similar content that will (hopefully) engage your audience even more. Ideally when you're looking at this report you want to see it in the green and growing each month.

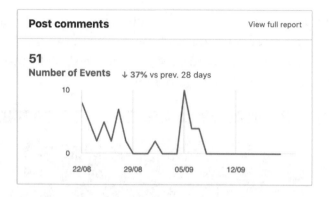

*Messages sent*

If you want your audience to be reaching out to you via messenger, then keep an eye on this one. Be warned though, messenger can be a rabbit hole that needs to be managed. I've seen a lot of small business owners end up with clients contacting them at all times of the day and night expecting replies.

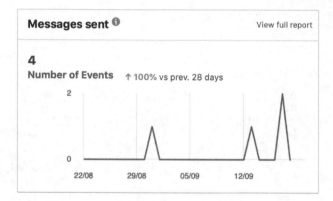

Okay, so, that's the basic overview of the analytics. But wait! Don't go diving for that stiff drink or 32nd coffee thinking that you're out of the woods because there is another way you can peek behind your Facebook page curtain and take a look at what's really going on. To do that you'll want to access your 'insights' via your Facebook Business page log in and not via the analytics page we've just been looking at.

To find your insights tab, log into your Facebook page via www.business.facebook.com/yourbusinessname.

Once you're logged in, you'll see your 'insights' tab located at the top of the screen (see following image).

Once you click on the insights tab, you'll be faced with an overview tab not dissimilar to what you've just seen.

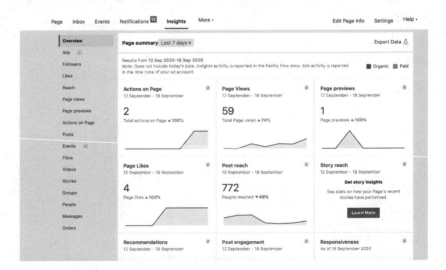

The first thing to note is that the date ranges will be set by default to the last 7 days. You can click on this to change the range to today, yesterday, last 7 days or last 28 days (see image below).

Now, my advice here is stick to the overview screen. You'll get everything you need to know from this one page. Just as we found with the analytics page, some of these insights will be far more useful to you than others.

Let's take a look at them individually so you can identify which ones will be of importance to you.

### Actions on a page

This tells us the number of clicks on your contact information or your call to action buttons.

## Page views

The number of times your page has been viewed over the set date range.

## Page previews

The number of times someone hovered over your page or profile picture for a preview of your page.

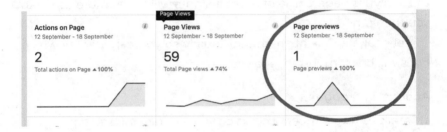

## Page likes

The number of new people who have liked your page over the assigned time period.

This one is worth keeping an eye on (you want your followers and base to grow) – but be aware that Facebook can average this number out, so it may not be entirely accurate. And please don't get caught up in the likes as a vanity metric; ultimately we want to see comments and shares on your content... that's what tells us your content is engaging.

### *Post reach*

The number of people who saw at least one of your posts across the assigned period.

Another one to keep half an eye on – this will give an indicator of how engaging your content is. Remember, if lots of people are commenting and sharing your posts then more people will see the posts.

### *Story reach*

This one will only register with data if you're creating Facebook stories on your page. If so, it'll show you the number of people who had one of your stories on their screen.

### Recommendations

I don't see data cropping up in this for many people. It tells you how many people have recommended your page.

### Post engagement

This is one you'll want to keep an eye on. It tells you the number of times people engaged with your content via a like, a comment or a share.

Ideally you want to see this number in the green and increasing. This will tell you the types of content your audience is looking for.

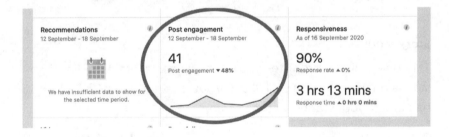

### Responsiveness

This one is all about the private or direct messages (pm or dm) you receive on your page. The percentage of messages you respond to and the time it takes for you to respond to a message.

I wouldn't bother with this unless messenger is part of your over-arching social media strategy.

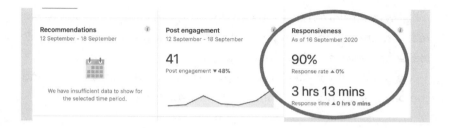

## Videos

You'll only see data here if you are releasing videos on your Facebook page. And, if you're not... *why not?* You really should you know; videos will produce some of the best engagement for you and build rapport with your audience.

This report will show you the number of times your video has been played for at least three seconds.

## Page followers

This is another handy one to keep an eye on. It'll show you the number of people who have followed (as opposed to like) your page over the assigned time period.

A quick note here on the difference between people who 'like' your page and people who 'follow' your page (as they are a little different).

You may have a friend who chooses to 'like' your page to support your business. If you look at their profile you will see their name attached to your business page – so it's visible to their friends list.

A follower is someone who wants to see your page updates (depending of course on the current Facebook algorithm) but not have their name attached as liking the page.

Now, a random thing you can do if you like a page but you're not really interested in seeing what they're posting is to 'unfollow'. This leaves you as a fan of the page, but you won't see the content.

By default if you 'like' a page you will automatically be following the page. You'll need to 'unfollow' to not see the updates.

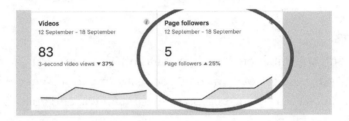

## Other things in insights...

### Your five most recent posts

This one compares your last five posts, and shows you at a glance what sort of post they were (video, text, photo, etc.) along with the reach the post received and the engagement.

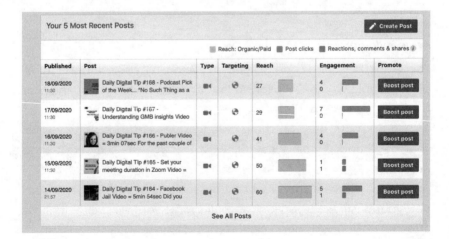

## People

You'll find this one on the left-hand side of your screen (see image below).

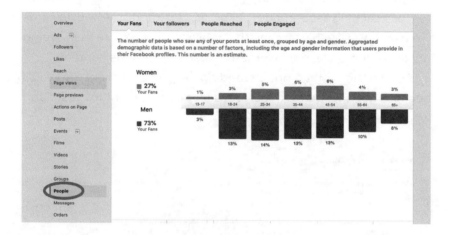

This one has some extremely useful information to keep an eye on, including a breakdown of information between:

- your fans
- your followers
- people reached
- people engaged.

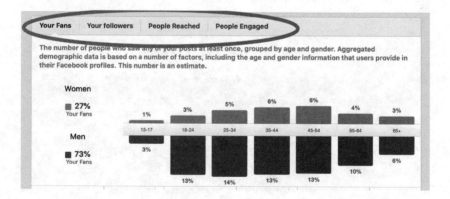

As you can see from the above image (I'm in the fan section) this graph gives me a split of the people who like my page as male vs female and their age range.

Having this level of understanding of your audience can be super helpful when it comes to creating content.

You can see with this example above the split is very heavily weighted towards men... but, when we look at the people the content is reaching (see image below) it's far more skewed towards women. Basically this tells me that while there are more men seeing my posts, there are more women interacting with the content.

Couple this with an understanding of your ideal client and you'll begin to get a very strong feel for the types of content to create and who to aim it at.

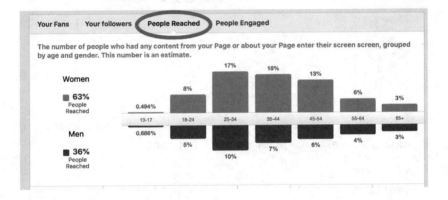

The last one I want you to keep an eye on is 'Posts' – again, you'll find it on the left-hand side of your screen.

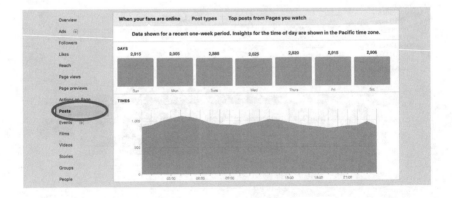

This tells you the number of people that are online by day and time. I'd suggest you marry this information with the 'active user by hour'

data we were looking at on the analytics site, and you're going to have a pretty strong guide as to the days and times your people are hanging around online.

If you're completely geeking out on all the analytics and insights you can get from Facebook (I know, I've only scratched the surface), then you can begin your next steps with further reading at: www.facebook.com/help/analytics/.

Or check out Facebook Blueprint, Facebook's online training platform – you'll find a whole lot more information on insights at www.facebook.com/business/insights.

## Creator Studio

*www.business.facebook.com/creatorstudio*

Now you've got a handle on your data and what it means, it's time we take a look at 'creator studio'.

At its core Creator Studio is about content. Everything you see through this site will in some way, shape or form revolve around your content.

I use Creator Studio to schedule all of my content for Facebook. And at its bare bones it is fabulous for doing that... but, there is so much more you can get from it if you know where to look.

It has a bunch of insights (yes, more insights) that can help you finesse your content even further.

When you first log in you'll be faced with your home screen.

On the left-hand side is your menu (just as we had with your Facebook business page). And, in the main area of the screen you'll see various options of things that may interest you.

From posting something new to your page, adding a story, uploading a video or going live.

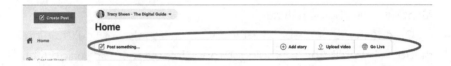

Your basic insights (focused on content) for the last seven days.

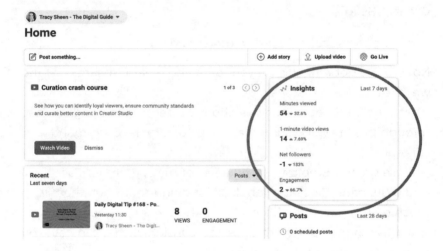

Suggestions of study you might like to do (and yes, Creator Studio works for Instagram also).

Your recent posts at a glance.

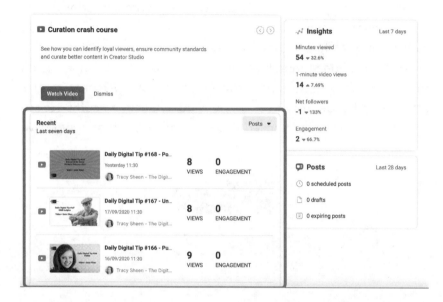

Additional post information such as anything you may have left in drafts or have scheduled to go out at a later date.

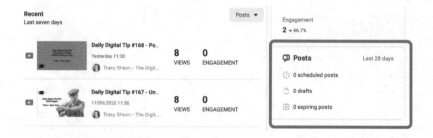

I'm not going to dive into the details of everything available to you through the left-hand side menu.

Instead I'm going to invite you to be brave and have a click around. A number of the things you'll find are also available to you directly through your business page. I find though by clicking around you'll become more comfortable with everything and learn where things live.

If you want more information on Creator Studio you can always go to: www.facebook.com/business/help/2160250460681592?id=203539 221057259.

And remember to put some time aside to go through the Facebook Blueprint training site... it really is a fount of wisdom.

Oh, one final thing I will say about Facebook, and this is all to do with security. Make sure you have two-factor authentication turned on and you understand all of the security options available to you through your Settings and Privacy tab in your personal profile. I shared further details on this in the 'security' section – suffice to say I've seen far too many hacked Facebook accounts that could have easily been avoided.

# 29. INSTAGRAM

Since we started with Facebook we may as well stay in the family and discuss Instagram. (Yes, for those who didn't know, Instagram is owned by Facebook.)

According to Statistica, as of July 2020, 13.9% of the globally active Instagram users were women between the ages of 18 and 24 years.

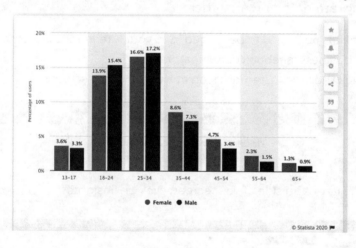

Believe it or not, Instagram only turned 10 in 2020 (I know, it feels like it's been around way, way longer than that... or maybe that's just a direct relationship to the number of breakfast photos I've had to wade through over those years).

It's a photo-sharing platform. Typically, I see clients doing well with Instagram in the following industries:

- health and beauty
- fitness
- travel
- fashion
- food.

I rarely see a professional services business using the platform with any great effect. To be honest I'm not a huge fan of Instagram but I have clients that l-o-v-e it and swear by what it's done for building their profile.

People who use Instagram spend a fair amount of their time on the platform. According to research by Sprout social, the average is just shy of an hour per day to be precise – so – if you're interested in maximising your Instagram usage here's what you need to know.

## Instagram data and analytics

First of all you'll need to be logged in to your 'Creator Studio' account: www.business.facebook.com/creatorstudio

Click the little Instagram icon at the top of the screen.

On the left-hand side of your screen click on 'insights'.

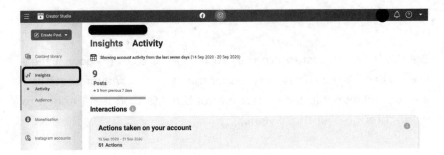

This brings you to your Instagram insights home page.

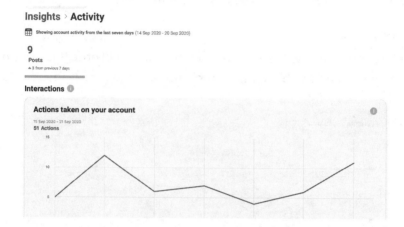

**The first report you see is 'Actions taken on your account'.**

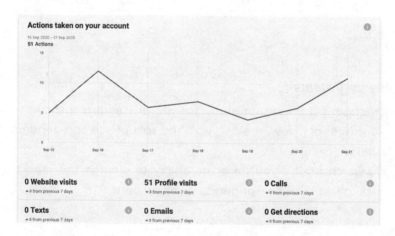

The report tells us:

- how many people clicked through to your website from the page in the time frame chosen
- the number of people who visited your profile in the time frame chosen
- the number of people that contacted you by phone
- the number of people that sent a text message
- the number of people that sent an email
- the number of people that asked for directions.

Based on the metrics you're interested in, you'll be able to decide which of these measurements you'd like to track.

### Accounts reached

This report will provide an estimate of the number of other Instagram accounts who saw your content over the selected time frame.

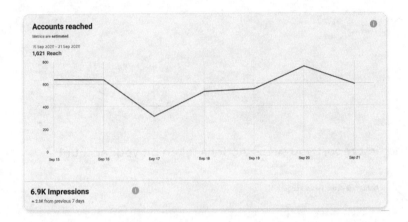

### Audience insights

This is the most important report for your Instagram. It shows your total number of followers along with the split of age and genders of your followers.

It's worth noting you have the ability to change the reporting metrics to just show age or gender or show both.

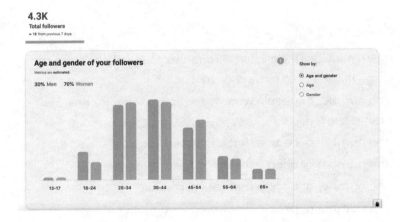

## *When are your followers on Instagram?*

This report gives you an idea of which days most appeal to your audience and can be a very helpful metric when deciding which days to post fresh content.

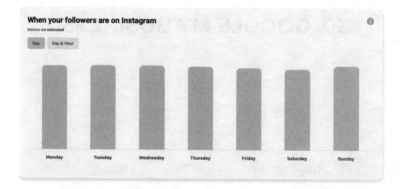

## Countries/Towns/Cities

It's difficult to keep Instagram content local. This report is worth keeping half an eye on to make sure your content is not being overshadowed by countries or areas you're not interested in servicing.

# 30. GOOGLE MY BUSINESS

*www.business.google.com*

In terms of bang for buck, we should all have a Google My Business (or GMB as it's known) profile.

Before you groan and roll your eyes, hear me out. GMB is owned by ... You guessed it, Google. And being owned by Google means they (Google) give it a little extra love. Used well (hang in there, I'll get to what that means) you'll get a kick along for your organic SEO (search engine optimisation) as well as it being a great place for clients to leave you a review.

There is one big difference you need to know about GMB before you really start using it as it is quite different to any other social media platform.

Any post you share will only be visible for 7 days. After that it is removed from your profile and no longer visible. Unlike your Facebooks or Instagrams, it is not as hungry for content from you (although it loves regular client reviews) so scheduling one post each week is enough to keep the platform happy.

Let's take a look at what your profile looks like once you've logged in. The first place you'll land is your 'home' screen. It will look like this. Note, I'm logged in via my desktop, if you log in via the 'My Business' app on your mobile device it will look slightly different.

The icons on the left-hand side of your screen are what drives the actions within the platform.

- **Home:** Your home screen. From here you can navigate to all areas of your profile

- **Posts:** Where you go to see all of your previous posts and to create a new post

- **Info:** All of the information related to your profile from your address, phone and website details to the areas your business service and the products or services you have on offer for clients

- **Insights:** Review your data and analytics to see what is driving traffic to your profile and your website

- **Reviews:** Houses all your client reviews and your replies

- **Messaging:** Your private or direct messages (pm or dm) similar to Facebook messenger

- **Photos:** Any images you or your clients have loaded to your profile

- **Products:** The area where you can add, adjust or delete any physical products you sell

- **Services:** Add, adjust or delete any and all of the services your business offers

- **Website:** GMB have their own website built in – please don't bother with this, it's pretty average (in my opinion anyway) and won't add any value

- **Users:** If you would like a social media manager to look after your GMB account, this is where you'll add (or remove) them.

I have created a GMB profile template to help you walk through everything you need to know about creating your own GMB profile. You'll find this (along with all the other templates) available for download from my website. For this reason, I'm not going to go into detail around setting up your profile here. While it's straightforward to do so, there are a few tips and tricks – so, it's worth your while to download and follow my guide.

If you haven't guessed by now, I am pretty focused on helping you understand the insights that these digital platforms offer your business. This is where I find technology can add huge amounts of value in understanding what type of content we should be creating on what types of platforms and for whom.

## Google My Business data and analytics

So, let's take a better look at what information you can take away from your insights ... shall we?

The first insight you'll see is:

### Queries used to find your business

This tells you what people are searching for to find your business. It's a handy one to keep (half) an eye on to ensure you're covering all the search terms when you're creating content.

For me, I usually just find people searching on my name (see image) – but I have a number of clients who have found some really interesting terms they would never have thought to include if they hadn't been on the lookout.

### How customers search for your business

You'll see looking at the image, this insight breaks up the information into how many people found you because they searched for your name (this is the 'direct' searching) vs how many people found you because they were looking for a business like yours (known as 'discovery' searching).

Ideally, we are looking for the 'discovery' search component to be growing. Meaning, we want more people to be finding your business because they were looking for someone like you.

Something worth noting is the adjustable time frame (as shown by the call out box on the left-hand side). You can adjust the searchable date range from one week to one month or one quarter.

My advice is to be checking on your insights on a monthly basis. You want to make sure you're tracking in the right direction.

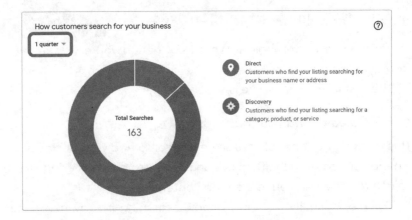

### Where customers view your business on Google

This tells us whether people have found us by looking at Google search or Google maps.

Now, I've chosen to not have a business location listed on my profile. I work from home and the vast majority of my work is either remote onsite with clients or via Zoom. For those clients who have a predominantly local focus on their business (think health, beauty, mechanics, cafes, etc.) then you'll absolutely want to have an address listed and you'll (hopefully) find the vast majority of your traffic will come via Google Maps.

Think about the last time you wanted to find a good coffee when you were out for a Sunday drive. Chances are you already have maps open and you simply ask Google for the best coffee shop nearby... that's one of the ways Google will give you a local SEO 'bump' if you list your business address correctly.

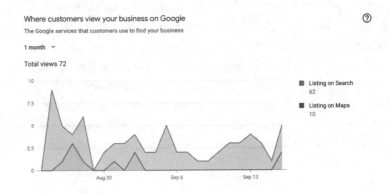

## Customer actions

This insight shows us the most common actions people are making when they visit your GMB profile. Do they jump off to visit your website? Do they call you or do they drop you a message?

This is a great insight to track if you're looking to generate phone calls for your business through posts (think hairdresser with a cut and colour offer as an example). By using an 'offer' post and tracking it I can see how successful that post has been.

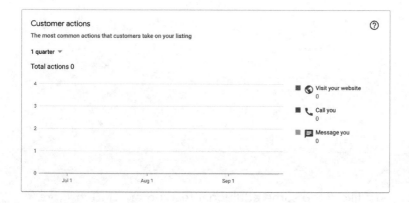

## Phone calls

Further information on the number of phone calls your profile has generated.

I haven't bothered to load my mobile number on my profile (I'd prefer to encourage email communication) – so my data is showing as 0.

If you're a locally focused business though, this is a great insight to keep an eye on.

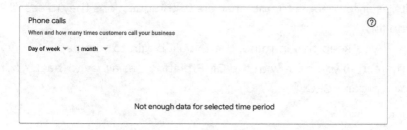

### Photo views

I find this insight is an excellent tool for food, fashion, beauty and real estate (as examples). Loading photos to your profile can draw a large number of people to your profile and then onto your website (or generate a call or message).

Tracking the number of views your photos are getting over your desired time frame is a great way to learn which photos are driving the traffic.

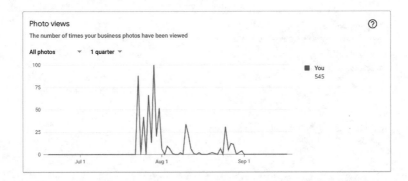

If you'd like to do some additional reading on GMB insights, you'll find some great information on the Google help site (the link will take you straight to GMB insights).

www.support.google.com/business/answer/7689763?_ga= 2.158743290.1378833957.1600560995-1500717747.1600560995 #searchqueries.

## Seven additional hacks to know in GMB

Google is looking to index all content you share. They do so to make it easier for people to find answers to the questions they're searching for.

If you keep this in mind, then you'll begin to think about every interaction you have with the GMB platform as a way to 'hack' your own organic SEO.

### 1. When you're completing your profile, think about the keywords and phrases that your clients use to find you

Make sure when you're building your services out (as an example) you are including those phrases.

As an example, I know when a corporate organisation or government body is searching for people who can provide training to small business owners, they are likely going to use the phrases:

· webinars
· training
· virtual training.

So, when I built my services section out, what do you think I used as each of my main service offerings? You got it... all of the words I know that they are using.

I'm making it as easy as I can for Google to match me against one of their search requests.

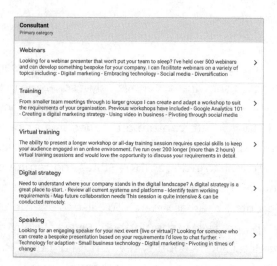

## 2. *When you're completing your Service Areas think micro and macro*

We all use Google to search in slightly different ways. Some of us say 'best hairdresser near me' and some will say 'best hairdresser in Sydney'.

If your business services Sydney (as an example) then think about what that might look like when people search. You can enter up to 20 service areas so you might like to create a list that looks something like:

· Sydney City (broad area)
· Greater Sydney (broad area)
· North Sydney (specific)
· Manly (specific)
· Parramatta (specific)
· Chatswood (specific)
· Hornsby (specific)
· Bondi (specific)
· Randwick (specific)
· Miranda (specific)

So now, if someone in Manly searches for 'best hairdresser Manly' I've got a good shot of showing up, conversely if someone in Parramatta searches 'best hairdresser Sydney' I'm just as likely to show. Thinking this way will allow you to capture a broader area as people search. And, if you're in a business (like mine) where you can service the entire country then I'd look to include all the States and Territories and fill in the remainder of the 20 areas from places where you know you have 'clusters' of clients ... or areas where you'd like to get more work.

My elderly parents live in the Northern Rivers of NSW, a little place called Evans Head (God's country really, but I digress). I'd love to get more work around there so I can visit them more frequently, so I've made sure to include the suburbs where I know I'd like work:

· Northern Rivers NSW (broad area)
· Byron Bay (specific)
· Ballina (specific)

It's giving me the best shot at popping up in someone's search from the region who is looking for services like mine.

Remember, these aren't locked in stone and you can delete, add or change the areas as often as needed (I suggest every couple of months). If you suddenly find yourself with a cluster of clients on the Gold Coast you can go back in and make sure your services areas are covering the surrounding suburbs.

### 3. Name all of your photos before you upload them

Okay, this is a super-secret hack that I'm not seeing many people do at all – and it's a cracker.

Before you load any photo to your GMB profile, make sure you name it with your business name and a location. This allows Google to index every single photo to your business and assign a location. So, when someone is searching for a hairdresser in Manly... BOOM there you are.

To give you a clearer idea, all of my photos are labelled as 'Tracy Sheen – The Digital Guide – location'. If it's a photo of me conducting a workshop or training then I'll make sure to include that as well 'Tracy Sheen – The Digital Guide – Google My Business workshop Surfers Paradise, QLD June 2020'.

Everything you're doing on GMB is to make it easier for Google to find you and put you in front of your ideal clients.

### 4. Use every character available to you and don't copy and paste from your website

As you complete your profile, you'll see each section gives you a character limit. Use them! Keep reminding yourself that Google is looking for content and a reason to put you forward as an authority on your subject.

By completing every section completely you're making it easier for Google. That's what we want to do... so they have a reason to organically promote us in search results.

The other piece to this is DO NOT copy and paste content from your website or other social media platforms. Google can see this as 'duplicate content' and it will actually do you more harm than good.

So, take the time to fill in each of the sections with new words ... You'll thank me a few months down the track.

### 5. Make sure you have your profile short name

This will make sense as you're completing your profile. One of the areas you'll be asked to complete is your profile short name. You have 32 characters here, and this bit is an absolute Godsend when you have a ridiculously long business name (like Tracy Sheen The Digital Guide).

Using your profile short name gives you a nice quick way to direct people to your page. As an example I've made my profile short name 'dig-guide' so now, when I want to share the link to my GMB profile for a client instead of having to send them to https://g.page/tracysheenthedigitalguide I can send them to: https://g.page/dig-guide – much quicker and much easier.

Remember... it's all about making it easier.

### 6. Collect reviews... as many as you can as often as you can

Google loves reviews, and so, by the way, do your clients. According to a HubSpot study, in 2019 88% of consumers trust user reviews as much as personal recommendations. And the average consumer reads 10 online reviews before making a purchase decision.

So, reviews... they are now your best business buddy.

Aim to be collecting 1 to 5 (depending on what type of business you're in) reviews each and every week. That way when anyone lands on your profile, they aren't seeing tumbleweeds drifting across the page with the last review from your mum two years ago.

Oh, and make sure you personalise each response to a review. Call the reviewer by their name (if you know who it is), acknowledge something they commended you on and sign off with your own name. You want the person who has taken the time to leave the review to feel acknowledged and thanked for their time.

I've popped an example of what I mean below.

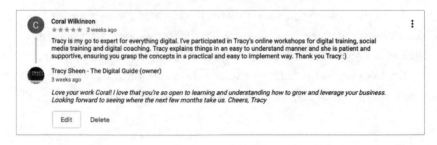

While we're on the subject of reviews, if you fancy a bit of a break from reading and you've found value in the information so far, why not share your experience with other potential readers and clients.

You can do so by following this link (note: you do need to have a Google account to leave a Google review): https://g.page/dig-guide/review.

### 7. *If you've not yet claimed and verified your GMB profile be prepared to wait*

One of the most annoying steps in creating your GMB profile is getting your account verified. If your business is in a commercial premises with signage then lucky you, you'll find the process oh so much easier. For those of us who work remotely or from home it can take weeks or months (mine took five months) for that wonderful little verification postcard to arrive in the mail.

I had three postcards arrive which all had incorrect verification codes on them. Eventually, when I thought all hope was lost, I was like Charlie with Willy Wonka's golden ticket.

In the meantime, while you're waiting DO NOT make any adjustments to your profile. Each tweak will cause Google to issue a new postcard and set you back another random period of time. So... do the basics, hit verify and then sit on your hands.

Oh, and if you are one of the ones who hasn't claimed your GMB page yet, you can do so by visiting this link: www.business.google.com.

# 31. LINKEDIN

*www.linkedin.com*

Okay. I'm not going to lie, I'm a big fan of LinkedIn. Out of all of the social media platforms, it's the one that makes the most sense to me. It's like a grown-up version of Facebook without the avocado on toast.

Seriously though LinkedIn kicks butt in the 'ways to bypass the gatekeeper' stakes. Business Insiders digital trust ranking has placed LinkedIn in the number one spot for trustworthiness three years running. And according to LinkedIn, four out of five LinkedIn members drive business decisions in their organisation.

Bottom line, if you're in B2B (business to business) then you really should be on LinkedIn. I'm not going to gush over the sales opportunities or the networking that can be done (although for the most part that is true). Instead, the thing I see most B2B businesses missing when it comes to LinkedIn is the SEO opportunity.

Hear me out with why I'm suggesting this.

Have you ever Googled yourself (go on, I know you have) and wondered why your LinkedIn profile appears as number one? And if it's not number one for you I guarantee it's top three.

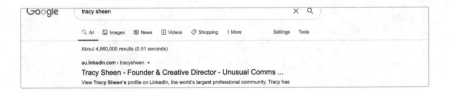

It's because Google considers LinkedIn to have as close to a perfect website as possible. It has millions of active users each day with fresh content being added to its site hourly (let alone daily).

All that equates to a fabulous SEO opportunity for us. We can ride on the coat tails of what LinkedIn has already created to bump our own organic search ranking.

Now, it means you actually need to take the time to properly complete your LinkedIn profile (yes, I mean every section with a headshot and a cover photo). And it means putting a bit of thought into what keywords and phrases you want to be known for or searched for. But hey, you've done that when you were updating or completing your GMB profile anyway, so the research is already done. I'm just asking you to apply the same research and thinking across your LinkedIn profile as well.

Again, with the eye roll huh?? I hear you, but, lucky for you I have another template to share. This one is my LinkedIn profile template. It gives you each of the sections that LinkedIn asks you for along with the character count and other bits and pieces to consider.

Just like the GMB profile, you can download your copy from my website. I'm a fan of getting clients to complete their profile into the template for a few reasons:

1. you can check your word count and see exactly how many characters you have remaining
2. you can spell check before you cut and paste
3. it gives you time to think about your keywords instead of writing the first thing that comes to mind.

## Social Selling Index

Once you have your profile sorted, LinkedIn has a fab little tool that you can use to track your progress. It's called the LinkedIn Social Selling Index (or SSI as it's sometimes referred to).

The SSI will give your profile a rating out of 100 across four different categories:

- establish your personal brand
- find the right people
- engage with insights
- build relationships

By monitoring your SSI (I suggest spending 5 minutes each month to review it), you'll very quickly see if there is an area within your LinkedIn strategy that you need to focus on.

Here's my SSI taken in September 2020 to give you an idea of what it shows you:

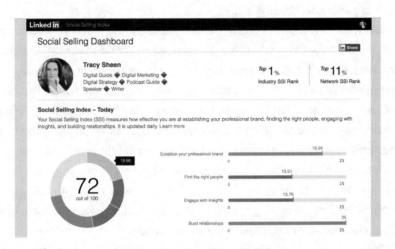

At first glance I can see that I've got the relationship thing nailed and my personal brand is doing okay (though I'd probably like to see it go up a couple of points if I'm honest). But I've really let the ball drop on finding the right people and engaging with insights.

I can tell you why immediately. I've done zero prospecting on LinkedIn (as in looking for people to reach out and connect with) for the past couple of months and I've dropped my posting consistency. Seeing these numbers will kick me back into gear posting (okay, I'll schedule that content, but you know what I mean) three times per week... and I'll take another look at people to connect with over the coming months.

Another cool thing is the SSI will rank me against other people in my industry and tell me how I'm doing as well as how I'm tracking compared to my overall network.

The point is, it's giving me direction, I know what I need to do.

If you want to check out your SSI, the link for you to find it is here: www.business.linkedin.com/sales-solutions/social-selling/the-social-selling-index-ssi.

## The three biggest pet peeves of LinkedIn users

### 1. Connecting

Anyone who uses LinkedIn with any kind of regularity has one big pet peeve. Getting a connection request with no idea why the person is connecting.

So, rule one of being serious in LinkedIn: Never send a connection request without including a personalised note.

To include a personalised note, click on 'connect'.

You'll then see a box pop up asking you if you'd like to personalise your connection.

Click on 'Add a note' and write your introduction. If you actually know the person, it's super easy… If you don't know them but you want to connect, look for common ground. Have you got mutual connections? Are you in the same industry? Have you read a post or an article they shared recently? Give the person you're reaching out to a reason to accept your connection request.

Want to practise that?

Drop me a connection request and tell me how you're enjoying the book: www.linkedin.com/in/tracysheen.

2. **Don't spam me!**

Rule number two of LinkedIn is don't connect with me and then immediately try to sell me.

I can guarantee if you connect with most people on LinkedIn and then send them a follow-up email or message that goes something like:

> *'Dear <first name>,*
>
> *Thanks for accepting my connection request.*
>
> *I thought I'd share a little bit about what I do as I thought it may be of interest to you....'*

... you will not be very popular.

Just. Don't. Do. It.

Remember the SSI we talked about a few moments ago? Put the hard yards in to build relationships. Share good quality content with me... wine me, dine me ... don't ask me to marry you on the first date.

I can't stress this enough... It's poor form and it p*sses people off.

Don't be that person.

3. **Don't export your contact list**

We've all had those emails land in our inbox that we wonder how the hell we made it onto your list.

There are a number of marketing agencies that advocate exporting all of your LinkedIn contacts (which technically you can do) into your database. I guess their hope is you'll win a few clients by doing this.

Here's the thing: it actually breaks LinkedIn's terms and conditions. Anyone who genuinely uses LinkedIn for good knows this, and we will report you to LinkedIn if you do it.

It's not worth it. It's poor form and you look like an idiot. And worse still it gives your business a really bad name.

Oh, and we'll probably report your email as spam, which means all your emails become tarred with the 'spam' brush.

## LinkedIn Company Pages

Okay... now you know how to maximise your profile and how not to annoy people while on LinkedIn, let's talk a little about LinkedIn company pages. Who uses them and why... and should you?

Over the years company pages (or 'pages' as LinkedIn calls them) have been the poor cousin to personal profiles. Only the super-big companies ever really bothered putting one in place, and often they'd go weeks or even months without bothering to post content to their page.

Recently though we've seen a bit of a push towards embracing pages by LinkedIn, and it would seem as though they may yet have a trick or two up their sleeves for promoting and leveraging pages as opposed to personal profiles.

So, is having a company page worth it?

Well... yes, and maybe no (sorry, I have commitment issues).

Here's my reasons for saying 'yes' to the company page.

If you have a number of employees within your business then, yes, absolutely go ahead and get yourself a 'page'. It is much easier to create brand alignment when your individual team members can be sharing and promoting your company content as well as giving your clients a place to come and see what the business (as opposed to each individual) is up to.

If you'll be looking for new team members at any point in your business, there's a reason recruiters hang out on LinkedIn. It's because they know it's filled with talented people looking for their next career opportunity. If your business is in the position now or in the future to recruit, a company page is a great resource to attract the right people.

If you have plans to grow the business beyond where it is now, Company pages allow you to create 'showcase pages' within your company page. These are a fab way to draw attention to a new product, business unit or project the business is working on.

So, a lot of positive reasons to have a company page ... right? There's one super-huge reason why you shouldn't though...

If you struggle to create regular content for social media (or blogs for that matter) – then either find yourself someone who can be in charge of regularly updating your page with content or don't do it.

You'll cause yourself and your business more angst by having a page sitting there that doesn't have regular updates. It's kinda like one of the old wild west towns you see in movies. If it's just you and the dog sitting on the porch whittlin' probably best to leave the idea alone.

If you do decide to push ahead and create (or perhaps re-engage) your company page then you'll be pleased to know that I have a template that you can follow to help you set your page up. Yep, you guessed it, it's available in the appendix or as a downloadable through the website.

## LinkedIn Company Pages analytics

The other thing you'll be pleased to hear is that pages offer some analytics for you to better understand how things are progressing. You'll see them in your admin view as you log into your page:

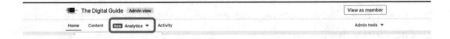

To be honest, the analytics are pretty rudimentary at this stage – it is one of the (many) things folks who use pages hope to see improvement on in the near future.

For now, though you can track:

· visitors

· updates

· followers.

### Visitor analytics

First couple of things to note is time is set to UTC. At this point you are unable to change it, so when you're looking through your analytics keep in mind (depending where you're based) you may need to do some time adjustment.

The other thing is (if needed) you can export your analytics. Super handy if you want to create a report or keep track of your progress.

### Visitor metrics

Shows the number of unique visitors to your page over the desired time period.

I do suggest you toggle the 'aggregated desktop and mobile traffic' switch on to give you a complete view of everyone hitting the page.

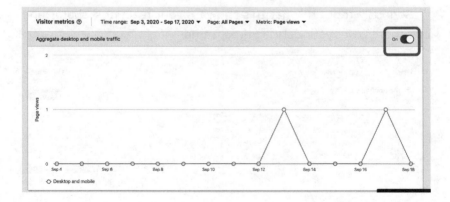

### Visitor demographics

Aggregates the members based on when they visited your page. Note that you can switch demographic views from:

· job function

· location

· seniority

· industry

· company size.

So, choose the option (or options) that best suit what you're looking to track.

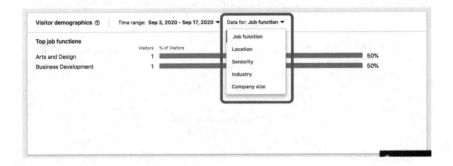

### Update analytics

Okay, I know as soon as you look at my screen shot, you'll scream that there is not an update in sight. This is one of those cases where I tout the old 'do as I say' moniker. I'm just a 'guide' remember, I don't claim to have it all working to perfection.

Seriously though, what this shows is your reactions, shares and comments over your defined time frame.

## *Update metrics*

Shows your engagement metrics (aggregated) over your set time frame. Note you can change the report to measure various different metrics including:

- **Impressions:** Shows the views when a post is visible to at least 50% of a reader's screen for at least 300 ms, or when it is clicked, whichever comes first.

- **Unique impressions:** The number of times your posts were shown to unique LinkedIn members who are signed into their account.

- **Clicks:** The number of clicks on your post, your business name, or your logo by a LinkedIn member who is signed into their account. Does not include interactions (shares, Reactions, and comments).

- **Reactions/Comments/Shares:** The number of Reactions (see image below) or comments, and the times your content was shared by members, including any ads or video posts.

- **Engagement rate:** Shown as a percentage the engagement rate takes the number of interactions, adds the number of clicks and followers acquired, and divides it by the number of impressions.

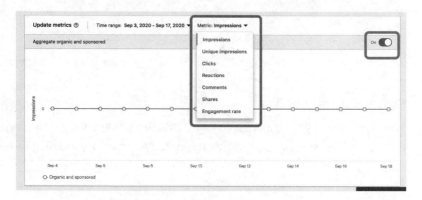

### Update engagement

Will show your engagement by individual post.

### Follower highlights

Shows you the number of total followers to your page as well as the number of new followers you've gained.

### Follower metrics

Shows you by date when you collected a new follower. If you're planning on doing paid advertising on LinkedIn, then you can aggregate the findings to show a mix of organic and paid followers.

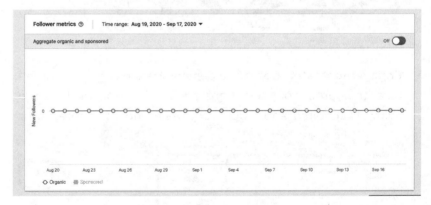

### Follower demographics

This will show you the breakdown of who's following your page based on five types of demographic data. You can drill down on the data to filter by:

- location
- job function
- seniority
- industry
- company size

Note: Currently, you're unable to view individual or specific followers of your Page.

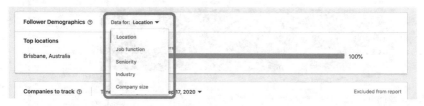

## Other useful things you'll find in 'Admin Tools'

Hiding under the drop-down tool on the right-hand side of your screen that says 'admin tools' you'll find a bunch of other useful resources worth knowing about.

- **Invite connections:** You can invite your individual connections to follow your Page.
- **Sponsor an update:** If you're considering running paid ads or sponsored posts you can do so here.
- **Post a job:** Got a job opportunity you want to share with your community? This is where you go to post a job.
- **Create a Showcase Page:** Showcase Pages are a great way to highlight a new product, business unit or project within the company.
- **Manage admins:** If you're looking to add (or remove) anyone to manage your company page you do so here.
- **Edit public URL:** Super important to do! Create your unique LinkedIn company URL to ensure continuity with your brand.
- **Deactivate Page:** Company page not working out for you? You can deactivate your Page through here.

- **View Help Centre:** Everybody needs a little help now and then; this is where you'll find the LinkedIn Pages information.
- **View Pages terms:** Want to know everything you can and can't do with your page? Look no further.

# 32. WHATSAPP

*www.whatsapp.com*

Another one of those 'owned by Facebook' platforms that is making big waves with small business, especially during the COVID pandemic.

WhatsApp is at heart a messaging tool. Use it for phone calls, video calls or text messaging – its popularity came about because of the ability to call internationally for 'free'. Of course, it's not really free; it relies on your WIFI data to make the call... Still though, better than the exorbitant international call fees we were all used to not that long ago.

The app will recognise people in your contact list and (if you choose) add them to your app. The idea being you never miss a call or message.

One of the best features around WhatsApp is their security. Offering high-level end-to-end encryption, similar to Apple iMessage. Meaning WhatsApp can't read your messages... even if they wanted to.

According to WhatsApp themselves there are over 1 billion people currently using the platform every single day, and with the introduction of WhatsApp Business the ability to communicate en mass to your client base has never been easier.

I like that you can create and verify a business account as opposed to having to manage things via a personal profile. I like the idea of labelling (so you know who you're communicating with and why) and that you can automate messages.

But, for me, the jury is still out on whether it's a value add or a time suck for small business. Personally, I have it on my phone but not my laptop, I'm not sure about having another method of communication available and open to my clients 24/7... It leaves me feeling like there is no division between work and life... But I have a number of friends who run businesses and have established successful and engaged groups using the functionality.

There was a change to the platform's 'terms of service' in February 2020 that gives parent company Facebook full and irrevocable access to share any of your information held on WhatsApp with Facebook and its subsidiaries. There is no middle ground here; you either accept the updated terms and allow your information to flow through to Facebook or you delete your WhatsApp account.

I have been using this app for a number of months; given this latest change though there are certainly other options on the market you could explore.

I'd put it in the 'one to check out' pile.

www.whatsapp.com/business

# 33. TIKTOK

*www.tiktok.com*

Ahhhhh TikTok, what would the millennials have done during the COVID pandemic if it were not for your dance challenges?

I'm going to be super clear here so as to leave no room for ambiguity. I do not like this platform. I see far too many security issues with it, and I will not download or use it for my business or advise any of my clients to use it.

There have been some great articles written around the TikTok security concerns (which I strongly suggest you read through). From a business standpoint though, if you are working with a younger client base then I can see the appeal of considering TikTok.

According to Hootsuite, TikTok had 800 million active users as of October 2019, and was growing fast, with average users opening the app more than 8 times a day ... That's serious eyeballs if you're targeting the younger demographic.

If you are considering TikTok as a platform to attract and engage a younger audience, there are a few do's and don'ts to keep in mind:

- Do keep it short. Around 15 seconds is perfect, and get straight to the point.
- Do keep it fun. Humour, dance, whatever it takes to keep it light.
- Do only use vertical videos.
- Do use music... TikTok is all about the music.

- Do start a challenge. TikTok loves a good challenge. Tagging 3 to 5 people you know will start it going for you.

- Do compete in other challenges. TikTok is all about inclusion.

- Do keep an eye on what's trending... then create something similar.

- Do be prepared to collaborate with influencers, brands, etc. Remember TikTok is about inclusion.

- Don't make your content feel like an ad.

# 34. SNAPCHAT

*www.snapchat.com*

If you're looking for a millennial market, then Snapchat could be an option you need to consider.

The platform started in 2011, and while it doesn't claim to have anywhere near the number of monthly users that Facebook enjoys, it does continue to engage with its desired younger audience.

According to research completed by Hootsuite in January 2020, Snapchat still drew over 218 million users to its platform every single day. That's millions of snaps created, seen and sent every day.

Further to their research, Hootsuite identified that over 80% of Snapchat's audience is under the age of 34. The really interesting thing with this information though is over one-third of the people on Snapchat won't be found on Instagram (which I'd usually suggest would be the platform you'd engage them on).

If you're trying to get your head around Snapchat, here's some language you'll need to know:

- **Snap:** An image or a video sent to one or more of your friends. Videos are maximum 10 seconds. Snaps are deleted once they've been viewed by everyone, unless you add them to a story... Unseen snaps are deleted after 30 days.

- **Story:** A place to house your images or videos you'd like to share with all your Snapchat friends. Stories are deleted after 24 hours.

- **Custom Stories:** Allows a group of your friends to create a story together. You can even geo-fence a story, which means people can only add content if they are in a certain location. Geo fenced stories can be added to by your friends of friends also, making your reach bigger.

- **Snapstreak:** Snap a friend within 24 hours for 3 days in a row... you're on a snapstreak. If you hit a snapstreak you'll see a flame appear next to your friend's name with a number correlating to the number of days you've had the streak running.

- **Snapchat lens:** Add animated special effects when creating your image or video.

- **Filters:** Overlay effects on an image or video which has already been created. Popular filters include locations, time of day and holidays.

- **Geofilter:** Filters that are unique to your current location. You need to activate geofilters by switching on location in Snapchat. You can also pay a nominal amount to create a custom geofilter. These are great for special events and building brand awareness.

- **Snapcodes:** Unique QR codes you can scan to add friends or access additional content and features.

- **Chat:** Snapchats version of instant messenger.

- **Snap map:** Shows your location and the location of all your friends. You can switch to 'ghost mode' by turning off location in your settings.

- **Friends page:** Swipe right from your camera to see this page. Your friends' stories and chats will live in this page along with people you may wish to connect with based on Snapchats algorithm.

- **Discover page:** Swiping left from your camera allows you to find content from other creators including anyone you have subscribed to.

- **Memories:** The camera roll that backs up your Snaps and stories.

- **Context cards:** Provide additional content to a snap, usually from a third-party provider such as Trip Advisor. You'll see these a lot in hospitality. To access a context card swipe up when you're inside a snap or story.

- **Bitmoji:** An animated icon representing you inside the app.

Snapchat do offer their business account users access to some analytics (though, not a whole lot to be honest). So you'll be able to see the age group most connecting with your content along with the gender split.

If you're considering adding Snapchat to your social media platforms then there are a few things you'll need to keep in mind.

- **Keep it short and sweet:** Snapchat users favour content between 1 and 2 minutes. And remember, Snapchat video only allows a few seconds of footage.

- **Mix it up:** Try promotional codes, behind the scenes, product reveals or consider partnering with Snapchat influencers.

- **Keep it raw:** This isn't a platform for highly edited content. Have a play with some filters but keep it authentic.

- **Sell the sizzle not the steak:** Snapchat is all about storytelling. While you may only have a few seconds via video, users enjoy engaging with content that's spread out over multiple posts.

- **You do you:** The big problem with a lot of Snapchat business content is it's the same as all the rest. Snapchat users are looking for something quirky and original. You'll need to up your game to get them engaging.

# 35. CLUBHOUSE

Clubhouse is the latest kid on the social media block. The point of difference here is it is an audio-based platform only. I think of it as talkback radio meets podcasting. Essentially you set up 'rooms' and host conversations. The rooms can be 'open' (meaning anyone on Clubhouse could drop in), 'social' (meaning the room is open only to your connections), or 'private' (meaning you set up a room with you and nominated people).

At the time of publication the platform was still in beta mode and only available to iPhone and iPad users. The talk on Clubhouse is the platform will open up to Android users in March this year. According to a story in *New York Times* in Decemebr 2020 there were only 600,000 users on the platform globally. There is a long waiting list and the FOMO (fear of missing out) is driving conversation globally.

There are some really big names already using the platform and some of the conversations I've been a part of have given me access to people I would have needed to pay thousands of dollars to hear speak previously.

At the time of writing, I've been using the platform for a number of weeks and spent a lot of hours figuring out what the hype is all about. It's become one of my favorite places to hang out and I see huge potential for a wide range of business owners.

If you own an iPhone and you're interested, download the app and secure your user name to get on the waiting list.

Clubhouse is definitely a platform you'll be hearing more about. My advice: download the app, secure your user name and get on the waiting list.

# 36. CUSTOMER RELATIONSHIP MANAGEMENT (CRM)

## Magic behind the scenes

When small business looks to leap into the world of marketing automation they typically think of automated emails, funnels and landing pages. Amazing bits of tech doing magic behind the scenes while they sit in a hammock drinking pina coladas.

Before we can get you to that point, the crucial first step into marketing automation is getting a good CRM system in place.

It's the CRM that does the heavy lifting for everything else that's to come. It's the bit that knows all of the information about your client, such as their name, phone number, email, web address, birthday. You can also capture information that is bespoke to your business like the date of last purchase or what they purchased, even their favourite ice-cream flavour if you are so inclined (Ben & Jerry's Phish Food in case you're wondering).

So, finding the 'right' CRM to suit your business should be at the top of the totem pole in terms of requirements. Get that right and the rest of your automation will start humming quicker than … well, let's just say it'll be a whole lot smoother.

There is a tonne of CRM systems available on the market. From the most basic using a spreadsheet to capture information, through platforms like HubSpot or Zoho, where you can snap a photo of a business card at a networking event and have the person loaded in your system pronto.

Here's the thing about CRM systems. Now, this is super important, so I need you to stop anything else you're doing and listen up … A CRM will only work if you work it.

'What do I mean?' I hear you ask … well, quite simply, deciding to start using a CRM system in an established business can be a right royal pain in the butt. After all, you've had a system for years – sure, it doesn't work great, but you have a system. Deciding to use a CRM means you, and by default the entire team, need to start using the CRM system.

That means every morning when you get into your office with your coffee and open the lid to your laptop you open the CRM at the same time. Every time a call comes in from a client you log the call in the system and update any details for the client that need updating. Any email you send, you send via the CRM. The more you use it, the more it'll get to know your business and the more it'll start adding value to you.

And it doesn't stop there. When you leave the office and you're in your car, if you need to call a client, you call them through the CRM… why? Because it'll log the call and you can leave notes.

In case you haven't got my point yet, it is that a CRM is a big commitment.

## How do you choose a CRM?

Well, I like to start by making sure it'll do the other bits and pieces that I was originally looking for (like email marketing, maybe landing pages and funnels). If it does all of that, it's a big tick. Depending on your business, if you have a sales or service team you might also like to make sure it'll have features your sales people are looking for like a deals or sales pipeline (I'll talk more about the CRM as a sales tool in the Sales section) and your service folk may like a job ticketing function or a knowledge base.

Now the CRM you're looking at may not tick every single box but it's a good idea to at least have a round table discussion with everyone first to see what would make their life easier. Then you'll be able to make a features vs cost decision when it comes to it.

In case you're wondering what I use... well, I went with a platform called HubSpot. I've tried many, many (God, so many) CRM systems over the years with various companies I've worked with and I've found some so painful I refused to use them while others lacked basic features and functionality I thought would have been essential to a CRM. Either way, after 30 years of doing this I opted for HubSpot a few years ago and I have to say considering their CRM section is free it's the best darn platform I've actually ever used.

You'll hear me bang on a lot about list segmentation and developing client personas, target markets, etc., because honestly, you need that stuff if you want your digital platforms to do what you imagine they're going to do for you. It's the CRM that will hold that variety of information and store it to ensure you're targeting the right person at the right time with the right piece of content.

As we begin to talk about marketing automation, you'll see I've done a comparison of a few of the better known platforms. Each of these have their own version of a CRM attached to them. Before you go 'all in' with one over another I'd strongly encourage you to either do a product demo and get someone to show you exactly what the system can do (even if you aren't ready for all the bells and whistles quite yet). At the very least, put a call out to your business buddies to see what they're using, what they like and what they wished they'd known before they committed.

'Cause once you do, well, I'm not going to say it's impossible to jump CRM platforms, but you'll need to be prepared to lose some data and enjoy another steep learning curve.

In this instance it's one of those occasions where my Mother would say 'less haste, more speed'.

# 37. MARKETING AUTOMATION

One of the things that originally piqued my digital marketing interest was the thought that I could automate certain aspects of my marketing. The idea I didn't have to manually respond to every single piece of communication that crossed my desk sent shivers of excitement down my spine.

Okay, that's probably too much information (TMI) and really does highlight:

· what a geek I really am
· I have no life outside of work

I've since come to learn that automation used well will enhance your customers' journey dealing with you, and used badly will create a bunch of very disillusioned or p*ssed off people.

So, let me step back. If you've not come across the term 'marketing automation' before, simply it is the ability to manage your marketing steps across a variety of platforms automatically.

As a basic example, think about the last time you signed up for a newsletter or to stay in touch with a brand or business you like. Chances are you popped your name and email on a form on their website (or maybe their social media) and within a few moments you received an email thanking you for signing up. Maybe it had an offer included, maybe it told you where you could keep in contact, but essentially you received a note of thanks.

That's marketing automation at work. The business you signed up with to stay in touch has a marketing automation platform that has a trigger which says, 'when we get contact details signing up to our newsletter, send them this email'.

In a more complicated scenario, marketing automation is the thing that sends you a series of emails over a number of days offering you free content (maybe an eBook, a blog, a template, a checklist... you get the idea) and then finally, somewhere around email 3 to 5 there'll be an offer to 'buy' or 'engage' with the brand. If you say no, you'll most likely be 'automatically' dropped into another email sequence to see if you'd like to buy something different... and around and around we go with (theoretically) our clients dropping in and out of various email sequences over a period of months or years.

Most marketing automation platforms are built around a CRM (Customer Relationship Manager) system which will collate and curate data on each of your clients. It's the understanding of your client interactions and behaviours that drives good automation.

As small business owners though we can use and implement some basic marketing automation to make our lives just that bit easier. Fabulous places to start are things like:

- **Thank you emails:** Signing up to a newsletter or recognising a client's birthday or anniversary with your business.
- **Onboarding:** It's likely you'll have a sequence of steps you take your new clients through, these onboarding steps make for great automated sequences.
- **Project updates:** If you're working with a client and have standard project milestones, these often work well in automation.
- **Abandoned cart:** Have you been shopping for something online and got side tracked? That's known as an 'abandoned cart' and they work exceptionally well as automations.

Okay, we get why we'd want to automate some emails, but if we take it one step further we can actually begin to automate content (like an ebook for example) to go out with the emails, or we can direct them to a landing page (which is just a fancy word for a single web page that they 'land' on... hence 'landing page'). Are you starting to see the power behind automation?

Now, the whole conversation about which automation platform is going to be right for you is a book unto itself (and there's been quite a few written on various platforms) and I'm not about to dive headfirst down that rabbit hole.

What I will share with you though are the questions you need to be asking yourself (and your potential automation platform) before making a decision which way you want to go.

### Why do you want to automate?

- What types of things are you looking to automate?

  Some platforms will allow you to automate:
  - tasks (if you have an internal process that needs to happen as a result of client interaction)
  - emails
  - content delivery

### How many contacts do you have in your database?

### What other information would you like to be able to track?

- website visits
- social media interactions
- calendar appointments
- internal tasks and processes
- sales pipeline
- service pipeline
- paid advertising (Google Ads, Facebook ads)
- SEO

I've worked with a lot of different platforms over the years and while I have my personal favourite, I think it's important to at least review and consider a few different options. So, I thought it would be worthwhile to share a few options to get you started.

| Product | Pros | Cons |
|---------|------|------|
| **MailChimp** | – Email automation<br>– Some easy to use templates<br>– Create contact lists<br>– Easy to schedule emails | – Used by digital marketing agencies to 'wash' client's data which means overall we tend to see more spam coming from MailChimp<br>– Once you start paying it is quite expensive for what it offers<br>– Not great with tutorials or help<br>– You need to understand MailChimp lingo to get going |
| **Ontraport** | – Drag and drop email creator<br>– Email automation<br>– Landing pages<br>– Marketing automation<br>– 2-week free trial | – Support is not great if you're based in Australia<br>– I've had issues with emails and content being delivered more than once or sending things out of sequence<br>– No free plans<br>– I found the CRM (database) clunky |
| **HubSpot** | – The free version is the best CRM I've found for a small business application<br>– Emails are easy to create<br>– Good reporting functions<br>– Great support – HubSpot academy, videos and knowledge base<br>– Great mobile app | – Landing pages and automations are on the paid plans and the jump to paid is a sizeable one<br>– Can be expensive, needs a cheaper plan |

| Product | Pros | Cons |
|---|---|---|
| **Active Campaign** | – Free version and good first tier of paid plans for SME<br><br>– Does all marketing automation requirements<br><br>– Reasonably simple to follow | – Reporting functions could do with some work<br><br>– Could do with a better help/support database<br><br>– No automation templates to start you off |
| **Agile** | – Reasonably intuitive to set up<br><br>– Great if you just want to do email automation<br><br>– Drag and drop functionality | – No landing page function<br><br>– Reporting is a little clunky |

I'm going to talk further about EDM (electronic direct mails... or 'email' as most humans refer to it) in a moment, as this is usually the first port of call when I chat with a client who wants to automate.

If you are thinking it's time to consider an automation platform I'd highly recommend gazing into your crystal ball and creating a 'perfect' picture for a few years down the road. Otherwise you could find yourself using an automation platform that you need to integrate (i.e.: tack on) with other bits of software ... and that's never fun. Nor is it fun to move platforms after you have your database set up and your emails automated, so best to do the leg work up front.

Oh, one last thing... Marketing automation is one of those bits of technology that I suggest you get some help with setting up and training. Trust me, it'll save you a whole lot of time, energy and angst.

## Automation funnels

Marketing funnels, sales funnels, conversion funnels... whatever you want to call them, digital marketers have long since salivated over the idea of 'funnelling' people through a series of steps in order to achieve an outcome.

The idea of the funnel is it catches a broad group of people at the top, and as you feed them content or information to take action they will move along to the next step until they have made a purchase decision.

*Sounds good,* I hear you say, and it is. It's also where your marketing automation platform will begin to earn its keep.... as long as you put the hard yards in while setting up your CRM. If you want an automation funnel to work, you really need to know your target market and client personas.

At its very basic level you begin to map out your funnel by following a few steps:

1. Define the problem you want to solve for your clients with this particular funnel.
2. Create some kind of initial offer (or 'lead magnet' as they're called) to entice people into the top of your funnel.
3. Begin to qualify your prospects and confirm they have interest in your product or service.
4. Begin nurturing these people (this could be with free high-value content, a free sales call, a free trial, etc).
5. Convert your prospect into a customer.
6. Analyse your results and refine the process.

The challenge with most clients these days though is they don't follow a traditional pathway. They may often loop around in the qualify and nurture stage for months, seeking more information, testing, questioning... the traditional funnel process just doesn't account for that.

During my time as a HubSpot partner I encountered their idea of moving away from a traditional funnel model and into a 'flywheel', where people are free to loop around wherever they like for as long as they like.

In moving our thinking to a more circular marketing strategy, we need to create content and have it available for our customers at every point of the marketing journey they're at.

Now, automation platforms can still do this for us, it's just a different way of looking at the process. Essentially though it still boils down to you needing to know... *really* know who your target client groups are.

There have been many hundreds of books written over the years about attracting clients through marketing and building funnels that work, so I'm not going to go into further detail about that here.

Instead I'm going to suggest before you consider taking on a marketing automation platform you read a couple of books: *Content Inc.* by Joe Pullizzi and *Building a StoryBrand* by Donald Miller.

Once you're clear on the types of content you're creating, building the actual funnel is no more difficult than drawing a flow chart.

# 38. EDM (ELECTRONIC DIRECT MAIL) AND EMAIL AUTOMATION

Most sane humans (read non-techy-marketing-type people) call EDMs emails. For some reason marketing techy people like to make things sound more complicated than they actually are.

When you start reading about or looking into email automation or EDMs, you may suddenly come across a bunch of other jargon that means nothing to you... that's okay, it's why you're reading this book! Let's take a look at some of the most common terms digital marketers may throw at you.

## Open rate

This is the term used for the percentage of your emails that were opened by your intended audience. E.g.: If you send an email to 100 people and 50 people open it, your open rate would be 50%. It's worth noting that open rates will vary greatly across industries (and even days!).

Think about how many emails are landing in your own email inbox each day, and then think about how many you actually bother to click on and open. Your goal is to create content in an email that your people 'want' to click on. You'll get much better results by working through segmenting your data and developing your client personas (remember back to the start of this section), because you'll be delivering hyper-targeted information to a smaller group of people with a bigger appetite for that content.

As a benchmark for all email campaigns, Campaign Monitor have reported across the board Aussies tend to open around 18.7% of emails. So, if you like comparing yourself to others, this would be the benchmark I'd suggest you work to.

And if you're interested in what day(s) are the best to send an email, well, that varies by industry too. Fortunately, Campaign Monitor collated that in their research too so I can include it for you here.

| **OPEN** RATE | SUNDAY Su | MONDAY M | TUESDAY T | WEDNESDAY W | THURSDAY Th | FRIDAY F | SATURDAY S |
|---|---|---|---|---|---|---|---|
| Advertising and Marketing Agencies | 16.20% | 17.90% | 17.10% | 19.30% | 18.10% | 18.90% | 18.90% |
| Agriculture, Forestry, Fishing & Hunting | 29.50% | 20.60% | 20.70% | 40.90% | 14.90% | 22.80% | 19.50% |
| Automotive and Aerospace | 29.90% | 32.00% | 27.00% | 37.10% | 30.20% | 33.50% | 28.10% |
| Construction, Contracting, and Manufacturing | 25.50% | 24.80% | 25.60% | 31.00% | 26.00% | 25.00% | 24.80% |
| Consumer Packaged Goods | 15.60% | 18.00% | 14.90% | 21.00% | 16.70% | 14.70% | 21.20% |
| Education | 28.30% | 29.70% | 31.80% | 33.30% | 31.50% | 32.40% | 31.00% |
| Engineering, Architecture and Design | 21.40% | 23.00% | 21.40% | 23.30% | 23.50% | 21.70% | 23.50% |
| Financial Services | 24.20% | 22.60% | 23.20% | 23.40% | 22.30% | 22.40% | 22.90% |
| Food and Beverage | 19.10% | 19.90% | 19.50% | 15.00% | 17.10% | 23.70% | 12.80% |
| Government | 30.00% | 31.30% | 30.80% | 30.50% | 31.80% | 30.00% | 28.70% |
| Healthcare Services | 23.50% | 25.40% | 23.10% | 26.40% | 26.00% | 23.10% | 25.20% |
| IT / Tech / Software Services | 20.10% | 18.90% | 19.00% | 18.10% | 20.50% | 18.20% | 20.30% |
| Logistics and Wholesale | 12.90% | 20.90% | 17.20% | 20.20% | 17.40% | 16.40% | 21.10% |
| Media, Entertainment, and Publishing | 15.90% | 18.20% | 17.30% | 18.90% | 15.70% | 17.40% | 19.00% |
| Nonprofit | 25.40% | 28.30% | 27.80% | 27.10% | 28.20% | 26.60% | 25.70% |
| Other | 27.90% | 29.90% | 28.60% | 29.80% | 28.40% | 26.50% | 30.30% |
| Professional Services | 20.00% | 21.10% | 21.60% | 24.50% | 20.30% | 22.10% | 22.60% |
| Real Estate, Design and Construction Activities | 19.70% | 19.50% | 19.50% | 20.20% | 20.70% | 20.20% | 18.30% |
| Retail | 13.30% | 15.20% | 14.60% | 15.60% | 13.80% | 14.50% | 14.90% |
| Travel, Hospitality, and Leisure | 17.40% | 16.80% | 16.00% | 16.50% | 18.60% | 15.30% | 18.00% |
| Unknown | 19.60% | 21.00% | 19.60% | 21.10% | 20.50% | 20.00% | 20.70% |
| Average | 18.30% | 19.00% | 18.40% | 19.40% | 18.80% | 18.40% | 19.60% |

## Click through rate (CTR)

If you pop a web link in your email that you'd like people to check out then your CTR is something you want to track. To get your CTR, take the number of people who opened your email (open rate) and divide it by the number that clicked on your web link. Voila ... CTR.

Again, if you're into comparisons, Campaign Monitor have reported that the average Australian emails in 2020 have a CTR of 2.8%.

If that seems low, I'd agree. Most clients I work with see anywhere from 10% to 20% ... but then I'm getting them to drill down on their segments and only send relevant information to relevant people.

Again, if you're into comparisons, Campaign Monitor has reported that Australian emails in 2020 have an average CTR of 2.8%.

| CLICK-THROUGH RATE | Su SUNDAY | M MONDAY | T TUESDAY | W WEDNESDAY | Th THURSDAY | F FRIDAY | S SATURDAY |
|---|---|---|---|---|---|---|---|
| Advertising and Marketing Agencies | 2.00% | 2.30% | 1.80% | 2.60% | 2.40% | 2.20% | 2.60% |
| Agriculture, Forestry, Fishing & Hunting | 5.10% | 3.60% | 2.70% | 9.80% | 2.10% | 3.00% | 2.50% |
| Automotive and Aerospace | 4.50% | 3.10% | 2.80% | 5.30% | 3.60% | 4.70% | 3.20% |
| Construction, Contracting, and Manufacturing | 4.30% | 3.30% | 3.60% | 4.60% | 4.50% | 3.60% | 4.00% |
| Consumer Packaged Goods | 1.10% | 1.60% | 1.40% | 1.70% | 1.50% | 1.20% | 1.80% |
| Education | 5.40% | 5.10% | 5.70% | 5.90% | 5.30% | 6.00% | 5.40% |
| Engineering, Architecture and Design | 2.80% | 3.00% | 2.70% | 3.40% | 3.50% | 3.00% | 3.10% |
| Financial Services | 3.10% | 3.10% | 2.80% | 3.10% | 2.90% | 2.90% | 2.90% |
| Food and Beverage | 1.00% | 1.60% | 1.90% | 1.50% | 0.90% | 4.50% | 1.00% |
| Government | 3.80% | 4.00% | 4.30% | 4.00% | 4.30% | 3.70% | 3.40% |
| Healthcare Services | 2.50% | 3.40% | 2.40% | 3.00% | 3.00% | 2.50% | 3.10% |
| IT / Tech / Software Services | 3.50% | 3.20% | 3.30% | 2.90% | 3.60% | 3.10% | 3.50% |
| Logistics and Wholesale | 1.20% | 1.80% | 1.40% | 1.50% | 1.50% | 1.40% | 1.70% |
| Media, Entertainment, and Publishing | 3.10% | 3.80% | 3.60% | 4.20% | 3.00% | 3.70% | 4.00% |
| Nonprofit | 3.50% | 4.40% | 4.40% | 4.00% | 4.10% | 3.90% | 3.30% |
| Other | 3.60% | 4.30% | 3.30% | 4.40% | 3.70% | 2.90% | 4.30% |
| Professional Services | 2.40% | 2.80% | 2.60% | 3.30% | 2.70% | 2.80% | 2.70% |
| Real Estate, Design and Construction Activities | 3.40% | 3.40% | 3.10% | 3.50% | 3.90% | 3.70% | 3.10% |
| Retail | 1.60% | 1.60% | 1.70% | 1.60% | 1.60% | 1.50% | 1.70% |
| Travel, Hospitality, and Leisure | 1.50% | 1.50% | 1.40% | 1.40% | 1.60% | 1.30% | 1.80% |
| Unknown | 2.80% | 3.30% | 3.00% | 3.20% | 3.00% | 3.00% | 3.20% |
| Average | 2.70% | 2.90% | 2.80% | 2.90% | 2.90% | 2.80% | 2.90% |

2020 Australia Email Benchmarks data

## Unsubscribe rate

We've all done it. Received one too many emails and hit the unsubscribe button. In fact, there were a couple of days during the early parts of COVID that I counted over 50 unsubscribes ... I think everyone suddenly went email crazy and were sending emails without a reason.

But I do say to my clients I'd rather have a list of 100 highly engaged people than 1000 that don't open or click through. So, if you lose a few people from your list every now and then, c'est la vie.

I hate to keep harping (I don't really), but if you keep your lists segmented and your content super relevant, your unsubscribe numbers will stay low.

And, I wouldn't have thought a particular day of the week would affect your unsubscribe rate, but thanks to Campaign Monitors research I now know I'm wrong ... here's what it looks like by industry and day.

## UNSUB RATE

| | Su | M | T | W | Th | F | S |
|---|---|---|---|---|---|---|---|
| | SUNDAY | MONDAY | TUESDAY | WEDNESDAY | THURSDAY | FRIDAY | SATURDAY |
| Advertising and Marketing Agencies | 0.20% | 0.30% | 0.20% | 0.30% | 0.30% | 0.20% | 0.30% |
| Agriculture, Forestry, Fishing & Hunting | 0.10% | 0.30% | 0.70% | 1.40% | 0.20% | 0.50% | 0.30% |
| Automotive and Aerospace | 0.40% | 0.50% | 0.40% | 0.50% | 0.50% | 0.50% | 0.40% |
| Construction, Contracting, and Manufacturing | 0.30% | 0.30% | 0.30% | 0.30% | 0.20% | 0.30% | 0.40% |
| Consumer Packaged Goods | 0.20% | 0.20% | 0.20% | 0.20% | 0.30% | 0.20% | 0.30% |
| Education | 0.60% | 0.20% | 0.30% | 0.50% | 0.20% | 0.30% | 0.30% |
| Engineering, Architecture and Design | 0.20% | 0.30% | 0.30% | 0.30% | 0.20% | 0.30% | 0.30% |
| Financial Services | 0.20% | 0.30% | 0.30% | 0.20% | 0.20% | 0.20% | 0.20% |
| Food and Beverage | 0.40% | 0.60% | 0.50% | 0.30% | 0.50% | 0.30% | 0.30% |
| Government | 0.20% | 0.20% | 0.20% | 0.20% | 0.20% | 0.20% | 0.20% |
| Healthcare Services | 0.40% | 0.40% | 0.50% | 0.30% | 0.40% | 0.30% | 0.40% |
| IT / Tech / Software Services | 0.20% | 0.20% | 0.20% | 0.20% | 0.20% | 0.20% | 0.20% |
| Logistics and Wholesale | 0.40% | 0.40% | 0.30% | 0.20% | 0.70% | 0.30% | 0.40% |
| Media, Entertainment, and Publishing | 0.10% | 0.20% | 0.10% | 0.10% | 0.20% | 0.10% | 0.10% |
| Nonprofit | 0.40% | 0.40% | 0.40% | 0.50% | 0.40% | 0.40% | 0.60% |
| Other | 0.50% | 0.50% | 0.40% | 0.40% | 0.50% | 0.40% | 0.40% |
| Professional Services | 0.20% | 0.30% | 0.20% | 0.30% | 0.20% | 0.20% | 0.20% |
| Real Estate, Design and Construction Activities | 0.20% | 0.20% | 0.20% | 0.20% | 0.20% | 0.30% | 0.20% |
| Retail | 0.10% | 0.10% | 0.10% | 0.10% | 0.10% | 0.10% | 0.10% |
| Travel, Hospitality, and Leisure | 0.30% | 0.20% | 0.20% | 0.20% | 0.30% | 0.20% | 0.30% |
| Unknown | 0.30% | 0.30% | 0.30% | 0.30% | 0.30% | 0.30% | 0.30% |
| Average | 0.20% | 0.20% | 0.20% | 0.20% | 0.20% | 0.20% | 0.20% |

2020 Australia Email Benchmarks data

## A/B split test

This is the ability to split your contact list and try a variation on an email across different audiences to see which gets the better reaction. A/B split testing can also be used in advertising on social media. You need a 'reasonable' sized database (in my opinion at least a few thousand) to bother with A/B testing.

## Abandoned cart email

The email that will trigger if a client has put items in their cart but not completed their purchase.

## Autoresponder

An automatic email that is triggered as a result of an action from a client. For example, an out-of-office email would be considered an autoresponder.

## Broadcast

A broadcast will go to every single person on your contact list as opposed to just a particular segment.

### Bounce rate

Essentially a bounce rate refers to the percentage of emails sent that were undelivered.

There are two different types of bounce rates to keep an eye on:

- **Hard bounce:** A permanent issue with the email address. Usually because the email is entered incorrectly, the person has cancelled their email or blocked your email address. You want to make sure your email automation platform does not attempt to continue resending emails to a hard bounce notification.

- **Soft bounce:** Often a temporary issue due to the email inbox being full or a problem with your client's email server. Your email automation platform should attempt to resend to a soft bounce email.

The average bounce rate in Australia according to Campaign Monitor is 1%.

### Call to Action (CTA)

The action you want your email recipient to take as a result of opening your email. It could be as simple as 'click to read our blog' or 'like our Facebook page' or a more sales focused 'buy this thing'.

Always remember to include some type of CTA in your emails (all marketing for that matter); it's a way your audience can repay you for your awesome content.

### Contact list

Another term used for your database or mailing list.

### Conversion rate

Every email should contain some type of call to action (CTA) as described above. Your conversion rate will measure the percentage of people who followed your CTA.

### Double opt in

Have you ever signed up for someone's newsletter and had an email asking you to confirm you wanted to join? That's a double opt in.

It's giving the user the opportunity to back out of the commitment. Once upon a time they were industry standard, we tend not to use them (as much) anymore. I think we (as an industry) realised we didn't want to put additional obstacles in the way of connecting with people, so it's rare you'll see a double opt in now.

### Email campaign

Also known as 'drip marketing', this is an email or series of emails that may be drip-fed over a series of days, weeks or months, taking your client on a content journey. The overall aim of this is to achieve some kind of marketing (or sales) goal.

### Email queue

When you send a bulk email to a group of contacts your emails form a queue in preparation for sending.

### Email service provider (ESP)

The company you use to 'host' your emails. For example, GMail and Apple Mail are ESPs.

### Email templates

A predesigned and pre-formatted email designed to serve a purpose. An example would be your email newsletter. You'd design the template once then update the content each time you wanted to send.

### Engagement

A catch-all phrase used to explain all interactions your clients have with your business, from opening an email to likes, comments and shares.

### General Data Protection Regulation (GDPR)

A law around the protection of personal data for European citizens. If you have clients based in the EU (even if you're in Australia), you need to ensure your email marketing platform is GDPR compliant.

### HTML Email (Hypertext Markup Language)

Essentially HTML is computer code. Using HTML allows you to create pretty design-based emails.

### IP Address (Internet Protocol)

The address of your computer. Your IP address is often used to identify you as a client or potential client when you visit a website. It will store information to advise the business you have visited before. It can also be used to whitelist (approve) for incoming emails.

### Landing page

A web page which is often hidden from your website navigation to capture information from clients when they click through from an email. It will usually contain additional information related directly to a particular product or service.

### List fatigue

A phrase used to describe a segment of contacts with declining engagement. This usually happens when a list has been emailed too frequently without valuable content.

### List growth

Refers to how quickly your list or database is growing and what actions you have in place to drive growth.

### List hygiene

Ensuring your contact list is current and contains correct information. List hygiene is super important to continue to do once you begin using an email marketing platform, as it makes sure you're sending the right information to the right person at the right location at the right time.

### List segmentation

Separate your contact emails into target market groups. Segmenting your lists allows you to create far more tailored content and marketing ideas directly relevant to each particular group of people. The more segmented you get, the more targeted you can get with your content. This usually leads to a higher open rate, CTR and conversion rate.

**We should ALL be segmenting our lists!**

### List washing

A term used to describe cleaning the data to ensure everything is current. It's particularly used when a list is very old or they haven't been contacted for a long time (i.e. 12 months or more). Typically, the list will be washed in a free email platform (like MailChimp, as an example) because we're expecting a higher bounce and unsubscribe rate. Once the list is washed by deleting bounced and unsubscribed emails, it's imported to the email marketing platform of choice.

### Newsletter

An update or bulletin shared with your contacts who have opted in to receive emails.

### Opt in

Otherwise known as 'Subscribe'. This is where a prospect agrees to receive emails from a business.

### Personalisation

Adding bits of information to your emails about your clients that you already know. This could be things like their first name, company name, birthday or product they've recently purchased as an example. This is done automatically in bulk by your software.

### Plain text email

An email which is sent without any HTML code. It's best practice to offer your clients a plain text option of your emails for better readability.

### Preview pane

Those two to three sentences we all see in our email inbox that help us to decide whether or not to click and open. Make sure your choice of email marketing platform will allow you to craft your own preview text... and make it as compelling as possible.

### Promotional emails

An email sent to promote a particular product or service.

### Re-engagement campaign

An email or series of emails sent to inactive users in the hope of re-engaging them with your content.

### Spam

Sometimes called unsolicited commercial email (UCE). I think we all know about and have been on the receiving end of spam. You can land yourself and your business in a lot of hot water sending emails to people who have not subscribed. Just don't do it... ever.

### Transactional emails

These are usually sent to confirm an order or reservation (as an example). Transactional emails typically have a higher open rate than promotional emails.

### Welcome email

The first email you send to a client when they onboard with you.

### Whitelist

An IP address your client considers 'safe'. Whitelisting emails means everything will land in the inbox as opposed to landing in junk or spam.

# 39. PODCASTING

I love podcasting. So much so, I very nearly wrote a book just about podcasting a few years ago. It's such a fun and fabulous medium to reach and engage your client base, and it's a never-ending source of content that you can repurpose and leverage.

Back in the early 2000s, I worked at an FM radio station in Coffs Harbour. I was there to sell advertising, which by default meant I got to create some pretty cool copy and do some pretty fun things with clients' ads. But when I wasn't on the road seeing people, I would often be found skulking about the presenters' booths and chatting with the music director. From there I got to do a few live broadcasts out and about, and the immediacy of radio got into my blood.

A few years later I moved back with my parents for a bit to take care of my Dad after a health scare. Looking for something to do to amuse myself when I wasn't in carer mode, I came across a community FM station. One thing led to another, and before I knew it I had my own show: 'A Trace of Insanity' (don't judge me... I thought it was cool). Something about the power of being able to tell the stories of the locals and play some tunes really filled a void. The show became quite popular around town, and we'd often have locals call in for a chat on air (no three-second delay, so we needed to be careful who we let on air... you only make that mistake once!) ... Not bad for a station with a total of three incoming phone lines, lol.

Anyway in 2005 when Apple added a podcast option to their iTunes store, I was hooked. Fast forward a few years and I started my first show: 'The Ex Corporate Hippies Guide to Wellness' (again with the judgey eyerolls). Not a huge hit, and not a passion area for me, but enough that I found my 'podlegs' and decided to give it another crack.

My next podcast though struck a chord. 'Not Another Business Show' (or NABS as it became affectionately known) was the first panel-style podcast show to be produced (to the best of my knowledge) anywhere in the world. The show took off, and I had people listening and downloading from places as far afield as Azerbaijan and the Maldives, with a good-sized audience in the US, UK and Australia.

What NABS taught me was that a podcast, done well, will deliver an audience.

Since those days I've spent a lot of my time helping business owners create and launch their own successful shows. I'm also a long-time judge for the Australian Podcast Awards, and I reckon I've helped launch well over 100 shows.

So... why am I telling you all this?

To highlight the opportunity and potential a podcast could have for your business. Don't be fooled though, creating a great podcast is a lot of (ongoing) work. And once you get going, you have to keep feeding the beast.

If you're considering a podcast, the first place to spend your time and energy is in your strategy. Yep, before you invest in a microphone or any other technology bits and pieces you need to get super clear on:

- why you want a podcast
- who you're creating it for
- what problem(s) you are solving
- what type of show you want to create
- how frequently you want to put an episode out
- how long you want each episode to be

Those things will ensure you create a show that will effectively deliver your marketing message.

Like I said, I almost wrote a book on podcasting, and probably half of it would have been on getting the foundations and your strategy right before you dive in.

Assuming you have a clear idea of your why, what, when and how, then you'll probably want to know about what technology you need to make it happen.

I'm going to contradict a lot of podcast mentors with what I'm about to say.

If you're starting out, all I want you to spend some cash on is a decent microphone. That's it. Don't worry about mixing desks, or software or sound dampening stuff yet. I've seen far too many people blow thousands of dollars on podcasting equipment, only to discover they didn't enjoy the process, or the show wasn't doing what they'd hoped quickly enough.

Podcasting is a long burn. If you don't expect to get anything out of it for the first 50 to 100 episodes, you're starting with the right mindset.

So, let's break down some of the essentials you'll need if you decide to give podcasting a crack.

## Microphones

First thing you need to ask yourself is, 'What type of podcast am I making?' If your show is going to be you sitting at your office desk each and every episode then you can check out a USB mic like the Blue Yeti or the Rode NT-USB mics. USB mics are typically 'plug and play', meaning there is little set-up required and they'll just work. My advice, this is your best starting option. Personally, I'm a fan of the Rode products. They're an Aussie company and have a fab range of microphones and podcasting kit. I should know, I've spent thousands with them (again, Rode, if you're reading this... very happy for endorsements). In saying that, I have a lot of clients who use the Blue Yeti and swear by it.

If you've decided you're serious about this podcasting caper and you want to drop a bit more coin on your mic then you'll be looking for an XLR connected mic. These mics mean you'll need some kind of mixing desk to plug into – and that's going to add additional expense. If you're okay with that then I'd suggest you take a look at the Rode Procaster (I use this) or the Audio-Technica AT2035PK.

On the other hand, if you've identified that you want to be a roving podcaster, showing up at people's places and interviewing folks then you'll want to look at something like the H5 Zoom handy recorder. It's a portable handheld recording device popular amongst journalists for capturing interviews.

One last thing on microphones: be mindful of connecting your mic via Bluetooth... it's just one more thing that can go wrong! To be honest, I find most of the reputable brands of microphone don't offer a Bluetooth option.

Additional microphone kit you may find useful:

### Pop filter

If you're someone who 'pops' when they say the letter P, you'll definitely want to grab yourself a pop filter when you get your microphone. It's extremely disconcerting for your audience to hear popping throughout your show, especially when it's easily fixed.

### Windsock

If you're going to be out and about recording, you definitely want to grab a windsock. It's just a fluffy fur thing that goes over the end of your microphone to shield the wind noise. (You've probably seen these on the news on TV.) I call mine 'The Donald' because I style him in the comb-over style we've become accustomed to.

## Recording

Once you've chosen your mic, you'll need to think about how you're going to record (not such a biggie if you're out and about). There are a couple of ways you can kick off nice and cheap while figuring out if you like this podcasting caper...

## Zoom

*www.zoom.us*

Yep, a number of podcasters record over Zoom. Just make sure you've switched off every other possible app in the background and no one in the family (or office) is streaming Netflix or music. Nothing worse than your conversation dropping out every second word.

Additionally make sure you have the session set to capture 'audio only' as an option... you'll need it when it comes to editing.

## Zencastr

*www.zencastr.com*

This has been my podcast recording go-to platform for years. And get this: it's free to use! Unlike Zoom, Zencastr is an audio-only platform so you won't get to see your interview while you're chatting. But it does have built-in latent redundancy, which is a fancy way of saying the program keeps recording if your internet connection (or your guests) drops out. At the end of the session you get two files, one for you and one for your guest. It also makes the editing process significantly easier.

It does take a little bit of learning though... so I suggest you schedule times to chat and test your setup with friends and family to familiarise yourself with all the features.

## Editing

After getting your strategy right, editing is the thing that will take up the majority of your time. Sure, you can have a conversation with a guest, throw your intro and ending over the top and whack it on iTunes, but what value is that really offering your audience?

No one wants to hear your five-minute conversation about the weather before you get into the good stuff, and we sure don't need to hear people stumbling and stammering over questions and answers.

Remember, your podcast is an extension of your brand. Don't half arse it and don't put out content you're not happy with. Take the time to edit your show properly … trust me on this one.

Now, all that being said, the easiest way I find to edit a show these days is to hire an audio editor on Fiverr (or find a musician looking for extra work) and ask them to do it. You'll need to tell them what to remove (I'll talk about that in a moment when it comes to transcripts) but once you hand it off, they can weave their magic.

If you really want to have a go yourself then use GarageBand (if you're an Apple user) or Audacity (as a PC user) and learn the ropes. To give you an idea of how long it will take, roughly one minute of unedited (raw) audio will take between four and six minutes to edit… You do the math on whether there are better things you can do with your time.

## Other things you'll need

### Transcripts

If you're handing your audio file to an editor, it's easiest to hand them a transcript of the show highlighted with the bits you want removed. You can use a program like Otter.Ai or Descript to create a transcript, or run it through a transcription software service like Rev.com.

Once your show is back from the editor, run a second transcript. Repeat the highlighting process to edit again until you're happy with the final result. Once you are, you'll want to load the transcript to your website with the podcast episode so Google can read it, index it and offer it as content to visitors. It's also wonderful to offer a transcript for any hearing-impaired clients you may have.

- Otter.ai: www.otter.ai
- Descript: www.descript.com
- Rev.com: www.rev.com

## Audio hosting platforms

Your audio host is where you'll house your podcast. It's not advisable to load it directly to your website as it will slow down the load speed time for people visiting – iTunes, Google, Spotify, etc. are just directories pointing people to the 'home' of your show. Instead, you'll need to find an audio host company you're happy to work with.

There are plenty around now; they vary wildly in pricing so before making a decision you'll need to know how often you'll be publishing your show and how long each episode will be.

A few audio host platforms I've worked or hosted with in the past are:

· Blubrry: www.blubrry.com
· Whooshka (an Aussie company): www.whooshkaa.com
· Libsyn: www.libsyn.com
· Podcast Co: www.podcast.co

One other question that's worth asking before you commit to one over another... Do they list your podcast on various platforms for you? Hint: you want someone that'll do that for you – it makes your life considerably easier.

## Music

Most podcast shows start with a bit of intro music. It sets the tone for the show and creates a nice mood before you get into the content. It's super important to make sure you're using copyright-free music for your podcast; the fines and legal exposure are not worth you trying to 'borrow' your favourite Ed Sheeran song.

My go-to music site for copyright-free music is Audio Jungle: www.audiojungle.net

## Voice over

You'll always want a little intro to start the show ('You're listening to Not Another Business Show, a weekly show for small businesses who think big'). Now there's nothing stopping you from reading and recording this yourself, but I like the 'Rockstar' intro (getting someone else to read the intro for you).

Make sure you choose the gender that will be representative of your target audience, and if your audience will be predominantly Aussie make sure to get an Aussie to read it… if you're going for a global audience then get an American or someone from the UK to voice it for you.

I use Fiverr – search for 'voice over': www.fiverr.com.

### Sound dampening

Okay, technically this isn't technology BUT if you get your sound proofing right it'll add a lot to the quality of your show. There's a few options when you're starting out:

1. Sit in a wardrobe and talk into your clothes.
2. Build a fort with pillows and cushions to talk into.
3. Put a blanket over your head.

Whatever you decide to do, the idea is to dampen the sound. It will be particularly noticeable if you're in a big empty space or a room with hardwood floors. Even the smallest amount of sound dampening will make a difference to your show.

### Cover art

Your show needs its own graphic, and it needs to conform to the various image sizes the podcast platforms like. The requirements change depending on the provider you're wanting to connect your podcast to. I advise you to Google requirements for podcast cover art to make sure you're getting accurate information.

Have a look at various podcast covers and see what you like and don't like. See whether the fonts work when they are small – can you read everything? How do the colours look? If you're using a headshot photo, make sure you don't look 'weird' in the cover art aspect.

Easiest way is to get a graphic artist to create this for you. Again, you could try a site such as fiverr for this: www.fiverr.com.

### Show notes

Each episode needs a written description to load to your audio host. These are called 'show notes'. You need to take your time crafting these as often it's how people decide to choose your show.

## Scheduling

If you plan on having guests as part of your show, you need a way of scheduling them into your calendar. Unless you want to play phone or email tag with days and times, the easiest way is to get yourself a scheduling tool.

A few of the options I've used or come across are:

· HubSpot: www.hubspot.com/products/sales/schedule-meeting
· Calendly: www.calendly.com
· Acuity Scheduling: www.acuityscheduling.com

## Promoting

How are you going to let the world know your podcast is available? There's over 18.5 million podcast episodes available to download or stream, so you need a plan to promote, leverage and repurpose.

\* \* \*

If you do decide to give podcasting a go, then my final piece of advice would be to set yourself a 'short run' season to begin. Somewhere between five and ten episodes will give you a good idea whether you like it and whether you have the time and energy to keep it going. Your audience is open to listening to a short season if you tell them up front, but if they subscribe to your show thinking it'll be an ongoing weekly event only for it to finish in four weeks, well, you're setting up yourself and your audience for disappointment.

# 40. VIDEO

According to a study by HubSpot, 54% of consumers want to see more video content. And a further study by Zenith suggests that the average person will spend around 100 minutes per day watching video in 2021.

We've all read or heard the stats and we've all agreed that video is an important tool small business owner's should be leveraging... So why aren't we?

Well, my straw poll of chats with clients and fellow small business owners suggest 'I hate being on camera' as a fairly regular response. To which I say... but it's not about *you*.

Your clients are asking for video. You're sitting on a mountain of valuable content... would you rather be creating videos and getting more leads or sitting around talking about how much you hate being on camera and lamenting how quiet business is?

When COVID first struck I was chatting with my business coach. I'd just lost every single client bar one from my digital marketing agency, and I was having a general bitch session about how tough things were getting. He listened for a while and then asked if I was ready to use the time to reinvent.

That conversation birthed 'The Digital Guide' brand as it is now. He challenged me to create one digital tip every day, seven days per week for the first three months of COVID. Nothing huge, just a few minutes each day chatting about a digital tip, trick, maybe a website or an app that I'd found and used that could help others.

I rolled my eyes and begrudgingly accepted the challenge (after all, I had the time). Within the first six weeks those videos were getting more views than anything else I had been putting on social media for years.

Because of those daily digital tips, I started getting leads with local councils to run training sessions, and picked up a few clients who consistently said, 'I didn't know you knew about that stuff'.

I now have 250 short, sharp digital tips available on my YouTube channel.

If you'd like to see my daily digital tips you can visit my YouTube channel www.youtube.com/c/TracySheenDigitalGuide

Did I want to do video? *Hell no.*

Do I see the value? *Sure do.*

## Creating awesome videos

Okay, so I'm not going to come at you anymore with 'you have to do video' talk. All I'm going to share with you in this section is a few super-useful things I've come across for creating awesome videos that make the process a little less cringeworthy.

### Loom

*www.loom.com*

This little app has been a game changer for me. I recorded all of my daily digital tips in Loom and then top and tail them using iMovie (an inbuilt video editor that comes standard with Apple).

You can record your screen; you can have the screen with a small image of yourself in the corner or you can record full screen. So, lots of options when it comes to recording.

I also use it when I need to brief a contractor on a project (I used it extensively recently to provide feedback on the new design of my website). Finally, I love being able to share quick videos with clients walking through how to use a particular piece of technology.

When I log into Loom I can see if anyone has watched the video, I can do some basic editing and people can leave comments.

You can start using it for free and then increase your pricing as your requirements change.

I can't recommend Loom highly enough as an easy way to slide into using video.

## Animoto

*www.animoto.com*

If you're really struggling with the thought of being on camera, Animoto could be a nice toe in the water of video for you.

The platform has a bunch of different templates where you can drag and drop images or short video clips, and the platform will curate them into a short video for you. It also has a stock library of music clips so you can add a great soundtrack to your video.

Get started for free or upgrade to remove the Animoto branding.

## MakeWebVideo

*www.makewebvideo.com*

Have you ever visited a website and seen a cool animated explainer video? MakeWebVideo helps you create these explainer-style videos for your business.

You choose the template, the voice over, the music and then write the script. The platform then turns your ideas into an explainer video. You even get to watch it and double check everything before you approve and pay! Happy days.

I really like this platform; it's super easy to use and I've helped dozens of business owners create great explainer videos for their own business.

## Wave.video

*www.wave.video*

This platform allows you to create videos but also edit and add subtitles. They also offer a place to host your videos if needed (I'd use YouTube over Wave, but the point is, they do offer the service).

It's another drag-and-drop platform, and one worth checking out if you'd rather use existing or stock images rather than creating your own.

There are other platforms available, ranging from free through to paid versions, I advise you to Google 'creating videos' for a bunch of options.

## Video hosting platforms

### YouTube

*www.youtube.com*

Not just for losing hours watching videos of cats doing crazy things, I see YouTube as one of the most underrated and underused marketing platforms for small business owners.

If you're posting content to YouTube, you're automatically getting the additional Google SEO love (in case you didn't know, Google owns YouTube). It is the second most used search engine behind Google, and has 2 billion logged in monthly users.

According to a study by Roy Morgan in 2020, YouTube is the most popular social network for the two youngest Generations, used by 91% of Gen Z (1981–1996) and 72% of Generation Alpha (2006–).

**Top Social Networks by Generation – February 2020**

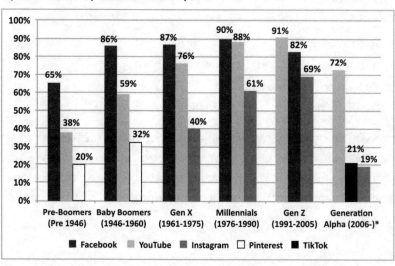

*Source 1: Roy Morgan Single Source, September 2019 – February 2020, n=25,379. **Base:** Australians aged 14+. **\*Source 2:** Roy Morgan Young Australians Survey, July – December 2019, n=1,047. **Base:** Young Australians aged 6-13 years old.*

If you're looking at the graph and your business is targeting Gen X, Millennials or Gen Z then they're hanging out on YouTube. Meaning you have a great opportunity to get your content seen on a YouTube channel.

Now, YouTube is not the only video hosting platform available to you, but it is the only one owned by Google.

I often have clients ask where they should be hosting videos and the answer is… it depends. It depends on who your intended audience is. The one big pet peeve people have with YouTube is (you guessed it) the ads. So, if your audience is going to be annoyed by having to sit through ads to view your content then I would suggest you look to another hosting platform (such as Vimeo, and I'll talk about it further shortly).

*But*… Please also load your content to YouTube. Why? Because it's owned by Google, and having your content there (whether or not you share it) means you can be found, indexed and offered as a solution to people's questions by Google.

If you don't have a YouTube channel and you're about to start creating video, it's worth setting up now as it can take a few days for things to settle.

To create a YouTube account, you need a Google-hosted email address. Once you have that it's pretty straightforward.

1.    Go to YouTube (www.youtube.com).
2.    In the top right-hand corner click 'sign in'.
3.    Click on the 'Create Account'.
4.    Choose whether it is for yourself or your business.

Once you've done that, you'll be able to create a YouTube channel. Your channel is where you'll go to upload videos. To create your channel, log into your YouTube account, then click on the option to upload a video. From there you'll be prompted to set up a channel if you don't already have one.

Google has some great instructions for these steps if you get stuck. You'll find everything you need to know at: support.google. com/youtube/answer/1646861

## YouTube data and analytics

As you may have guessed what I find interesting in this platform (apart from the Google love that abounds) is the analytics you can access. To see your insights, you'll want to log into 'YouTube Studio': Studio.youtube.com

Once you're logged in, you'll be taken directly to your home screen and your insights 'overview'.

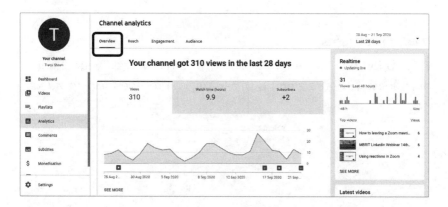

Everything around your insights will be found through the 'insights' tab on the left-hand side.

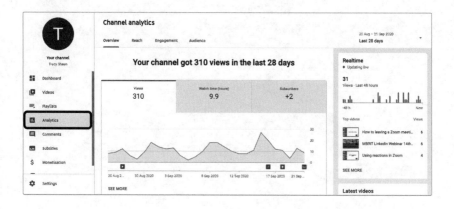

The first insight shows you how many views your channel has had over the past 28 days, how many hours of viewing and the number of new subscribers your channel has picked up.

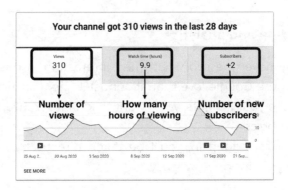

### Realtime insights

This option provides information on who has viewed your channel in the past 48 hours, along with a list of your top-performing videos.

## *Top videos for this period*

This will provide a list of your top-performing videos over your set time period. It will also show you the average view time and the number of views.

| | Video | Average view duration | Views |
|---|---|---|---|
| | **Your top videos in this period** | | |
| 1 | How to leaving a Zoom meeting<br>10 Aug 2020 | 0:35 (60.4%) | 103 |
| 2 | Using reactions in Zoom<br>10 Aug 2020 | 0:27 (31.6%) | 57 |
| 3 | #68 Delete LinkedIn messages<br>2 Jun 2020 | 0:56 (31.1%) | 44 |
| 4 | Muting & unmuting yourself on Zoom<br>10 Aug 2020 | 0:28 (18.4%) | 18 |
| 5 | ASBAS Logan Webinar Content Marketing | 11:04 (17.7%) | 16 |

## *Channel analytics: reach*

Now click on the 'Reach' tab next to 'Overview'. This will take us through all the information on the reach of our YouTube channel.

## What does it all mean?

### Reach overview

The reach analytics provide us with the following data:

- **Impressions:** This is when your video thumbnail is shown to someone on YouTube.
- **Impressions click through:** The number of people who clicked on the thumbnail to watch the video.
- **Views:** The number of people who watched your video.
- **Unique viewers:** The estimated number of people who watched your videos during the selected time period.

### Traffic source types

This tells you how people are finding your content. Ideally you want people finding you by searching in YouTube, purely because you'll be getting that additional Google love through YouTube searches.

### *Impressions and how they led to watch time*

This gives you a visual representation of how many people saw your video thumbnail and then went on to watch it.

### *Traffic sources: external*

This is an insight I like to keep an eye on. It shows who the top referring sites are, and how people are finding your content outside of YouTube.

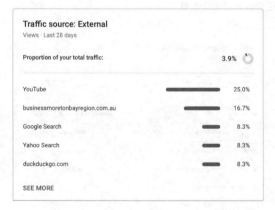

### *Traffic Source: YouTube search*

This will tell you what content people are searching for when they find your answers (very helpful when it comes to content creation ideas). It also shows you what percentage of your total YouTube traffic is made from YouTube searches.

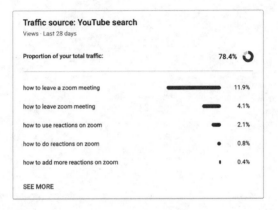

### *Traffic Source: Suggested videos*

This shows what traffic is being driven by the other 'suggested videos' that come up at the end of viewing a video on YouTube. It will also show you what percentage of your overall YouTube traffic is driven by suggested videos.

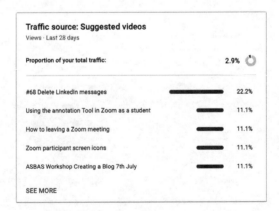

### Channel Analytics: engagement

This section tells you how long people are engaging (hanging around watching) with your videos.

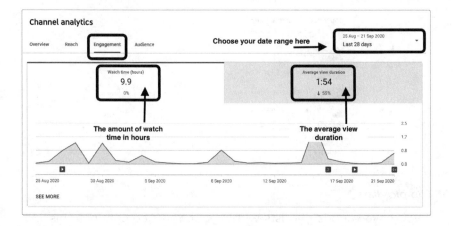

### Top videos

This tells you the top-performing videos on your channel according to how long people are watching them in hours over your selected time frame.

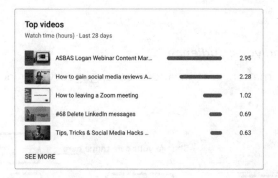

### Top videos by end screen

If you have chosen to put an 'end screen' on your YouTube videos, this will show you the top performing videos from your end screens.

### Top playlists

If you have various playlists within your YouTube channel, this will showcase your highest performing playlists.

### Channel analytics: audience

Shares information on the audience engaged with your YouTube Channel.

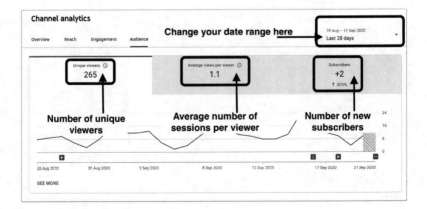

- **Number of unique views:** The estimated number of people who engaged with your content during the selected date range.
- **Average views per viewer:** The average number of times a person watched any video on your channel.
- **Subscribers:** The number of new subscribers (followers) to your channel over the selected date range.

There are a range of other metrics available for your YouTube channel which may show 'not enough data'. This means your channel does not currently have enough viewers for YouTube to provide that information, or your audience is predominantly viewing your videos from a device that is not signed into YouTube. Some of these reports will include:

- when your viewers are on YouTube
- other videos that your audience watched
- viewer age and gender
- top countries
- top subtitles

## Other things worth knowing

If you're interested in learning more about YouTube, whether it's becoming a YouTube creator or the analytics, you'll find excellent resources at:

- support.google.com/youtube/topic/9257532?hl=en&ref_topic=9257610
- creatoracademy.youtube.com/page/lesson/using-analytics

I've compiled a list of the most useful analytics to grow and improve your YouTube channel. In no particular order:

- Audience insights:
    - How long are people watching?
    - How many videos are they watching?
    - Number of views
    - Number of new subscribers

- Traffic sources:
  - How are people finding your videos?

Remember, if you want your videos to rank in YouTube (and Google) then you need to think about things a little differently:

- Rethink your keywords to video keywords:
  - Use the search bar in YouTube to search for videos like yours and let it 'autocomplete'. You Tube will only show popular phrases. Meaning, these are what people are looking for. Optimise your videos around these keywords.

Make sure you're completing each of these areas when you upload a video:

- Description:
  - make sure this is at least 250 words long
  - put your keyword in the first 30 words
  - include your keyword 2 to 5 times.
- Video tags (not as important, but handy to know):
  - use for your audience (e.g. small business)
  - one for your specific keyword (Ranking videos in YouTube)
  - include a couple of others around the keyword (e.g.: SEO, link building)
  - targeted tags help your video show up more in the right-hand side recommended videos.
- Remember, Google typically shares video content for certain types of keywords – this is important because you want to make sure you're putting Google-friendly keywords in the video description or title as well:

- How to (how to rank for YouTube videos)
- Funny videos (kittens do funny things)
- Fitness or sport (Yoga workout)
- Reviews (Apple iPhone review)
- Tutorials (Setting up a YouTube channel).

· Videos with high audience retention rank:
  - Make sure your videos are the best quality information you can offer.

· Ask people to comment or subscribe after watching:
  - People liking and subscribing sends a big signal to YouTube your video (or channel) is worth watching.

· Ask people to share your video to their social media.

· Create awesome thumbnails and titles:
  - Click-through rates help you rank.

· Longer videos (typically) rank better.

· Make sure you say your keywords in your video – preferably at the start:
  - YouTube can now subtitle your videos, so by saying the keyword or phrases you're giving YouTube a very clear indication you want your video to sit with these keywords.

· Make sure your video titles are at least five words long – and try to include your keyword up front:
  - E.g. 'Ranking videos in YouTube; everything you need to know in 2021'.

· Promote your videos.

· Put a link to your YouTube channel in your email signature.

One final thing on YouTube that I'm often asked... How do I make money from my YouTube Channel?

It is true that YouTube will pay content creators with a large audience to insert ads within their content. Each time an ad is watched the content creator receives a small payment. My advice in using your YouTube channel as an additional revenue source is this: don't. Instead treat your channel instead as a base for providing super useful content to your audience without asking for anything in return. Do that, and it'll turn into cash for you at some point.

But, if you're still interested in what it takes to earn cash from your channel you should know YouTube requires you to have at least 1000 subscribers and have 4000 hours of watched content.

## Vimeo

Let's agree on the fact that YouTube will help our Google rankings just by having videos present on the channel (okay, so there's a little more to it than that, but you get the idea). Vimeo is another video hosting platform. The main difference I see with Vimeo is there are no ads. So, if you're looking to send a video to a client and you don't want them getting interrupted by pesky ads, Vimeo could be a good option for you.

Another of the nice features in Vimeo is the ability to brand your videos and embed your logos.

What started as a platform for artists to share content has now grown to a viable alternative for businesses wanting to connect with their audience without subjecting them to advertisements.

According to Statistica, Vimeo had 1.39 million viewers as of 2nd quarter 2020 vs 2 billion on YouTube. So, if you're looking for a platform where you're likely to stand out more, then Vimeo could be for you.

There are some great analytics available to you on Vimeo, but I'm not going to spend time on them here because, well 1.39 million vs 2 billion viewers... I think you need to spend your time and energy understanding and tweaking your YouTube channel before biting off Vimeo analytics too.

The big thing to watch out for according to all the reviews I've researched is the Vimeo customer support, which seems to be about zero. I had a Vimeo account for a while and had a similar experience... to the point where I cancelled my account because I was getting stuck in a loop that wouldn't fix itself.

# 41. QR (QUICK RESPONSE) CODES

A QR code is like a barcode but it's formatted in a matrix style. If a person scans a QR code they will be delivered information or (most commonly these days) taken to a page on a website.

I've created a QR code for you to scan. This will take you directly to the book resources page on my website, where you'll find all the templates, etc. we've been discussing in the book so far.

While QR codes have been around since 1994 they went through a resurgence during the COVID pandemic as cafes and hospitality used them as a way to direct patrons to a page where they could register their attendance for dining.

The marketing uses for QR codes for small business are endless as they allow you to drive traffic to a very specific location.

Consider using a QR code as an easy way:

- to ask people to sign up for a newsletter
- for customers to locate you

- to capture additional client information
- to deliver people directly to a website or social media page
- to deliver a promotional offer

Don't write off the humble QR code; added to your marketing mix it becomes another wonderfully engaging tool.

# 42. APPLYING THE DATA

It's one thing to be looking at our insights, data and analytics, but what do we actually do with this info other than stare blankly at a screen?

For me, data is knowledge, and knowledge is power.

When we understand the data we can manipulate the back end to tweak the numbers in our favour.

For example, let's say you're a dog breeder. By looking at your Google Analytics popular pages and your Facebook content insights, you would know that your posts about what to feed puppies under six months old got the highest interaction. So now you can create a bunch of additional content breaking down the information even further. Maybe you create a running series of what to feed your puppy from six to eight weeks, then eight to twelve weeks, then twelve to fourteen weeks, and so on. You take those blogs and you turn them into short videos for your Facebook, YouTube and social media, you get lots of cute photos of puppies and put one fact that you mentioned with each puppy photo and push that out to your socials also.

You're now beginning to play the system. You know you're creating content that your audience wants to see, and you're doing it in ways that are going to encourage your audience to follow you around the internet (dare I say, like a puppy). From your Facebook to your Instagram to your website to your YouTube channel ... Leaving breadcrumbs for them to follow along the way.

**Data is knowledge and knowledge is power**

Another example is that because you've familiarised yourself with Google Analytics and your Facebook Insights, you've learned the days and times when people are most active on your page.

Because of that you change the day you post your blog and the time that you share your content on Facebook. That leads to a further increase in traffic and greater reach on your Facebook page.

That's when the data has become our knowledge, and the knowledge is being used in a powerful way.

So, you see, to me the data is a means to an end. We all want more eyeballs and interaction on our website, and we all want greater reach on our social media pages. Google and Facebook are giving us that very information... for free! I mean, it's right there. All you need to do is take the time to learn and understand what the various bits of data actually mean and where to find them, and then you can begin to apply this value information in ways that will undoubtedly grow your business.

Part of what I love about watching people digitise their business is seeing the light bulbs come on when they learn just how powerful some of these free analytics can be.

Lean in... learn the data... understand what it's telling you, then make the tiny tweaks needed and measure your results.

It really is as simple as that.

## Where does advertising fit?

I can't tell you the number of times I've had a small business schedule a session with me, and the first thing they ask me is, 'How do I run a Facebook ad?'

After a little discussion (usually) I find out that they aren't getting the sales or traction they've been hoping for online, and there is a belief if they throw some cash at Facebook (or Google, or any of the platforms) that people in turn will start throwing cash at them.

Sorry if this is about to burst a bubble ... It doesn't work like that.

If you want advertising to work, you need to be super clear on:

· your why

- your client persona
- the problem you're solving
- how your solution is the thing that will change their world

And, you need to be able to articulate it in around 30 seconds (often far less).

While I agree there is a place for advertising, and I've seen clients get some amazing results with Google Ads and Facebook advertising, I'm not going to address the details of how you go about it any further in this book.

Until you nail the basics we've discussed, and you've tweaked your data to within an inch of its life, then you're not going to get the results you're looking for by throwing more cash at it.

If you don't believe me and you want to learn more about Google Ads or Facebook advertising, then the best places to start are:

- Learndigital.withgoogle.com (search for Google Ads). This is Google's own learning platform with a tonne of courses and certifications.
- Facebook Blueprint (www.en-gb.facebook.com/business/learn). This is Facebook's own learning platform; you'll find plenty of information about setting up and running your own ad campaign.

* * *

Hey, look at you, you made it to the end of another section!

That was one hell of a section, huh? So much info and data to take in and think about. I did warn you.

As we do at the end of each section, I'd really like you to take a few moments and reflect on the things that stood out for you. Have you made a to-do list of things you want to check out? Is there anything you could download, purchase or review today that would help you to get started?

Often when I'm chunking down a huge to-do list with a client, we'll make a priority list. So, pick your top three things from this section you want to take further, then put one action beside them to further it along (do you need to download it, buy a book, watch a YouTube video?) and give yourself a due date to have it done.

Once you've done that, schedule those dates into your calendar or pop them as a task list in your CRM so they get actioned.

Sadly, while I can give you a lot of information via osmosis, I can't improve your bottom line without your input. So, make sure you follow through.

Okay... one last thing before I want you to close the book and take a big break (trust me, your brain needs it).

Grab a piece of paper... any piece as long as it's around A4 size.

You're going to make a paper aeroplane.

Scan the QR code below and you'll go to a YouTube video tutorial on how to make a paper airplane.

And if you don't have any paper around you, I want you to go to your app store and search for a Paper Toss game. Once you've found one and downloaded it set a timer on your phone for 15 minutes.

... you're welcome.

# SECTION SEVEN

## SALES

**WHATEVER BUSINESS YOU'RE IN** there's one thing we all have in common. We need sales or we don't have a business, and whatever your thoughts are on the sales process a common denominator is the need for more leads.

More leads, more clients. More clients, more money.

Typically, a small business owner has no idea how many leads they need to win a client. They don't know how much time it takes someone to move from lead to prospect and prospect to client. Key insights that could drive the sales process and provide certainty around required capacity are not in place, and mostly unknown. Sure, there may be a few back-of-the-envelope numbers and an idea of how long things take, but no real data to support or contradict the gut feelings that most small businesses operate on.

Couple that with how quickly technology has evolved and it's no wonder we're feeling overwhelmed and out of step with our own businesses. It's left many feeling like they've completely missed the boat and are at risk of becoming obsolete.

Technology used well can provide solid data for you to begin tracking sales numbers, make the process smoother for your team and your clients and give you control over your business.

How much of a blessing would it be if you could look three months down the track and have reasonable confidence in what work was going to come in? How better prepared could you be in terms of cash flow and capacity? It's not a big leap to expect that you could have this level of comfort with a few small additions or tweaks to your current operation.

And that's exactly what we're going to talk about in more detail now ...

# 43. CUSTOMER RELATIONSHIP MANAGEMENT AND SALES PIPELINES

If you read the section on marketing, you would be familiar with my thoughts on the intrinsic value a CRM offers. Not only will it keep a record of all interactions you have with your contacts (whether they're clients, suppliers, staff or prospects) but used with a sales mindset it can help you develop a sales pipeline, tell you how long the sales process (actually) takes and how your sales team is tracking against quotas.

Whether you are a team of one or managing a sales team of hundreds, your CRM is the life blood of key sales insights for your business.

Before I get down into the tech aspect, let's make sure you're familiar with the concept of a sales pipeline.

Essentially a sales pipeline is the steps a potential buyer goes through with your company before they become a client. It usually goes a little something like this:

· Outbound cold contact – phone, email or LinkedIn outreach.
· Leads coming in via website, phone or email.
· Setting appointments to meet with prospects.
· Email conversations.
· Sales proposal.
· Quote.
· Sale won/lost.

Now I get that that's a simplistic way of viewing your clients, but for a salesperson they think in pipelines.

Now, add in your CRM and suddenly you have a way of tracking as a business owner how many people are sitting at each stage of the pipeline and which salesperson holds the responsibility for the lead.

You'll also quickly know if anyone else within the team is involved in the process in any way (maybe service had to respond to a technical question for you, or logistics had to confirm stock). You'll even see at a glance the last interaction a lead had with the company.

When looked at from a sales pipeline perspective, your CRM is giving you:

- metrics that you can easily and accurately measure
- sales team management (with everyone using the same system and remaining accountable to the process)
- sales forecasting (what is likely to close when)
- pipeline health (you need to know your pipeline is growing, not shrinking and you need to make sure each salesperson is constantly identifying new opportunities).

Industry standards suggest a good salesperson will often be working with around 1.5x more opportunities (read cold to warm leads) than deals. The only way you can accurately track that is by using some kind of sales pipeline in your CRM.

There are many, many different CRMs that will have a kind of sales pipeline feature built into the system. Just as we discussed in the marketing section, it's important to get your sales team onboard with your choice of CRM … this is especially important if you're looking to implement a CRM to an existing team. Don't get me wrong – I'm sure your salespeople are fabulous, but, speaking as a former salesperson myself, if I had a company for which I didn't have to report or track or measure what I was doing with my days and the number of opportunities I was currently working… Well, let's just say I might be a little resistant to suddenly needing to report on those metrics. For the most part though, if your CRM and pipeline removes some of the thinking and work for your sales team, they will embrace it with open arms.

I'm going to give you a couple to look at to start your search. This is by no means an exhaustive list so please do a little Googling and have a chat to a few different providers before making your decision.

| Product | Pros | Cons | Platforms |
|---|---|---|---|
| **HubSpot** | – The CRM is amazing<br>– Basic sales pipeline included in free version<br>– Assign tasks during the pipeline to other team members<br>– Sales teams can update from their mobile on the road<br>– Meeting scheduling included | – If you have a detailed sales process you may need to go to the paid version to give you the functionality required<br>– If you do need the paid version the price jumps are significant from free | – Cloud based<br>– Windows, Mac, iOS, Android, and Windows Phone |
| **Pipedrive** | – Free 14-day trial<br>– Manage activities through the calendar<br>– Meeting scheduler | – Poor customer service<br>– Can be buggy | – Cloud based<br>– Windows, Mac, Linux, iOS, and Android |
| **Monday** | – Free trial with unlimited users and boards<br>– Visual representation of sales process and team members | – Not really a CRM<br>– Not rated well for customer service | – Cloud based<br>– Windows, Mac, iOS, Android Phone |

Let me be clear with what I've just shared. I use HubSpot, so I can easily talk about the pros and cons of their system. I've tried a lot of different platforms over the years and (for me) I find HubSpot just works, however I have other business friends though who are not HubSpot fans at all.

My point is your CRM and your sales pipeline software will be a subjective choice. There are a few questions you'll need to consider when investigating your pipeline options:

- How big is your sales team?
- Does the team vary through the year or is it a set number?
- Do you need the software to integrate with anything else? E.g.: emails, accounting software, proposal software
- Would you like something with a mobile app?
- What measurements would you like to monitor?
- Does the platform offer a free trial?
- Does the software have tiered pricing? If so, what does that look like?
- What are the broader business requirements?

It's my sincere belief if you are looking for one big bang-for-buck thing to digitise your business, it's getting a CRM.

You implement a CRM that works across your sales, marketing and other areas of your business and you will see a huge difference to the way your business operates internally and with your clients ... And, you'll be all over your key metrics.

# 44. VIDEO

We covered video from a marketing perspective in the marketing section of the book, but what about using video as a sales tool?

One of the smallest changes that had the biggest impact in my business was sending prospective customers a video after our initial phone call. As soon as I jump off the phone, I'll open up Loom (check out the marketing section if you're unsure what I'm referring to) and record a quick check in.

It only needs to be a couple of minutes to quickly touch on the key things discussed on the call and any follow-up you need to do. Super quick, but I get so many comments on those couple of minutes.

Then, if the client progresses to the proposal stage, I'll share a video along with the written document talking them through my recommendations and why I'm suggesting what I am. In a video a client can hear the tone of your voice, they get the inflection and they can see your smiling face. Emails, especially in the sales process, are so often subject to interpretation and leave way too much wiggle room for miscommunication. You don't want any reason to put up an objection or barrier to someone spending money with you.

That ability for your client to connect with you eye to eye, even in a pre-recorded video, is powerful. Super powerful. And yet, I rarely see small businesses take advantage of the amazing connections we can build with our customers.

My challenge to you is this. Next time you have an initial call with a prospect, jump straight on your camera and record a quick thank-you-for-your-time video. Cover the points you discussed and finish with the next steps.

I guarantee it'll make a difference.

# 45. WEBINARS

Webinars are a fantastic way to educate your potential customers and move them further along the pathway to purchase.

We were all bombarded with the number of free webinars that happened during the start of COVID and, like a lot of things when we have too many of them, we became fatigued and worn out to Zoom land.

During 'normal' business cycles though I've seen webinars used exceptionally well to take a group of people from prospect to clients.

Personally, I tend to make my webinars a 'sales free zone' and just try to offer as much value to the folks on the call as I can because I know everyone who signed up for that webinar has had to do so with an email address. That email address goes straight in my system and now I can send each person further information and chat to them about other products and services that are aligned to what we were discussing on the webinar.

Remember, sales are a numbers game.

7, 11, 4 – remember when we discussed those numbers and the Zero Moment of Truth that Google identified?

Webinars are a great way to help your audience 'rack up' those numbers, moving them ever closer in the sales pipeline.

In terms of technology and what you need to run a webinar, there really isn't that much to it.

· You need a killer slide deck.

- You need to hold the audience's attention for the duration of the webinar. Remember, there will be little to no interaction from your audience.
- You need to keep your energy levels up and constant.
- You need a software platform that will host webinars (more about that in a second).
- You'll need an email platform to send everyone a note after the webinar thanking them for coming and providing a link to your offer or to the recording.

In terms of your software platforms, I use Zoom, as do most of my friends who regularly run webinars but it's not the only option. To get you started I've put together a list below.

| Feature | Zoom | Go To Webinar | Webinar Jam | Webinar Ninja |
|---|---|---|---|---|
| Cloud based | ✓ | ✓ | ✓ | ✓ |
| Share screen | ✓ | ✓ | ✓ | ✓ |
| Chat function | ✓ | ✓ | ✓ | ✓ |
| HD video quality | ✓ | ✓ | ✓ | ✓ |
| Automated recording | ✓ | ✓ | ✓ | |
| Polling | ✓ | ✓ | ✓ | ✓ |
| Pre record and schedule | | ✓ | ✓ | ✓ |
| Call to actions | | | ✓ | ✓ |
| Number of presenters | 4 | 6 | 6 | 4 |

**The big questions to consider before choosing a webinar platform are:**

- How many guests do you think you'll be presenting to?
- Do you want live webinars, evergreen, auto scheduled or a mix?

- Evergreen are webinars that are available to watch on demand.
    - Auto scheduled means they 'go live' at certain days/times.
- What branding is available?
    - Registration pages.
    - Emails.
- Can people dial in via phone as audio only?
- Can people join from any device?
    - Phone.
    - Tablet.
    - Laptop.
- What reporting and analytics does the platform offer?
- What recording options are available?
    - Local.
    - Cloud.
- How long does the recording last?
- Does the platform integrate with social media platforms?
- What's the process like for a client to register?
- What attendee engagement options are available?
    - Live chat.
    - Polling, etc.
- Can you send reminder and thank-you emails through the platform?
- Does the platform integrate with your CRM?
- Can you run paid webinars?
    - What integrations for payment gateways are there?
- What help is available to set everything up once you sign up?

If you do decide to start running webinars (and I highly recommend you consider it) then here's a few tips to running a great webinar:

- Focus on your content before all else.
    - You want to make sure you're delivering outstanding value.

- Always do a dry run.
  - Get some friends to join for a walk through to check your timings and explanations.
- Use a good-quality microphone or headset.
  - Your audio quality needs to be top notch.
  - No jewellery that could bump the mic, etc.
- If your platform allows, set the webinar to auto record.
  - Nothing worse than being halfway through and realising you haven't hit the record button!
- Promote the hell out of it.
  - Start a minimum of seven days out and don't stop talking about it till you're about to go live.
- Take your time in writing the webinar sales page – it's what will get your clients to register.
- If you're having presenters, make sure you include bios and headshots of them.
- Use polling and chat during the webinar to create engagement.
- Look through the attendee list before going live, see who you know and make sure to reference a few people directly during the webinar.
- Restart your computer around 60 minutes before your webinar (just to make sure everything is fresh).
- Don't do any software updates an hour before the webinar.
- Minimise possible noise or interruptions:
  - No one on other internet devices (especially streaming).
  - Kids and animals otherwise preoccupied.
  - Close every other app your computer could be running.
- Start on time.
- Have pre-prepared questions ready for Q&A.
- Finish on time.
- Steel yourself that stuff could go wrong.

I remember the first webinar I ran for the Federal Government's Australian Small Business Advisory Service (or ASBAS as we affectionally call it) – not long after we kicked off the council turned up in the park that backs onto our house to cut down a tree! We had chainsaws and blokes yelling for the entire hour we were online.

I've had power outages in the middle of webinars and I've even forgotten to hit record during one of them, which meant I had to put a call out to my socials for a handful of people to jump online and immediately re-run the thing to get a recording!

Things happen … you'll need to go with the flow, but if you're looking for a great way to build your sales pipeline and increase your authority with your audience then webinars could be just the thing.

# 46. ONLINE (OR VIRTUAL) SUMMITS

Pre COVID the virtual summit was a pretty rare beast, but thanks to the pandemic there were a bunch of planned live events that scrambled for a way to go ahead while meeting the new requirements of COVID.

Think of them just like attending a live, in-person one- or multi-day event. There's a line-up of speakers, maybe some panel discussions, perhaps some breakout rooms for workshops, and usually some kind of trade exhibition or stands for suppliers and sponsors to spruik their wares.

The online summit is exactly the same thing... except the attendees are dialling in from the comfort of their own home.

There are considerable benefits to online summits:

- No travel or accommodation costs for guests or speakers.
- No venue costs.
- Your audience will gain valuable content with little effort required from them (just an internet connection).
- Your speakers are gaining valuable exposure to new audiences and you get to leverage their contact list to gain them as attendees.
- Your business gets to build its authority, credibility, and contact list.
- Your business increases its network and partnership potential for ongoing referrals and warm introductions.

Sounds great, doesn't it? But before you go all 'green light' on your first virtual summit, there's a number of things you want to consider (and the technology is just one part).

## Why do you want to host a summit?

Are you looking to build a partner referral network to increase warm leads?

Are you wanting to build your potential sales pipeline?

Do you want to build your authority and credibility in your industry?

Whatever your reason, you need to be super clear and laser focused before you go any further. A summit without an intention is never going to achieve any of your desired outcomes, and could have the opposite and more damaging effect on your business and brand.

Take the time here to think about:

- How many attendees would you like to have?
- What's the outcome for them attending?
- How long will the summit run?
- How many speakers would you like?
  - What will they talk about?
  - Will they be cross promoting or offering a sales pitch?
- Will you need any sponsors, partners or affiliates for your summit?

## What type of summit model will work for you?

If you're looking to build your sales pipeline and increase the size of your database, then you'll probably be considering a 'Free' summit.

This is where attendees exchange an email address for a pass to the summit. The idea being if you add a tonne of value during the summit, you'll turn at least some of your newly acquired contacts into clients further down the road.

The next option for hosting a summit is the 'Freemium' model, which allows attendees to register for free but pay to attend certain sessions within the summit.

The risk in this model is ensuring you're adding a tonne of value to your free attendees (remembering it's a numbers game, and we're going to hopefully convert a few of these to clients at some other point in time).

The final model you can consider is the 'paid' version. Typically, this only works with an existing base of clients that recognise and appreciate the value you bring to the table. Out of the three, this is probably the least popular option for people to choose.

### What's your summit going to be about?

Choosing a theme for your summit is critical to the success of the event. You need to choose something that is aligned with your overarching business objectives, and that contains enough interest to entice speakers to join your line-up and attendees to register to attend.

Remember, you'll be reaching out to speakers to engage with your potential clients, so the theme of the summit needs to have enough depth to it that your speakers won't be overlapping on content or ideas.

Just as we did in the marketing section, now is the time you want to be thinking about the persona of people you want to attract; what their big problem is they're trying to solve, and how this summit is going to resolve that problem for them.

### What software will you need to host your summit?

Similar to considering webinar platforms, you'll need to find a virtual summit platform host. The main difference between webinar platforms and summit platforms is that your summit platform will permit each of your speakers to log in and create their own profiles and branding kits, as well as having some additional technical capabilities in the back end.

You'll need to consider if you'll purchase a summit domain name as a place to house the event. This can be a worthwhile activity to drive traffic back to each of the speakers, as well as giving your business overall branding rights. If so, you'll need to purchase the domain name and either build a website or have one built for you.

While we're on websites, you'll need to consider landing pages as a way to direct and engage signups for the event. You'll probably want to create several different formats and designs for use across various platforms and at various times.

You'll need a good email platform and possibly some automation to be in constant contact with your attendees and speakers in the lead-up to the event (email platforms and automations were discussed in the marketing section of the book).

If you'll be scheduling interviews or doing pre-promotional activities with your speakers in the lead-up to your summit, then you'll need to also consider a calendar scheduling platform (we covered these off in the productivity section of the book).

You'll probably want to create some videos in the lead-up to the event to help promote it. If that's the case, then you'll also need to consider video editing software (or getting someone to edit for you).

Finally, for the event itself you'll need decent audio and visuals, so think about what sort of microphone, web camera and lighting you'll be using.

Recap of software and tech requirements:

- online summit platform (we'll cover that separately)
- summit domain name
- website
- landing pages
- email automation
- calendar scheduler
- video editing
- microphone
- web camera
- lighting

### Select your list of speakers

You've already put some thought into who you'd like to have join you on your online summit, hopefully you've made those decisions based on:

- Knowing they'll deliver great value to the attendees
- Having a reasonable database they can promote the event to
- Alignment with your brand and the theme of the summit

Assuming all of that is organised, it's time to reach out to them and gauge their interest in being involved. At this point you'll need to be super clear on:

- your expectations of their involvement
- how much you'd like them to promote the event
- whether they can sell, or cross promote
- time slot allocation
- any pre-summit interviews or promotions

### Get promoting

The majority of the work is about to start. You'll want a bunch of pre-written emails ready to go to your speakers, who will also help you to promote the event. Each of the emails provides them with a pre-written script so they don't have to think too hard to promote the event and it's easy to share links and hashtags.

Don't forget to be sharing your content on:

- social media
- emails
- newsletters
- media releases

If you can get any guest spots on people's podcasts or guest blog posts it's worth taking those opportunities up as well.

Now, before we move away from the concept of Virtual summits, I promised I'd share a few virtual summit host platform ideas to get you started:

- Hey Summit
- Big Marker
- Accelevents
- Airmeet
- Brandlive

I'm sure you've figured out there are a lot of finer points to creating a successful summit that I've glossed over – again there's enough in 'just' running a summit that people have written books on. The big take away I'd like you to consider when it comes to a virtual summit is this:

They have potential for huge payoffs ... But they also will take months of planning and many hours of promotion. Make sure you have the skills in-house or the contractors to support you before you take the concept on. This may be one of the times you choose to partner with a company that specialises in the area you are tackling.

You need this to work well for you or the consequences for your sales opportunities could be disastrous.

So, where would I put the idea of hosting a virtual summit on your list of sales priorities?

Well, if you have a team to back you up and you've successfully hosted webinars, workshops and events before then an online summit could be a great option for you to consider.

If, however, you've already had four Gin and Tonics while reading this section, then park it for now and focus on the quick wins.

\* \* \*

You made it.

I completely understand this section may have felt like a slap in the face with a wet fish (that was wrapped around a brick). Sales is one of those areas where people either completely freak out and turn to Gin and Tonics as they weep for their future, while others see the opportunities that the tech platforms offer them for understanding and building their sales pipeline with more control.

If you're looking for that one place to start that will make the biggest difference, it's the CRM.

Find the CRM that suits you best and get that implemented in your business. And by implemented, I mean that everyone is using it... everyone, each day, for everything.

If you have the CRM nailed and you're looking for 'the next' thing, bite off the webinar idea and start slow. Build your list and your webinar muscle.

Right, I don't know about you, but I feel like I need a lie down. Let's set our watches or our phones for a 45-minute power nap shall we, and we'll get back to it with a clear head.

# SECTION EIGHT

# CUSTOMER EXPERIENCE

**IF THE COVID PANDEMIC** taught me anything it was this. The customer experience will make or break businesses. Being forced to work remotely and having our economy effectively shut down for a period of time saw a huge swathe of business owners looking for ways to pivot and diversify. Two words that became synonymous with what the pandemic actually meant if you were in business.

We saw bakeries offering sourdough starter kits to cook at home, restaurants transitioned to virtual cooking lessons and gyms providing home-based workouts.

Business owners rapidly discovered what 'Zoom' was, and the words 'you're on mute' became the catch cry of Zoom calls throughout the country.

Throughout all of this our relationships with our customers needed to be maintained. We recognised the power that came from developing real relationships with our customers and we frantically searched for ways to navigate the unprecedented times together.

The lessons we took away from our time in lockdown are ones we all need to work on maintaining and growing as COVID becomes a distant memory. As business returns to 'normal' (whatever normal was for us), being able to maintain the customer at the centre of everything and strive to excel in every interaction has never been more important.

In this section I'm keen to show how technology can be used to improve our customer interactions to create the strong bonds between your customers and your brand. This will future proof you against whatever the next few years have in store for us all.

# 47. WHAT DO YOU ACTUALLY SELL?

If I asked you this question five years ago you possibly would've looked at me like I was a sandwich short of a picnic. The common responses being I'm an accountant, a plumber, a hairdresser, a lawyer... you get the idea.

And then, COVID. Suddenly everyone found themselves in a very different business. We all became in the business of connection, of providing security, of providing laughter. Whatever you did for your clients during the COVID pandemic speaks more to the character of your business, the 'soul' if you will than the actual physical product or service you thought you offered.

It's those deeper emotional connections that bond a client to your business. It's knowing that Mary lost her beloved dog Harry last week and will probably take longer to respond to things right now that make Mary feel like she can trust you with her time, her problems, and her money.

So, how does that 'woo-woo' approach to customer experience and relationship building lend itself to a discussion around technology? Well, it's all about leaning on the systems you put in place to help you manage your business as a holistic entity that will allow you to grow and take care of more people like Mary.

It's using your CRM system to pop a note on Mary's account when you spoke to her and learned about Harry (the dog) with a follow-up task to just check in in a week's time and see how she's doing.

It's having an automated email go out to Anh because it's his 1st anniversary being one of your clients, with a voucher for a free lunch at your local cafe to say thanks.

It's being able to send Andrew a video walking though a solution to his problem because that's easier to understand than trying to sit on the phone and have him getting frustrated.

It's having a sales pipeline in place that captures Priya as an opportunity and connects her to Sam as her salesperson because he'll be the best 'fit' to build a relationship.

It's capturing reviews from your happy customers so other people looking for your services can see you're a company who cares about their people.

The point is, by now you (hopefully) have found at least a couple of platforms or digital accessories you feel would add value to your business, and (hopefully) you're on your way to implementing and learning them. If you can commit to spending the time to really embed them into your business, then the customer experience knock-on effects will happen by default.

# 48. HOW DO YOU SELL?

In April 2020 5.2 million Australian households shopped online (stat courtesy of the Australia Post 2020 eCommerce industry report).

Think about that for a moment... We're a country (just shy) of 25.5 million people and one in four of us opened our computers or phones and purchased something from an online retail store.

In April 2020 alone 200,000 new shoppers entered the world of online retail, purchasing something online for the first time, and over a third of all new shoppers went on to make multiple purchases. For those who were well versed in the online retail environment their numbers also increased their purchase frequency, with over half of them buying online more than twice in April 2020.

We were already seeing big shifts towards e-commerce (the ability for businesses to sell their products and services online) with the likes of Black Friday and Christmas, but the pandemic gave everyone a whole new baseline to consider.

Wine and alcohol proved to be a hot favourite for Aussies during the pandemic, with online sales peaking during March and April, reaching an extraordinary 160% growth on the previous year. Department store purchases also grew by 400% over the previous year across the Easter week.

Consider your own household for a moment. My family moved to grocery shopping online and I moved my elderly parents (80+) into placing their grocery order through their iPad. We purchased Lego and exercise equipment online for the first time. We had never considered making such purchases online before COVID.

Think of this as your line in the sand moment. I really want you to stop and evaluate how you sell and deliver your goods and services.

No one could have predicted what 2020 served to us and nobody would have expected online shopping to jump a massive 80% year on year... (and that was just in the first eight weeks after the WHO declared the pandemic!) but it did... and here we are faced with a decision.

Do we embrace the ways our customers are purchasing, or do we join the list of business owners closing their doors for the last time?

I don't want you to think this is all doom and gloom. It's not that difficult for most business to meet their customers in an online environment, but it does take learning and commitment to making the process as simple as possible.

Let's take a look at a couple of case studies to showcase what I mean.

I love to cook. It's my happy place. It relaxes me to create food for family and friends and I can easily lose a day (or three) buzzing around the kitchen trying new recipes.

During COVID I needed to buy my cooking spices online from Gewürzhaus (www.gewurzhaus.com.au). These are my go-to folks for herbs and spices, and seriously if you love to cook you really need to check them out (and Gewürzhaus, if you're reading this I'm open to sponsorship). Now, until COVID I was travelling to Sydney or Melbourne each month for work, so I'd simply duck into their retail outlets and grab what I needed.

Some things that I immediately noticed when I jumped on their website:

1.  They were offering free shipping on any order over $50 (guess who always makes sure their order is over $50?).

2.  They have an amazing recipe section on their website showcasing various herbs and spices, giving you ideas of how you could use their products.

3. They set up a fabulous Facebook group for their community where they would go live answering questions about products, sharing live cooking demonstrations and generally encouraging activity and sharing from their community of home cooks.

4. They have a regularly updated blog which highlights various things around and related to their products that their community would find interesting.

5. Their ordering process is super easy, with the ability to search for the product, the cuisine or the main ingredient you're cooking with or you have the option to shop the entire range if you fancy more of a meander through their online store (which I always do as I love reading the descriptions to figure out how else I could use the products).

6. Their imagery screams *yummy*.

7. Once you order, you receive regular updates and super-quick delivery via tracked post.

8. Their packaging (all their herbs and spices are sold in glass jars) is superb and I've never had any issues with loss or breakage.

So... why do I share this?

To highlight the ease this business has provided in the customer journey. They've identified what I'm likely to want to look at (based on a CRM system that holds records of my previous purchases). My movement through the website is easy; I don't feel like I'm being 'sold' to.

Usually, I'll jump on the site thinking I need to pick up 'just one or two things' and leave having invested another couple of hundred dollars in what has become my Gewürzhaus addiction. Then I post about what I've just ordered in their Facebook group, and ask for recipes or share a photo of my heaving spice rack as it's my kitchen pride and joy.

This is what a great customer journey, a great customer experience and a great online sales experience looks like.

How could you make that work in your business?

Now, let's look at the ongoing debacle I have every time I try to order from a well-known liquor outlet.

Like most Australians, hubby and I may have enjoyed a few too many glasses of our favourite red when news of the pandemic first started hitting home. We usually have a reasonably stocked wine rack, not because we drink excessive amounts but because we enjoy finding and trying new wines, and of course wine pairs well with good food and great company. We may not have been able to continue having the friends over, but the food and wine... well, a girl has to eat, right?

Anyway, it reached a point where we decided it was probably easier to just jump online and get a case or two of wines delivered and stock up in case this COVID thing got really bad (some people went for toilet paper, we opted for wine and coffee... we figured it would have high barter value if needed, lol).

What a shambles.

First of all, I had to change my password three times because it wouldn't recognise me (I'd just signed up for goodness sake!).

Then I tried to search on Pinot Noir NZ, and it showed me a bunch of completely unrelated options... including several white wines from Chile.

Finally, I selected a few wines to add to the shopping cart and the site crashed, forcing me to log in and start over again.

Three times I tried using different browsers (I thought maybe they didn't like Safari) ... each time I got to checkout – bang, I'm booted out.

In exasperation, I asked Peter to do it ... same thing.

Guess who didn't spend several hundred dollars with said liquor outlet? Guess who has told everyone (including you, my dear reader) about the horrid online experience, and guess who will not be giving their online portal a go anytime soon?

The thing about moving into the world of online retailing is this.

The process has to be seamless for your client. Don't make it difficult for them to spend money with you. Sure, it needs to suit the back end of your business too, but you won't have a business to worry about if you make the process to purchase so convoluted that people give up in exasperation.

So, if you're thinking about moving your business into an e-commerce solution, ask a few of your clients what they would like to see. Get a mockup created and check that it all makes sense, and that everything is working from every possible device you can think of. It's no good to just get it working and looking good on a desktop. What about mobile and tablets?

According to Global Stat Count, online shopping from a mobile phone overtook shopping from a laptop in 2019. In 2020 approximately 76% of online shoppers used their mobile vs 45% using their laptop.

Really take the time to stress test your solution before going live. Better to delay by a few weeks or months and get it humming than launch early and annoy your people. Then lean on the data your site will be providing and be prepared to tweak as needed. Things will change, new clients will onboard, new products will launch and you need to be able to move things around to suit your clients and how your business is changing.

If you're still struggling to grasp the concept of a customer journey, *Harvard Business Review* define it like this:

> *A diagram that illustrates the steps your customer(s) go through in engaging with your company, whether it is a product, an online experience, retail experience, or a service, or any combination. The more touch points you have, the more complicated — but necessary — such a map becomes.*

So... where to start in mapping your customer journey for an online platform?

Well, it all begins with the work you did on your customer personas (remember that from the marketing section?). Once you understand which of the personas you'd like to focus on first, then some questions to consider include:

- What channels is the client likely to interact with on their journey? Social media/website, etc.

- What are the possible touch points for your client? E.g. Facebook messenger, live chat on the website, email, phone.

- What are the common problems your customers experience that could be solved by your product or service? How did your clients solve their problem before they knew about your product or service?

- What are the common events or triggers that cause customers to begin searching for a solution? What words or terminology might your clients use when talking about your product or service? What keywords or search phrases do your clients use when they begin looking for a solution?

- What are the key values of your business? What are you known for? What are the most important features to your clients that are provided by your product or service?

- What are the different ways in which your clients would use your product or service? How difficult is your product or service to use or implement? Do your clients require any prior level of knowledge or skill before utilising your product or service?

- How does your sales model typically work? Will it require any tweaking to transition online?

- What is your pricing structure? Is there anything that will need tweaking to transition online?

- What's the typical length of your customers' pathway to purchase?

- What are the typical objections you encounter during a sales process?

- Who within your business is usually involved in the sales process, and what is their role?

- Is your competition currently offering an online solution? If so, what's working and what isn't? Have you purchased something through their site to experience the process?

- What areas of your business are your greatest assets when compared to your competitors?

- Where are you lacking?

- Are there any trends happening in your industry?

- Are there any third-party software platforms you will need to integrate to make your product or service sellable online?

- Does your solution work across all platforms and all technologies? Have you made transactions using different platforms and devices? Where could you improve, and what worked well?

- What opportunities for on-sell, cross-sell or upsell are there?

Like many of the things we've talked about during the book, start slow, ask lots of questions and be prepared to take an objective look at how your business could provide a better customer experience... whatever that may look like.

# 49. SEGMENTATION

We spent a fair amount of time discussing the value of creating your client personas, and really becoming super clear on who your target audiences are.

The true value of this exercise for your clients becomes very targeted, extremely relevant information they can engage with. This narrowing down of your data is known as 'segmentation'.

Since we're talking about customer experience in this section, it's a good place to discuss the value that segmenting your data adds to your business.

During the first couple of months of COVID it seemed as though every business that I had ever interacted with decided it was time they sent me an email. Initially every email was concerned about how I was doing, then we moved into chatter about the 'unprecedented times' and within a week or so they moved to trying to sell me something. Every. Single. Email.

One Saturday morning I'd had enough of another 'checking in with how you're going' email and snapped. Within a two-hour period I had unsubscribed from (almost) 50 emails. Week in week out, since my initial 'snap' I've unsubscribed to a further 5 to 10.

All because they were either no longer relevant to me or they were completely untargeted.

The worst are the emails where they don't even try, and you end up with a Dear <insert first name>, like they couldn't even be bothered to keep their contact list populated with first names.

Peter (my hubby) often signs up for emails as 'Poo' just to see if any company bothers trying to clean the list... we often have a giggle at the 'Hi Poo' emails.

Anyway, my point is this. You're not the only person emailing me. In fact, according to *Harvard Business Review* the average number of emails in a person's inbox... 200. If you're trying to connect, engage or sell to an office worker, they're getting around 120 emails per day. And as an overall stat, just to remind you where your one email sits in the grand scheme of things... According to Statistica there are 306.4 billion emails sent daily in 2020, with the number expected to rise to 347.2 billion by 2023.

So, before you send another email to your database, ask yourself:

- Am I adding value?
- Am I making myself the one email my client enjoys opening?
- Am I sending targeted and relevant content?

If the answer to any of those questions is no then step away from the keyboard and have a good hard think about what you can do to become someone that people look forward to hearing from.

When you're starting down the segmentation pathway here's a few questions to ask yourself:

- What are the best customer segmentation areas for our business to identify (Remember the work we did on customer personas earlier in the book)?
  - Demographics: Age/Gender
  - Geography: Is it best to send information based on an area?
  - Would it work better to segment by industry?
  - What about things like interests or personalities?
  - What about segmenting on your product or service?
- What does each of my audience segments need from me? Starting from a position of adding value will always win out in the long run.
- What do you want the audience to do? You may want a potential client to take a different action than an existing client.

- How segmented do you want to go? Be very clear about any crossover between your groups. You don't want to cause confusion by sending communications that may only have part relevance to a group of people.

- Where's the low-hanging fruit? Which segment is more likely to respond and purchase from you most quickly and easily?

- Which segment has the highest dollar value? You need to know who is worth the most to your business in $$$. They may take longer to convert, but it's important to continue sending relevant content to them.

You'll need to check every month or so that your data is accurate. If you start seeing your unsubscribe rate increase or your open rate drop (we talked about the various email metrics to measure in the marketing section), then you definitely want to give the segmentation a good look and a bit of an overhaul. And make sure you do this if you launch a new product or service.

# 50. READING YOUR DATA

Okay, we've got some segmentation in place. While you're pondering the move to an online selling platform (in whatever shape that looks like for you), it's worthwhile talking about what data you're going to want to track.

Thankfully, you'll have all of the systems already in place, they're things we've covered off in previous sections. Now it's time to start pulling them all together and understanding the overall picture.

## Website

Google Analytics and Google Search Console are the two main mechanisms we'll rely on, as well as Hotjar.

The main reports you'll want to track month to month are:

### Behaviour

You definitely want to know how your site content is tracking. This lets you see all the pages, blogs, web pages, everything. I'd suggest you compare this month to month to see if any pages are declining in performance – you might need to pop in and freshen the content up or add a few new keywords.

### Site speed

You absolutely need to keep an eye on whether your site speed is slowing down for any reason. A slow site will dramatically affect your rankings, and the number of visitors. It's also helpful to look at any pages in particular and see if they're slow for any reason... particularly if you're trying to see from your site. Remember, it's all about your customer experience and a slow site = a poor customer experience.

### Audience overview

You need to know most of the things in this report. From the number of sessions to the number of average pages visited per session and the average length of a stay on your site. You also want to keep an eye on your bounce rate.

Remember, Google is looking for more time spent on your website and more pages viewed. It's also a good indication the content on your site is engaging and relevant to your audience if they're hanging round and clicking through a bunch of pages. So, you basically want to see these numbers increasing month to month.

Add in your Hotjar report and you've got a very good understanding of how your clients and potential clients are interacting with your content.

## Social media

Insights. All of them on whatever platforms you use. Some offer higher value than others (I pretty much think the LinkedIn ones are useless). Facebook, Instagram and Google My Business all give you great insights, so check them out month to month and see what's working.

I particularly like to see the times and days people are visiting, along with which pieces of content had the most interaction. Both super valuable pieces of information that you can leverage across other platforms.

## Emails

Lean on your CRM, it's your best mate.

Each time you send an email, have a look at what the data is telling you 24 hours down the track. Keep an eye on your:

- open rate
- click through rate
- conversion
- unsubscribes
- bounce rate.

Monitoring those things will tell you what emails hit the sweet spot and what crashed and burned. Do your clients like short punchy emails, or do they prefer to curl up with a cuppa and catch up with what's been happening in your world? You'll only know if you start reading your data.

\* \* \*

I understand this can all feel like a lot to take on board. But once everything is in place, realistically it's probably 30 to 60 minutes once per month.

Of course, one very important thing I need to mention when it comes to tracking the data on how satisfied your customers are is analogue: you need to talk to them and, more importantly, listen to them. They'll tell you if they don't like a change you've made (if you ask them) ... just beware the survey of one. Always ask a good sample size of people the same question so you can accurately gauge the importance of their responses.

# 51. VIRTUAL MEETINGS ARE NOW PART OF THE CUSTOMER EXPERIENCE

For a while there in 2020 we had no choice. The only way we could keep going in business (if we weren't completely online) was to lean into Zoom, Teams (formerly Skype) or one of the other virtual conference platforms.

While Zoom hasn't actually confirmed how many new subscribers they picked up during 2020 they did acknowledge over 100,000 schools began using the platform and over 300 million meetings per day were conducted via the business. And Microsoft acknowledged that total 'Team' calls were up 1000% in March 2020.

So, what does this tell us about the customer experience?

In this instance I'm going to stretch you to think about your own team as being 'customers' in a way. We all suddenly had to shut up our physical presence and set up around dining tables or in a corner of a bedroom. So, how did our team members and customers feel about interacting with us from our home environments?

Well, the first thing we realised is that it allowed our customers a peek behind the curtain. There was no getting away with a four-year-old screaming down the hallway or the dog deciding to lose its mind at the postman (maybe that's just my dog). We couldn't hide the cat jumping up on the keyboard or our partner walking past in the background eating lunch.

And here's the thing... customers and our team members (for the most part) loved it. It humanised our businesses in a way we've never seen before, and allowed us all to bond over the strange year that was. From home schooling to lockdown, masks to second waves, we all had common ground.

According to a report by Gartner, around 74% of businesses plan to continue with remote working, in some way for the reason that 35% to 40% of workers said they felt more productive working from home.

Now, I love working from home. I was lucky enough to be a part of a team in my final corporate role with Telstra which permitted working from home, and I would get far more work done, and often would work longer hours just because I was comfy and uninterrupted.

So, the first thing you need to consider is how did your team feel about working remotely? Did you notice any decline in productivity or deliverable actions? If not, maybe it's time to consider whether you need full-time office space or even as much room as you previously had. More and more I'm hearing businesses tell me they plan to reduce the size of the office and rotate the days the team members come into the office. I take that as a win for the ability to quickly digitise.

But what about our customers? Well, it seems as though they're quite happy with us working wherever, as long as it doesn't interfere with the delivery of their goods or services. The stigma that was once felt around having a home office has certainly diminished thanks to the pandemic, and it's my belief we will only see increased reliance on platforms such as Zoom to connect with clients and team members to ensure business continuity.

The other flow-on effect I see with leveraging platforms like Zoom is the potential reduction in costs for our clients. BC (Before COVID) there was very little chance I would get a client to agree to conduct a strategy session 'online', their preference was always in-person. And while I'll never discount the value of in-person meetings and connections, if I don't need flights and accommodation my clients can save.

I'll certainly continue to provide virtual options to people, and I think that's the big take-away: we all need to give our clients the best customer experience however they choose to work with us.

# 52. AUGMENTED REALITY (AR), VIRTUAL REALITY (VR) AND THE ROLE OF FUTURE TECH

The one thing we know for sure (apart from death and taxes) is that the technology space will continue to grow and evolve.

New things will be released on a weekly basis. Apps and software will make the things we've discussed obsolete (or at least seem outdated) and the ways in which we interact with our clients will continue to move and grow.

One of the most exciting things on the small business horizon I see is the evolution and price drop around AR and VR.

It was only late 2019 that Lego leased a temporary space in London to partner with SnapChat to deliver a fashion store with no clothes.

Customers would enter the otherwise empty space where a Snap triggered portal took them into a virtual world of DJ booths, a Lego bouncer, arcade machine and most importantly a range of Lego branded clothing to select from.

Lego has also gone on to incorporate AR into the Lego sets with the release of 'Hidden Side' where you build a traditional model then, through the use of AR, can hunt and trap ghosts, adding a whole new layer of play to the existing Lego set.

Gucci and Adidas have released the ability for consumers to virtually try on a range of sneakers. Ikea Place allows customers to virtually place Ikea furniture into spaces to get an idea of how things would look. Dulux gives you the ability to see what your walls will look like once painted in a particular shade. And makeup brand Sephora has an app that allows its customers to see what a lipstick or eyeshadow shade would look like on them.

There are so many examples now of larger brands incorporating technology into their customer experiences. Because of this, we will continue to see a price drop in the cost of rolling out similar features in smaller businesses, allowing you to get even more connected with your clients.

So, be prepared. This technology is coming to small businesses in the very near future. It's up to all of us to consider the implications and ways in which we can use and adapt this newly emerging sector for our benefit and the benefit of our clients.

# 53. REVIEWS

Reviews, recommendations, testimonials. Whatever you want to call them, they are as valuable to consider in the customer service section as they are in the marketing section.

Collecting and curating reviews allows your clients to sit in the driver's seat of your business, sharing their experiences with other potential clients. The value we place on reviews (also known as social proof) is immense and should not be overlooked. According to Wyzowl 79% of people have watched a video testimonial to find out more about a company, product or service and 37% of people believe testimonial videos are effective because they're more authentic than a business's own pitch. When you're thinking about collecting or requesting reviews from your existing customers, put some thought into some framing questions that will assist your clients to create a review that will add value to potential clients. Things like:

- Asking your client to expand on what drew them to your business initially.

- What their specific problem was when they employed your services?

- The outcome the client received working with your business.

By providing context to your clients in requesting the review you are setting up the client and your business with the best possible outcome... and the one most likely to assist potential clients when reviewing your business.

We discuss reviews further in the marketing section, however it's important to recognise they need to be a part of your overarching strategy when considering your customer experience.

\* \* \*

Alright, before you move onto the next section I want you to take some time to think about what you currently have in place to capture and track your customer experience and what you would like to be doing this time next year.

Take the time now to put the book down, pour yourself a big glass of water (you need to stay hydrated to think) and make some notes around the things that triggered for you in this section. Things to investigate, things to implement or things to stop doing. Whatever they are, they're all helpful... if you capture them now while they are fresh in your mind.

Once you've done that, get up, have a big stretch and take yourself outside for 10 minutes to breathe deep and give your eyes (and brain) a rest.

I'll be here when you get back.

# SECTION NINE

# HEALTH AND WELLNESS

# Egon in the room

**AT FIRST GLANCE** you may wonder why I've even bothered to include a section on health and wellness in a book about business technology.

To be honest I never considered *not* including it.

As small business owners we have a tendency to be 'on' 24/7. We live, eat and sleep our business, often to the detriment of our health.

It's my belief we all need to become a little more focused on maintaining a healthy mind, body and spirit, in order to continue to build a better business and service our community.

And that is the reason we're about to chat health and wellbeing.

Oh, one more thing before we get into this section, I'm going to let you in on a little secret. Well, not so much of a secret as something that the majority of my digital clients don't know.

I have qualifications as a food and wellness coach.

I've had some health issues for a good part of my life, and I wanted to get a better understanding of what was going on with my body and, make better choices.

I share this with you now to give you some back story on how interesting I find the whole health and wellness section. How I've found the combination of technology with health and wellness a Godsend for collecting, curating and understanding data around my own health. I'm not going to lie – mixing tech with health and wellness... is my happy place.

Over the years I've gone down just about every health and fitness tech rabbit hole there is. I've got the smart sleep equipment, the blood pressure monitors, the smart watch and numerous apps. I'll share them all with you in detail throughout the section.

According to Statista, revenue from the top 10 health and wellness apps increased by 61% in 2019 to reach $327 million globally. Add to that, the number of fitness app users is expected to surpass 353 million by 2022.

However you look to use technology in your life, one of the first and obvious places I find people let their tech guard down is when it comes to health and wellness.

While you may notice this section is somewhat shorter than the others in the book, it's no less packed with some of my favourite things that will make a difference to you as a human, which (the hope is) will make you a better businessperson. Jump on to your app store of choice and you'll see literally hundreds of health and well-being apps tailored to your area of interest. There's audiobooks and podcasts you can download and listen to as well if that's more your thing. Most of them are fairly straightforward to use, and I won't go into details on the great options available, but I will call out a few to start you on your search.

So, be prepared to open up and – who knows – you might find something that changes your life... literally.

# 54. WEARABLE TECH

We can't even begin to talk about adapting technology into our health and wellness without talking about wearable tech. It is estimated by Gartner that the global wearable tech market will be worth more than US$87 billion in 2023.

But let's step back for a moment and talk about what wearable technology is. If you've ever owned a Fitbit or a Smart watch you've worn wearable tech. Essentially, wearable technology is just a piece of technology you wear that will provide data for you in real time.

The number of steps you've taken in a day. How many calories you've burned, or that data could be what your heart rate is like just before you give that big presentation.

These devices may connect to a WIFI network, or may have a sim, others still connect to another device (like your phone) through Bluetooth. They will all in some way connect you as a human to your health and wellness goals, whether that's to lose weight, stay active or track a medical condition.

The more popular wearable tech options available include:

## Smart watches

The Apple watch has dominated the landscape when it comes to the smart watch category, and effectively now they are a mini version of your phone (Dick Tracy flashbacks anyone?). From a health and wellness point of view my Apple watch allows me to track:

- my daily steps
- whether I'm standing often enough through the day
- what my heart rate is doing
- my workouts (down to whether I've done Pilates, cardio or strength training).

I can set challenges with friends and family if I'm looking for a little extra motivation, and I can check out the number of calories I burned during a workout as well as my average heart rate and heart rate range during my workout.

There are a bunch of preloaded workouts built into the watch, which know what calorie rates to burn at; I need only click on my workout for the day to get a full breakdown of information.

It syncs all this data with my phone and (because I'm an Apple user), places it into a health app which will then give me ongoing data across days/weeks/months. For me, and for my hubby, it's been an invaluable tool to be able to share during GP visits and to feel connected to and in control of our own health.

Apple is not the only player in the smartwatch market though. Google and Samsung both have their own versions (and their own health tracking apps to support). As with most things in the tech space your choice of provider will come down to what else you're running and ease of connection.

## Fitness trackers

If you don't want a watch but you'd still like to track your daily activity, a fitness tracker might be a better option for you.

There are way too many options on the market to get into here, although Fitbit remains the best known.

Typically, fitness trackers offer better battery life than their smart watch cousins; they are also cheaper than a smart watch.

According to a survey conducted by Gallup, 90% of American consumers said that they are currently using a wearable fitness tracker. The same percentage said they were also using a health app.

## Health and wellness apps

According to IQVIA, there are over 318,000 health apps available in app stores worldwide. And over 200 more apps are being added daily. If you've ever ventured into the health and wellness section of the app store, you'll quickly realise there are apps for a wide range of requirements, including:

- food and nutrition
- fasting
- sleep
- meditation
- mindfulness
- mental health journals
- running
- yoga
- strength training
- habits
- heart rate
- brain training
- goal planning
- weight loss
- addiction
- fertility
- cycling
- hiking
- water tracking
- macro counting
- motivation
- first aid
- baby health
- toddler health
- teenage health
- elderly health
- men's health
- women's health

... you get the idea. The point is, if you want to track or monitor any aspect of your health and wellness for you, your family, your employees or your health professionals you have a myriad of choices available.

I've done a little research for you, and to give you a heads up I thought I'd share some of the most popular health and wellness apps for 2020 based on a few of the major segments.

## Food and nutrition

This was my first foray into an app within the health and wellness space. I was looking for something that I could use as a food diary and I was looking for something that would help me track my Macros (for me that meant protein, fat and carbs). There are some really specific food apps available for those who need to track certain things (like diabetes or celiac for example) but if you're just looking for a good basic overall app to get you started here's a few of the more popular ones:

| App | Pros | Cons | Available |
|---|---|---|---|
| **My Fitness Pal\*** | – Best app for logging food<br>– Huge food database<br>– Bar code scanner for quickly entering food<br>– Create your own recipes and meals<br>– Will track exercise and water intake as well as food<br>– Integrates with other health apps | – Takes some learning<br>– Need to pay to unlock some of the features you're likely to use | – Apple<br>– Android<br>– Web |
| **Calorie Counter** | – Stand-alone food diary<br>– Pre plan meals to understand macros<br>– Easy to learn | – Not as many food options as My Fitness Pal<br>– In app purchases to unlock some features | – Apple<br>– Android |
| **Lifesum** | – Builds in motivation<br>– Inbuilt recipes<br>– Works with a variety of diets (keto, paleo)<br>– Offers kick starter plans to help you get started | – No community features<br>– One diet only available on free version<br>– Food database not as large as My Fitness Pal | – Apple<br>– Android |

\* This is the app I use… daily. I mean I track everything for every meal. If you count macros (by macros I mean protein, carbs, fats etc) and really want to understand your food, this is my recommendation.

## Meditation and mindfulness

In the words of Frank Costanza from Seinfeld we could all use a little more 'serenity now'! The mindfulness and meditation space has exploded with offerings over the last few years, and during the COVID pandemic this segment was the most talked about amongst my small business clients.

Whether you've been meditating your whole life or you're looking for a way to test the meditative waters, there is bound to be an app that suits your requirements.

A few of the more popular ones are:

| App | Pros | Cons | Available |
| --- | --- | --- | --- |
| **Headspace** | – Great for beginners<br>– Easy to use<br>– Choose your session length | – Super limited as a free version<br>– Sessions can feel repetitive after a while | – Apple<br>– Android |
| **Insight Timer** | – Over 35,000 free guided meditations<br>– Bookmarking your favourite session makes it easy to return to<br>– Premium version available offering new content daily | – Anyone can upload content, so choose your session wisely | – Apple<br>– Android |
| **Calm** | – Recommends content based on your goals<br>– Masterclass sessions available<br>– Wide variety of content available | – More expensive than the other apps | – Apple<br>– Android |

| App | Pros | Cons | Available |
|---|---|---|---|
| **Ten Percent Happier** | – Different content offered for different experiences (eg: sleep, guided meditation)<br><br>– Lots of short meditations<br><br>– Great for beginners | – Only available on subscription | – Apple<br>– Android |

## Exercise

There are those who walk among us that find exercise a stress reliever and actively seek out the ability to work out... Weird, I know, but true!

Whether you are one of 'those' people or you're an average time-poor business owner looking to snatch a few moments to stop your body from falling apart then there is a huge range of exercise app options available to you.

I can't possibly even scratch the surface of what's available (particularly if there is a particular exercise genre you're interested in), but I can share some of the more popular or better rated ones to get you started:

| App | Pros | Cons | Available |
|---|---|---|---|
| **Les Mills on Demand\***<br><br>**(Group Classes)** | – Huge range of workout options<br><br>– New workouts loaded regularly<br><br>– If you're familiar with the Les Mills classes in gyms you're going to feel right at home<br><br>– Good support via social media from the community | – Free trial but expensive as an annual subscription<br><br>– Can feel a little overwhelming knowing where to start<br><br>– The app can be a little glitchy | – Apple<br>– Android<br>– Web |

| App | Pros | Cons | Available |
|---|---|---|---|
| **Peloton Digital (Group Classes)** | – Live streamed classes daily<br>– iOS users can download workouts<br>– Variety of classes from strength to yoga, spin to meditation | – You need the internet for it to work<br>– Some of the classes use jargon which newcomers may not understand<br>– Many of the classes not suitable for beginners | – Apple<br>– Android (far more limited features) |
| **Glo (Yoga)** | – Over 3500 classes<br>– Good for beginners through to experienced<br>– Downloadable sessions | – Only suitable for Yoga fans<br>– Talk of issues when looking to cancel subscription | – Apple<br>– Android (appears to be clunky)<br>– Web |
| **Runtastic (Runners)** | – Accurate tracking measures<br>– Keeps a detailed history<br>– Audio updates at checkpoints<br>– Play your music inside the app | – In app offers can be distracting<br>– Takes some set up<br>– Freemium – so you'll be asked to upgrade… a lot | – Apple<br>– Android |
| **Strava (runners and cyclists)** | – Keeps track of segments without logging them<br>– Ability to share a running route<br>– Challenge others | – Need to go pro to access many of the features<br>– By default your GPS data is made public | – Apple<br>– Android |

\* This is the app I have a subscription to. I use it in combination with in-person gym visits. It sure did get a workout (see what I did there) during COVID though.

## Sleep

I've tried quite a few different sleep apps over the years. I've come to figure out if you really want to track your sleep, you need to get a device (like a sleep mat or a fitness tracker) that will sync with an app. Relying on something just on your phone is never going to give you reliable data.

With that in mind, the best sleep apps I've come across lately are:

| App | Pros | Cons | Available |
|-----|------|------|-----------|
| Headspace | – 'Sleepcasts' designed to help you get to sleep available on the free version<br>– Good to help you wind down | – You need the paid version to gain variety<br>– Doesn't actually track sleep | – Apple<br>– Android |
| Rain Rain* | – Variety of different white noise options<br>– Good variety on the free version<br>– Create combinations of sounds | – Doesn't actually track sleep<br>– If you want to use it all night make sure your phone is plugged in | – Apple<br>– Android |
| Sleep cycle | – The microphone will detect and track snoring<br>– Alarm wakes you at optimal time | – Animals can trigger the microphone<br>– No detailed sleep cycles captures | – Apple<br>– Android |
| Fitbit | – Provides detailed heart rate and movement information<br>– Provides sleep cycle suggestions<br>– Smart alarm | – Subscription required for full information<br>– Not all models provide sleep tracker | – Fitbit |

| App | Pros | Cons | Available |
|---|---|---|---|
| **Withings sleep tracker mat*** | – Non wearable – goes under your mattress<br>– Measures deep sleep, REM sleep and light sleep<br>– Heart rate tracking and snore detection<br>– Shareable health reports | – Designed for one person<br>– Needs to be positioned correctly | – Apple<br>– Android |

\* I use both the Withings sleep tracker mat and 'Rain Rain'. I like the white noise to fall asleep to, and also value the amount of data I'm able to retrieve from the sleep mat.

It's worth noting at this point that my favourite health app would actually be the Withings Health Mate app. I've become quite the advocate of the Withings products (no kickbacks mind you, although Withings if you read this, I'm certainly open to endorsements).

Their app is available on either Apple or Android, and through this one little app I can monitor my:

· activity
· sleep
· blood pressure
· weight
· heart rate

It connects to other health apps like My Fitness Pal and the Apple health app. When it combines the data, the app provides insights into how my health is tracking, and allows you to download and share this data with your health professionals.

## Health tracking devices

I've already given you some insight into one of the tracking devices I use on a daily basis but the range of available options to keep on top of your health and wellbeing is growing by the week. And we've already talked a little about some of the wearable tech that is available in the market right now. Let's take a look at some of the other options available to you in the health and wellness space.

### Blood pressure monitors

According to the Australian Institute of Health and Wellness around 1 in 3 Australians over the age of 18 have high blood pressure. For many the need to track and monitor how their blood pressure is doing is vital.

Fortunately, we now have access to 'smart' blood pressure monitors that will automatically update the readings in an app and allow you to share this information with your health professional.

In case you're wondering, we have the Withings blood pressure monitor at home (my hubby is one of those with high blood pressure) and we both frequently track our readings.

### Smart scales

Okay, very few of us are on speaking terms with our bathroom scales, I get it. But having a set that is at least accurate and can track your weight is a must have. There are a number of scales on the market now you can sync with your phone to collect your data... and yes, we use the Withings brand.

... I really should be getting a kickback from the company by now – don't you agree?

### Sleep

So, you already know I'm using the Withings sleep pad but it's not the only one available on the market.

If you feel as though you're struggling with good quality sleep or even wondering how much sleep you're getting, investing in a sleep tracking device could be an investment worth making.

### Meditation

The 'Muse' headband has been around for a while and has made significant improvements over the past couple of years. Essentially 'Muse' is designed to train you how to meditate, providing real-time feedback and assisting you to achieve calm.

### Smart watches

From Apple to Samsung, Garmin to Fitbit and many others in between, the smart watch has become the ubiquitous wearable health tech device.

If you're looking to start your foray into wearable technology then a smart watch is definitely the place to begin.

## Other wearables worth mentioning

Wearable tech in healthcare is a booming industry. COVID certainly did assist in the escalation of adaptation of technology throughout the population (really, who else had a telehealth appointment before COVID?) but there is a lot of inroads being made into very specific use case requirements including:

- ECG monitoring
- Diabetes/ blood and glucose tracking
- Biosensors for collecting real-time information like respiratory and heart rate
- Epilepsy – monitoring of brainwave activity
- Parkinson's – brain inserts for controlling muscle shakes and movement.

It's a brave new world, and something that will continue to evolve. I fully suspect by the time I'm my parents' age (mid '80s) we will be in a position to monitor and upload just about every conceivable piece of information our health care professionals would ever need.

\* \* \*

Congratulations on reaching the end of another section. Before moving onto the next section, take a few moments to find an app, a podcast or an audiobook that interests you and download it to your phone.

Then before you continue on, get up, stretch and get outside for some fresh air. Maybe take the dog for a walk or kick the footy with one of the kids... Whatever you choose, make sure your watch is tracking your activity.

# SECTION TEN

# OTHER HANDY THINGS TO KNOW

**THERE WAS A BUNCH OF STUFF** when I was outlining the book that just didn't seem to have a natural home but were still relevant and important for you to know about.

Rather than try to make them fit somewhere, I thought it easier to just give them a section of their own.

So, this is for all the misfits and random tidbits that could come in handy one day and you don't want to throw away (kinda like the third drawer in your kitchen).

There's no order … So, don't bother trying to look for one, just enjoy the randomness of the way my mind gathers information and know that some day one of these tips will come in handy.

# 55. BACK IT UP

No, not a reference to a random hip hop track – a reminder that now you're all over your tech stuff you're going to want to make sure you've got a good backup and storage solution in place.

Working in an Apple environment, I have the ability to back up each night to my iCloud account (which I do), and working in Google or Microsoft you'll find you have the ability to save things directly to your cloud (so please make sure you've taken the time to set everything up to do just that).

If you're not backing up to iCloud or you work in a PC environment, you're going to need to do some research on backup solutions. In the old days (read 5 to 10 years ago) you would most likely backup to a hard drive kept on site; these days it's easier to look at a cloud-based solution, and potentially having a secondary solution as an onsite external drive to keep everything secure.

Cloud backup solutions tick so many boxes it really is a no brainer to organise. Having your data backed up to the cloud is:

· convenient
· secure
· automatic
· flexible
· reliable

Awesome. So, what do you need to consider when you're setting up a cloud-based (or any kind of) backup solution? Well, I'm glad you asked …

## What do you need to back up?

While you may be using Google or Microsoft to maintain the majority of your productivity tools, remember, it's your responsibility to secure your data. Now, I'm not saying anything will happen to your stuff sitting on Google's servers… but what if it did?

It's a smart move to back up anything you can't afford to lose:

- emails
- productivity tools (Microsoft or Google data)
- accounting information
- HR data
- any other critical information

### Where is our data getting backed up to?

Who stores your data and where is it stored? Is it important to you to have it stored in Australia (because a lot of cloud solutions aren't Aussie based)? It's not something to lose a lot of sleep over, but it's worthwhile having an understanding of where everything is actually kept.

### How often do we need to back up?

I've got my system organised to automatically back up every night. Every. Single. Night. That means if I have an outage or anything goes down, the worst case is I lose one day's worth of data. While I wouldn't be happy (especially if it had been during the writing of the book), I could deal with the consequences of a one-day loss.

How much data could you afford to lose? Answer that and you have the answer to your question 'how often do we need to back up?'

**What happens if we need to retrieve our backup?**

Do you know how to retrieve your backup if needed? If you were hacked and being held to ransom, could you just laugh it off and restore all your computers without issue?

You need to know what the process is in case you ever need to restore your data. It's also worthwhile checking the integrity of the backup every now and then. Just to be sure.

These days your data really is your business lifeblood. This is something you don't want to muck around with. If you are still the slightest bit nervous or unsure about what to do in this area, find yourself an expert in backup solutions and network set up. It's worth paying the money to have this done professionally.

## Checking for updates

This one is kinda up there on the importance scale with the backup set up. The more digitised our businesses become, the more updates you'll need to do across hardware and software.

Clicking the 'install later' option might be a solution for right now, but it's not a long-term viable option. So, take the time to create a policy and procedure around how you're going to handle updates.

When it comes to my hardware (laptops, phones, etc.) I usually set these to automatically update. That means as soon as a new update is available, I'll be notified. At that point I tell the device to complete the update overnight. When I come back to it in the morning all there is for me to do is give it a restart and I'm good to go.

Software can be a little tricker, as sometimes the platform will tell you that you need to update before you can use the system again. This is especially true of software that isn't used every day. Sometimes you need to roll with the punches on those things and click the update button as needed … Besides, it gives you a good excuse to go make a coffee or call someone for a catch-up.

Websites are a whole different ball game. I can't tell you the number of times I've had someone tell me they did a WordPress update only to find they now have three things no longer working on their site.

When it comes to websites my advice is, find a company that offers a maintenance service and get them to do the updates. There are so many security patches and other bits and pieces coming out all the time, it's just easier to let someone else handle that and keep your site operational. You don't need the headache of trying to fix a broken site on top of everything else you have going on.

So, set up automatic updates where possible. Take the odd 'update now' message as an excuse for a break and leave the website updates to someone who has the patience and knowledge to keep things ticking along.

# 56. TIPS, TRICKS AND HACKS

Every day people share with me their favorite piece of software, or the latest digital tip, trick or hack. You can imagine over 30 years just how many I've collected. These are a few of my (current) favourites worth checking out.

## Copyright/royalty free image sites

I get a lot of questions about where to go to find images for blogs or social media. My first piece of advice is, make sure you're accessing images that are royalty or copyright free. Nobody needs to be worrying about someone knocking on your door for breaching copyright.

Never just Google an image and use that. Again, you have no idea what copyright is on the image.

There are quite literally dozens, if not hundreds of websites devoted to copyright and royalty free images that you can use throughout your marketing. Some you may need to acknowledge the photographer; most are free for you to just use.

Here's a list of some of my favourites in no particular order:

- Albumarium: www.albumarium.com
- Death to stock: www.deathtothestockphoto.com
- Foodies Feed: www.foodiesfeed.com
- Unsplash: www.unsplash.com
- Life of Pix: www.lifeofpix.com
- Pexels: www.pexels.com
- Pixamatic: app.pixamattic.com/auth/login
- Pixabay: www.pixabay.com
- Pic Jumbo: www.picjumbo.com
- Gratisography: www.gratisography.com

If you couldn't find anything you liked in that list, then just Google 'Royalty Free Images' and have fun losing hours to find that perfect shot.

## Removing the background from an image

Sometimes you'll find a photo and think how perfect it would be if it didn't have the background. That's where Remove.bg comes into play: www.remove.bg

Upload your photo and the computer will remove the background for you. I've found this works best on images with people in it that aren't too complex.

If you have something complex, then I suggest using Fiverr.com to get someone to remove the background and tidy the image up for you.

It won't cost much, and it's a better use of your time.

## How to organise your iPhone home screen

If your iPhone screen is a jumbled mess of random apps that make no sense, or you can't find what you need when you need it, then you probably need to organise your home screen.

You have two options to organise your screen.

If you're using the current ios14 on your iPhone you can swipe right (you may need to swipe a few times) and Apple will suggest folder groupings for your apps.

If you'd prefer to create your own groupings simply press and hold on an icon (this is called a 'force touch'); you'll feel a haptic response and everything on the screen will start jiggling.

Right about now I like to think this is the apps getting nervous you're going to delete them.

Anything with a 'X' you can delete (so get rid of those apps you haven't opened in months).

If you press and drag an icon you can move it onto another app that is similar to create folders.

For example, I have a 'Weather' folder created that houses my various weather apps.

I have a 'fitness' folder that houses my exercise and fitness apps.

I have a 'productivity' folder that houses my Google shortcuts and time tracking apps... you get the idea.

Take some time while you're watching TV to organise your home screen. By having things in folders you'll find everything is much easier to find and you won't be scrolling through four pages of home screens looking for that one news app you want to read.

## My must have apps

These are the apps I can't do without and will access on my phone if not every day then certainly on a weekly or regular basis.

· Podcasts – I listen to around 2 to 3 podcasts every day, so this gets used a lot

· Navigation – because I couldn't find my way out of a paper bag without them:

- Google Maps
- What 3 Words – I mentioned this earlier in the book
- News – because I want to read the news on my terms:
  - ABC
  - Apple News
  - Guardian
- Health:
  - Fernwood – I book my gym sessions and check class times through the app
  - Activity – Apple native app, tracks daily activity
  - Health mate – Withings app, curates all my Withings health devices
  - Health – Apple native app, tracks overall health information
- Social Media:
  - LinkedIn
  - Facebook
  - Facebook Pages
  - Messenger
  - WhatsApp
  - YouTube
- Productivity:
  - Google Docs
  - Google Sheets
  - Pages
  - Numbers

## Questions I ask before choosing an app

Over the course of the book we've talked about a number of different apps. There will come times when you'll be needing to find an app for yourself to suit a particular identified problem; when that happens, how do you choose the best app?

I thought I'd share the questions I run myself through before I choose an app to plug an identified gap.

### What problem am I hoping to solve?

If you can start with this question top of mind, then you'll be approaching the apps with a view to resolve the big issue.

### What support is available?

At a minimum I try to look for apps that support both iOS (Mac) and Android. That way if I need or want to collaborate with anyone, I can recommend the app without being concerned about people's operating systems.

If they have web support as well, I'm pretty well hooked. I do a lot of work each day on my laptop or desktop, so allowing the app to just sync to the phone is the easiest way for me to operate.

### Will the app sync between devices?

Following on from the previous one, it's worth knowing whether your app will transfer and sync data between your phone, tablet and laptop/desktop.

### Up front and ongoing costs

Look at the initial set-up cost of the app along with any ongoing expenses. You need to do your maths and ensure its ticking the boxes within your budget.

### Do you need to be able to back up the data in the app?

Now that we understand the importance of having a solid backup solution, consider if you need to back the data up that is stored within each app.

### Do you need to connect the app to other apps or software solutions?

Often the app we're choosing is part of a solution for a single (or multiple) problem. Understanding how (or if) the app will connect into other apps or existing software solutions can be a make or break for the choice of app.

### Set a timer

Once you've identified you need an app to solve a problem you could lose hours going down various rabbit holes trying to find the 'perfect' solution.

Set a timer. Give yourself that allotted time to review and read about the various apps. At the end of your allocated time choose the best app based on everything you've learned.

One final thing I'll say on choosing an app is the follow through is just as important. You'll need to make time (put it in your calendar) to learn, embed and begin using the app in order for it to provide value to you.

# SECTION ELEVEN

# WHAT'S NEXT

**IF YOU'RE STILL READING,** congratulations, you made it! It's been a marathon effort to work your way through each area of your business and your life through the prism of digitisation.

There's been a lot of information to take on board, so now it's time to begin working your way through all the 'ah ha' and the 'that's a good idea' moments you collated along the way and get them into some kind of order.

Hopefully during the course of the book there were a couple of areas that really stood out to you as a priority. Things that you looked at and had an immediate *I need to do that* feeling gnaw at your stomach.

In this section we're going to cover how you:

· get your digital ducks in a row
· figure out when it's time to look for or implement something new
· choose a contractor to work with to help
· choose a software solution
· introduce the new technology to your workplace.

This, my friends, is where the rubber hits the road. It's time to stop making paper airplanes and patting puppies ... it's time to digitise your business.

But first, maybe one last game of paper toss...

# 57. GET YOUR DIGITAL DUCKS IN A ROW

Before you begin signing up for new software, setting time aside to learn that new app or buying new hardware, it pays to take a few moments and get your metaphorical digital ducks in a row.

I mentioned in the intro that most likely you found one (or possibly a few) sections that leapt out to you as you read them, knowing these were the things you needed to do. These will arm you with the knowledge to streamline the business, or maybe scale it to the next level.

Whatever those things were it's time to put pen to paper (or start creating tasks in your to do list) so you can prioritise.

Think about:

- What's going to have the greatest impact on your business?
- What's required to make it happen?
  - Time?
  - Money?
  - Resources?
  - Buy in from the team?
- What is the quickest win you can have (we all need a quick win now and then)?
- What requires additional research?
- What can you do yourself and what will you need some assistance with?

Give each of your identified areas a score out of 10 in terms of overall impact to the business in order to create your priority list.

Then it's time to gather the team together and share your thoughts. You're now moving more into a 'change management' stage. There are several steps to help make it a success throughout your business.

## You need to build momentum

It's very important that your team is 'along for the ride' if you want your resolution to digitise the business to be successful. Remember, your team has been doing it the 'old' way for many years, and human nature says we don't like change.

You need to let them know why you're looking to make the changes now. That you've listened to their feedback and you understand there's a better way to do things... but you need their help for it to work.

It's time to paint the vision you have for the business and what you see happening if you don't embrace the digital world now.

At this point you'll uncover any resistance and any hidden talents simmering within the team that you need to manage or foster. Any of your identified priorities that directly impact team members will need their buy-in.

You can ask them to get involved by conducting the research or sharing what they believe would make life easier, less time consuming or provide a better customer experience.

You'll find the process of implementation and embedding significantly easier if the decisions are made in consultation with your team... and if the team gets to involve themselves in the process from the beginning.

With the team buy-in you may find that your priorities have altered slightly. There may be something they've identified that would be a quicker win or make more sense to address ahead of something else you'd determined. If so, shuffle the list around until it makes sense.

With your digital priorities in hand, it's time to move to the next stage.

## Do you really need something new?

It's not uncommon for a business to get to the stage where they've identified their priorities and realise that they purchased a piece of software two years back that would resolve that problem, but no one had the time to learn it, so it got shoved to the bottom of the 'to do' list and gathered dust.

If that's the case, then it's time to pull it out and take a good look at it. Knowing what you now know, do some research and see if it's still the best solution for you. If so, great, then open your calendar and schedule some time in to begin learning everything it can do... or, speak with your team member whose area of responsibility it is and task them with prioritising the learning.

If you can build momentum around the required change, you have a far higher chance of the change sticking.

## It's time to find your 'change champion' for your project

Your change champion becomes your ally in helping to continue the momentum. Part of your change champion's new role is becoming the lead learner for the software change. They will create any procedures of how to use it for the business along the way. As they learn, they can teach you and other team members. This embeds their learning and makes it far more likely the new solution will stick across the organisation.

You'll want to schedule regular check-ins with your change champion and listen to what they're telling you about the process. Allow them to take the lead in helping embed the process throughout the business and continue to paint the picture of why the change is happening.

Setting the expectation throughout the business allows everyone to stay connected to why the change is happening. It also strengthens the chances of the team following and embedding the new procedure. The earlier you can make the new piece of software mandatory for everyone, the quicker improvements across the company will be seen.

The final step to ensuring a smooth transition to your new software is to remove any obstacles you or the team may have in using the platform.

This may mean you need to look at working with a contractor to help with the embedding process.

I'll talk a little further about what to look for when selecting a digital contractor (or choosing a software platform), but for now just be mindful to be on the lookout for any resistance popping up around the embedding process.

You want to remove any and all obstacles as quickly as you can to ensure the uptake of your required change doesn't stall.

With the support of a contractor, or maybe some online learning, you're setting up your business and the team for a successful integration of your first digital priority.

Don't forget to celebrate the quick wins along the way! This keeps everyone motivated and encouraged to move on to the next digital project once the dust has settled on the initial one.

## How to choose a new software platform

So, you've identified a gap within the business and you now know that there is a software solution that will help you plug the gap. That's great, but before you jump in feet first with the first software provider you find, here are some handy questions to ask.

### What's the big problem we're looking to solve with this software?

Being very clear on what the problem is that needs to be solved goes a long way to helping you identify the right software for the job.

### What does the business need vs what does it want?

Way back in the beginning of the book we talked about getting clear around understanding the difference between your digital wants and needs. Before you decide on any software solution it's vital you understand what the system needs to be able to do for you vs what would it be nice if it could do.

While you may get a platform that does everything it's more important it ticks off your 'needs' boxes than your 'wants' boxes.

## What are you looking to achieve by implementing this software?

It's a good idea to have your metrics identified for what you need the software to do. After all, you need to be able to measure whether or not implementing it was a success.

It doesn't need to be a monetary metric – it could be an increase in productivity, better customer experience or better visibility over an area of your business. Whatever it is, be clear on how you'll know it is successful.

## What growth room does the software offer?

If your business scales in capacity, can the software accommodate it? Are there additional charges or a change in plan to consider? If so, what does that look like?

## Have you got the right resources in the team to implement?

Does the software require a new skill set you don't currently have? Is it something you could upskill a team member on or is it something you could instead outsource? What capacity does your team have to learn and implement new software?

It's also worth finding out what an accurate representation of implementation looks like and if the software provider has anyone that will assist you with onboarding.

## What support does the platform offer?

Do they have phone support? Live chat? Contractors who can visit? Where are they based? Can you get the support you need at the time you're likely to need it?

## What's the budget?

While $5 or $50 per month may seem 'doable', you need to consider how many of those small amounts you're paying to various software providers. Make sure you're getting value for money in your budget decisions.

### Do they offer a free trial?

While you may believe you've found the perfect solution for your business, it pays where possible to get a free trial. Nothing is going to give you a truer indication of how the software is really going to fit in with your business like trying to fit it in with your business.

### Do you know anyone else using the software?

It always pays to have a chat with others who are using (or have used) the software. You'll get an accurate report from people about:

- how long it really takes to implement and learn
- what they wish they'd known when they first started using the software
- what they don't like
- what customer support is like
- how long they've been using the software.

If you don't know anyone directly, put a shoutout in a few social media groups; you'll find people are usually pretty happy to share their personal experiences with you if you ask nicely.

### Tips to make sure you successfully implement your new software

Once you've chosen your platform and you've got your digital ducks in a row, knowing who'll be responsible in the team for championing the change and implementing the software you still need to set yourself up for success.

There are a few key tips that will make any software implementation run a little smoother:

### *Make sure you know your responsibilities for installation*

Depending on the size and scope of the software you've chosen, you may find the company will assign an onboarding and implementation team to assist you with setting things up.

It's crucial that you find out what your responsibilities are during this onboarding time and make sure you allocate sufficient time to complete all of the tasks assigned to you.

### Understand your implementation timeline

As a follow-on to the above, you'll need to map out the full instal-lation and make sure you're clear on the time requirements you'll need to set aside for training and for implementation.

### Assign your change champion

Make sure you've chosen a team member whose responsibility it will be to sit through the training and implementation. They will be the change agent within your business to help embed the new software and bring the remainder of the team along the journey to using the new software.

It's important to choose someone who would normally be across the process the software is supporting. That way they are empow-ered to make the decisions around the best way to set up the software for your business.

### Don't skip the foundational decisions

The way your software is set up will impact the way it interacts with your business. The most important time with your software is right at the beginning of its implementation. Taking the time to under-stand how the software works and interacts with your business will mean you're best placed to make the foundational set-up decisions accurately.

### Train your team during the set-up phase

Whoever the software will be impacting needs to be trained in the platform during the set-up phase. Waiting for the system to be live before training your team is asking for a poor experience for your team and a greater chance of disaster for your software success.

### Test and tweak before going live

You need to test various scenarios to see how they play out across your business – this allows you to tweak and adjust before going live.

### Celebrate your achievement

Implementing a new software system in any small business is no mean feat. Take the time to celebrate what you've achieved and make sure to report to the team on how its implementation has positively impacted the business.

## How to choose the right contractor to work with

Throughout the book you probably identified a number of actions you'd like to take in your business but maybe you feel they are tasks best outsourced to someone who specialises in that field.

Perhaps you want to overhaul your website, get some SEO work done or outsource your content creation or implementation. Whatever you're looking for, it's a minefield out there looking for a tech expert you can trust to do the job and deliver good value for money.

Here are my tips to finding yourself a contractor you can trust (note: not all questions will apply to every project):

- How long have they been in business?
- How long have they been in their industry?
- Have they got case studies or clients you can speak to?
- Can you see a sample of their work?
- How long do they typically take to complete a project like yours?
- Do they charge by the hour or by the project?
- What types of industry do they enjoy working with?
- Do they do the work in-house or do they outsource it?
- How do they stay up to date with their industry?
- How do they handle disputes?
- Who will manage your project? Who do you deal with?
- What information will you need to provide them?
- Are there any time/resources you'll need to allocate?
- What is their backup if they get sick? Who will look after your project?
- How many revisions do they allow?
- Do they offer ongoing support if needed? At what cost?

I find if you put a call out to your community for a particular type of contractor (web site, SEO, etc.) you'll get swamped with replies. So, make sure you ask your connections:

- Why do they recommend them?
- How long did their project take?
- Was there anything that didn't work?
- Would you work with them again?

# 58. WHERE TO NOW?

You've got your plan, you've got your team on board, you've identified what software or what contractors you need to tick the things on your priority list.

The only thing left to do is to take yourself back through the digital audit we started with and see how you're feeling about everything.

If you've followed all the advice in the book, you'll be well on your way to digitising your business and best of all – whether you've realised it or not – you can no longer call yourself a technophobe.

I'd love to hear how the book has changed the way you look at technology and I've made sure that you have access to all of my social profiles along with an email address at the close of the book. So please reach out with your success stories.

Thank you so much for coming on this journey of technology with me. I hope now you face the digital world with confidence and will continue to update and learn as things continue to change.

For now... Get up, stretch and take the dog for a walk.

You've earned it.

# GLOSSARY

No matter how hard I tried throughout the book to keep the jargon to a minimum, the very nature of the topic often includes acronyms and jargon.

With that in mind, I've put together a glossary of terms which you can lean on while you're reading the book.

This glossary can also be found on my website, and will be updated as new terms and applications become available.

**A/B Split Test:** The ability to split your contact list and try a variation on a message.

**Abandoned Cart Email:** The email that will trigger if a client has been in your shopping site but not completed their purchase.

**Active Campaign:** Cloud-based customer experience software.

**Acuity:** Cloud-based scheduling software.

**Adware:** Unwanted software that presents advertisements on your computer screen when visiting a site.

**Agile CRM:** Cloud-based CRM, marketing, sales and automation.

**Agra:** The heaviest book ever written weighing in over 2000kg.

**Alexa:** Amazon's virtual assistant.

**Algorithm:** Procedures search engines or social media platforms go through to rank content.

**Android:** A mobile operating system for non-Apple devices.

**Answer the Public:** A keyword tool to help create content.

**Any.Do:** A productivity app designed to help people stay organised.

**App Store:** A distribution platform for distributing Apple software.

**Apple Home Pod:** Apple's smart speaker.

**Apple iCal:** A personal calendar application operating on Apple devices.

**Apple iPhone:** The smartphones developed and operated by Apple.

**Appointlet:** Cloud-based scheduling software.

**AR:** Augmented reality. Integrating digital information with a user's existing environment.

**Asana:** A web- and mobile-based application designed to assist with project management and organisation.

**Audiobook:** A voice recording of a book.

**Autoresponder:** An automatic email that is triggered as a result of an action from a client.

**Back link:** A link from one website to another.

**Basecamp:** A web-based project management tool.

**Bit:** The speed data is measured in. There are 8 bits in a Byte.

**Blaq Wolf:** Business that creates physical objects you can attach to items, allowing you to track your items in case they are lost or stolen.

**Blogging:** The process of creating articles to generate content of interest for your clients and potential clients.

**Bluetooth:** Wireless technology used to transfer data.

**Bounce Rate:** The percentage of emails sent that were undelivered.

**Broadcast:** An email that goes to everyone on your contact list.

**Brute Force Attack:** Trial-and-error approach to infiltrating your data.

**Byte:** How data downloads are measured. Each increment is 1000x larger than the one before it.

**Calendly:** Cloud-based scheduling software.

**Captcha:** A computer program designed to determine the difference between a human and a machine accessing information.

**Chatbot:** A software application that responds to questions based on text responses.

**Clubhouse:** A social media platform designed around voice only.

**Contact List:** Another term used for your database or mailing list.

**Content Strategy:** Developing, planning and managing content required in business.

**Conversion Rate:** Your conversion rate will measure by percentage the number of people who followed your CTA.

**CoWorking:** Shared office space within a single location.

**CPC:** Cost per click. What a business pays each time a user clicks on an ad.

**Creator Studio:** Post, manage, measure and monetise your Facebook and Instagram pages.

**CRM:** Customer Relationship Manager.

**CTA:** Call to action. The action you want your email recipient to take as a result of opening your email.

**CTR:** Click through rate. To get your CTR take the number of people who opened your email (open rate) and divide it by the number that clicked on your web link.

**Cyber Security:** Security related to anything internet- or computing-based.

**Cybersecurity Insurance:** Insurance to protect a user if they are subject to cyber attack.

**Domain:** A domain is your website address (e.g.: www.tracysheen. com.au)

**Drag and drop:** The ability to drag one piece of information to another part of the screen.

**Duck Duck Go:** An alternative internet search engine that does not store or utilise your data.

**E-Commerce:** Electronic commerce. The ability to sell and transact in an online environment.

**EDM:** Electronic direct mail.

**Email Campaign:** Also known as 'drip marketing'. An email or series of emails that may be drip fed over a series of days, weeks or months, taking your client on a content journey.

**Email Queue:** When you send a bulk email to a group of contacts, your emails from a cue in preparation for sending.

**Email templates:** A predesigned and preformatted email designed to serve a purpose.

**Encryption:** Encoding information to mask its original information.

**Engagement:** A catch-all phrase used to explain all interactions your clients have with your business

**ESP:** Email Service Provider. The company you use to 'host' your emails.

**Everhour:** A time tracking and organisation application.

**Excel:** Microsoft spreadsheet software.

**Expensify:** A cloud-based expense management system.

**Facebook Blueprint:** Facebook's own online training platform.

**Facebook Insights:** The analytics platform available through Creator.

**Facetime:** A video-based calling service developed by Apple.

**Fat Joe:** A website where you can get content created, link building and SEO assistance.

**Fax:** A primitive form of communication.

**File Sharing:** Sharing information via files between computers.

**Firewall:** A security device that monitors internet traffic and protects your computer from danger.

**FOMO:** Fear of missing out.

**Gb:** Gigabyte – a measurement of data storage.

**GDPR:** General Data Protection Regulation. A regulation based in the EU protecting privacy of computer users.

**GMB:** Google My Business.

**Google:** American-based multinational technology company specialising in internet-related products. Best known for its search engine site.

**Google Ads:** An online advertising platform developed by Google.

**Google Analytics:** A web analytics service offered by Google that tracks and reports website traffic.

**Google Assistant:** Google's artificial and virtual intelligence.

**Google Calendar:** A time management and scheduling system operated by Google.

**Google Chrome:** Google's own internet browser.

**Google Chromecast:** A device that plugs into your TV allowing you to stream content.

**Google Docs:** Google owned word processor software.

**Google G Suite:** A range of cloud-based applications, productivity and collaboration tools owned and managed by Google.

**Google Maps:** A web-based map and navigation tool owned and managed by Google.

**Google Meet:** A video communication platform owned and managed by Google.

**Google Nest:** The brand used to market Google's IOT devices, including speakers, lights etc. Formerly known as Google Home.

**Google Pixel:** A brand of phone developed and operated by Google.

**Google Search Console:** A web service offered by Google that helps optimise visibility of your website.

**Google Sheets:** Google owned spreadsheet software.

**Google Slides:** Google owned presentation software.

**Google Tasks:** A cloud-based task management system owned and managed by Google.

**GPS:** Global Positioning System. A satellite-based navigation system.

**Gusto:** A cloud-based payroll system.

**Gyroscope:** A productivity-based application for Apple users.

**Hacker:** Somebody attempting to infiltrate your computer or website.

**Hard bounce:** A permanent issue with an email address.

**HD:** High definition.

**HDMI:** High Definition multimedia interface. A cable allowing connection between TV and other devices.

**Hot Desking:** Multiple workers sharing a single desk rotating through days/times.

**Hotjar:** A cloud-based software platform that provides a visual representation of how people travel through your website.

**HourStack:** A time tracking application that allows you to track and manage your time in a visual way.

**HTML:** Hypertext Markup Language. Essentially HTML is computer code.

**HubSpot:** CRM and full suite of marketing, sales and administrative software tools.

**iCloud:** Cloud storage solution offered by Apple.

**Inbound Marketing:** Marketing activities you do within your business that cause clients or potential customers to reach out to you.

**InDinero:** Cloud-based start-up accounting software.

**Internal Data:** Information relating to the business such as company reports, sales figures, etc.

**Internet Browser Extension:** An add-on that allows you to get additional information or more functionality from your web browser.

**iOS:** iPhone Operating System.

**IOT:** Internet of Things. Refers to devices with sensors (e.g.: TV, speakers).

**IP:** Intellectual property.

**IP:** Internet protocol. The address of your computer.

**JOMO:** Joy of missing out.

**Keap:** Email marketing and sales-based platform.

**Keychain:** A password management system used by Apple on Macs.

**Keyloggers:** A software program that records the keystrokes on a computer. Often used to gain access to financial information.

**Keynote:** Apple owned presentation software.

**Keyword:** A word your clients use to find your services.

**Krisp:** A cloud-based noise cancelling virtual microphone.

**Landing Page:** A dedicated web page. Used in response to a marketing campaign.

**Last Pass:** A password management system.

**Link Building:** A process in SEO that aims to increase the number of inbound links aimed at your website.

**LinkedIn SSI:** Social Selling Index. It measures your online social presence across four platforms and provides a score out of 100.

**List Fatigue:** A phrase used to describe a segment of contacts with declining engagement.

**List Growth:** Refers to how quickly your list or database is growing.

**List Hygiene:** Ensuring your contact list is current and containing correct information.

**List Segmentation:** Separating your contact emails into target market groups.

**List Washing:** A term used to describe cleaning the data to ensure everything is current.

**Loom:** A cloud-based screencasting software.

**LSI:** Latent search indexing. A term Google use to determine 'other' phrases people may use when searching for your products or services.

**Mail Chimp:** An integrated marketing platform to assist small business.

**Malware:** A computer virus. Intentionally designed to cause damage.

**Marketing Channels:** The way content gets to clients. Examples of marketing channels are direct selling and social media.

**Marketing Funnel:** The idea of the funnel is it catches a broad group of people at the top and as you feed them content or information a smaller percentage of these people would funnel through to the next step until eventually they drop out the narrow end as a client.

**Mb:** Megabyte – a measurement of data storage.

**MBPS:** Megabits per second.

**Messenger:** Also known as Facebook Messenger. An online instant messaging service with inbuilt video calling.

**Metadata:** Data about other data. Examples of metadata include the date something is created.

**Microsoft 365:** A SAAS – solution-based software based around office required activities. Formerly known as Office 365.

**Microsoft Exchange:** Microsoft email server.

**Microsoft Office:** Part of Microsoft 365. Refers to the known Office bundle of Word, Excel and PowerPoint.

**Microsoft Teams:** Microsoft based communication platform.

**Microsoft To Do:** Cloud-based task management system owned and managed by Microsoft.

**Mint:** Cloud-based personal financial management software solution.

**Monday.com:** A web-based project management tool.

**MYOB:** Cloud-based accounting software solution.

**Newsletter:** An update or bulletin shared with your contacts who have opted in to receive your emails.

**nTask:** A free task management system for Android users.

**Numbers:** Apple owned spreadsheet software.

**OK Google:** The command used to wake a Google Nest device.

**OntraPort:** Cloud-based business automation software.

**Open Rate:** The percentage of your emails that were opened by your intended audience.

**Opt In:** Otherwise known as Subscribe. This is where you agree to receive emails from a business.

**Pages:** Apple owned word processor software.

**Password Manager:** A software program which allows users to securely store and generate passwords for software and computer logins.

**Pathway to Purchase:** Often called the 'buyer's journey'. Refers to the steps a prospective buyer makes on the road to becoming your client.

**Payment Gateway:** A merchant service provided by an E-Commerce application. Also known as a Payment Processing Solution.

**PayPal Here:** A mobile payment services provider.

**PC:** Personal Computer. Typically, anything that is non-Apple is classified as a PC.

**Personal Data:** Information related to the individual, things like your name, email, phone number, etc.

**Personalisation:** Adding bits of information to your emails about your clients that you already know.

**Phillips Hue Lighting:** A brand of smart home lighting.

**Phishing:** A fraudulent attempt to gain access to information.

**Plain text email:** An email which is sent without any HTML code.

**Podcast:** A digital audio file. Think of it like radio on demand. You listen to what you want when you want it.

**Pop Up:** A message which appears on your screen when visiting a website.

**POS:** Point of Sale.

**PowerPoint:** Microsoft owned presentation software.

**Productivity Owl:** A Chrome-based browser extension that monitors your online productivity.

**QR (Quick Response) Code.** A type of matrix bar code that directs people to a particular web page.

**QuickBooks:** Cloud-based accounting software solution.

**Ransomware:** A type of Malware that attempts to hold the computer owner to ransom unless a monetary amount is paid.

**Re-engagement Campaign:** An email or series of emails sent to inactive users in the hopes to re-engage them with your content.

**Receipt Bank:** A cloud-based receipt management system.

**Rescue Time:** A web-based application designed to highlight where you spend your time while you're online.

**SAAS:** Software as a Service. A delivery model where software is licenced to the user on a monthly or annual basis, rather than purchased outright for a single fee.

**Safari:** Web browser developed by Apple.

**Samsung Galaxy:** The brand of smartphones developed by Samsung electronics.

**Schedule Once:** Cloud-based scheduling solution.

**Screen Shot:** Also known as 'screen capture' or 'screen grab'. A digital image taken showing the contents of a computer screen.

**SD:** Standard Definition.

**Search Engine:** A software system designed to carry out internet-based searches.

**Secure Pay:** Cloud-based payment processing software.

**Security Plugin:** An additional piece of software to plug a security gap.

**SEO:** Search Engine Optimisation. Improving the quality, quantity and frequency of visitors to your website via improved 'organic' search engine performance.

**SERP:** Search Engine Results Pages. These are the pages that are served to you after you submit an enquiry through a search engine.

**Shopify:** A brand specialising in e-commerce websites.

**SIRI:** Speech Interpretation and Recognition Interface. Otherwise known as Apple's virtual assistant.

**Skype:** A Microsoft-owned company specialising in video calls between computers. A competitor to Zoom.

**Slack:** A channel-based messaging and communication tool.

**Smart Home:** Also known as home automation. Refers to houses which have internet-enabled devices such as lights, speakers, etc.

**Smart Phone:** A mobile phone that combines that ability to call with various computer-based technologies.

**Smart Watch:** A watch that combines traditional timekeeping with some computer-based technologies.

**Soft Bounce:** Often a temporary issue due to the email inbox being full or a problem with a recipient's email server.

**Spam:** Sometimes called unsolicited commercial email (UCE).

**Spear Phishing:** a fraudulent attempt to gain access to information often using the information from a trusted source.

**Spyware:** Software that allows the user to obtain information without another person knowing.

**Square:** A mobile payment services provider.

**SquareSpace:** A drag-and-drop website builder.

**Squirrel Street:** A cloud-based receipt management system.

**SSL Certificate:** Secure Sockets Layer. Essentially it's encryption software that protects the user on your website.

**Stripe:** Cloud-based payment processing software.

**Sync:** Short for 'synchronisation'. Meaning all of your data is shared and up-to-date across your devices.

**TB:** TeraByte – a measurement of data storage 1 TB = 1000000000000 bytes.

**Telco:** Telecommunications.

**TFA:** Two Factor Authentication. Two layers of security to pass to enter a software system.

**Tiles:** A physical device you can attach to something which allows you to track it in the event it's lost or stolen, usually via Bluetooth.

**Timely:** Android application that allows you to track calendars, appointments and messages on the road.

**Timeneye:** A time tracking application.

**TL:DR:** Too long, didn't (or don't) read.

**Todoist:** A productivity tool based around a to-do list.

**Toggl:** A time tracking application.

**ToodleDo:** A productivity platform that incorporates a range of tools, including to do list, notes and habit tracking.

**Trello:** Web and mobile based kanban style application to assist with project management and organisation.

**Trojan:** Anything which misleads a computer user about its intent. E.g.: A photo that hides a computer virus.

**Unsubscribe:** Removing yourself from a mailing list.

**URL:** Uniform Resource Locator. It's the address of your web page.

**USB-C:** Transmits both data and power.

**USB:** Universal Serial Bus. Industry standard cable for connecting devices and computers.

**Vimeo:** A video hosting platform.

**Virtual Summit:** A digital lead generation tool. Gathering a group of people online to host a summit as you would in person.

**Virus Protection:** Software that protects your computer from unwanted attacks.

**Virus:** A computer program that infects the system, rendering it inoperable or leaving it compromised in some way.

**VPN:** Virtual Private Network. It extends a private and protected network across a public domain.

**Wave:** Cloud-based accounting software solution.

**Wearable Tech:** Smart electronic devices worn close to, or on, the skin that collect or transmit data.

**Webinar:** An online meeting or presentation held online.

**Website Hacking:** Gaining access to a website for nefarious purposes.

**Website Hosting:** Website hosting is akin to paying a landlord for your office rental.

**Welcome Email:** The first email you send to a client when they onboard with you.

**Whale Phishing:** A term used when a phishing attack goes after a wealthy or prominent person.

**What 3 Words:** A navigation application based on 3 words finding your location anywhere in the world.

**Whitelist:** An IP address your client considers 'safe'.

**WIFI:** Wireless fidelity. A wireless network allowing devices to interface with the internet.

**Windows:** Microsoft operating system.

**Wix:** A drag-and-drop website builder.

**Woo Commerce:** An open source e-commerce plug in.

**Word:** Microsoft owned word processor software.

**WordPress:** A website builder. Currently the most popular website platform builder.

**Worms:** A computer virus that replicates itself in order to spread to other computers.

**WTForecast:** A mobile-based weather application PG through to R rated content.

**Xero:** Cloud-based accounting software solution.

**YouTube:** A video hosting platform and the world's 2nd most popular search engine. Owned by Google.

**Zencastr:** A web-based online audio recording platform.

**ZMOT:** Google's research paper 'Zero Moment of Truth'. That moment we all reach as consumers when we move from thinking about purchasing to actually committing to buying.

**Zoom:** American telecommunications company providing video conferencing, webinar facilities and online chat services.

# NEED MORE TRACY SHEEN IN YOUR LIFE?

Would you like to work with Tracy? There are so many options, from going to her website to social media and email.

You can also follow her on Facebook at 'The Digital Guide', through LinkedIn (Tracy Sheen) and YouTube (Tracy Sheen The Digital Guide).

Or open your camera and hold it over the code below – you'll be magically transported to Tracy's website.

# LOOKING FOR QUICK DIGITAL TIPS?

Tracy has released 250 digital tips covering everything from productivity to marketing, sales to health and wellness, including geeky gadgets.

You'll find all 250 of these tips on her YouTube Channel (plus bonus content!).

Scan the below QR code to go directly to the YouTube page (don't forget to subscribe).

# LOOKING FOR A PRACTICAL, EMPOWERING GIFT FOR YOUR SMALL BUSINESS CLIENTS?

Strong digital literacy for business owners means long-term viability and adaptation.

If your organisation has small business owners as clients, then *The End of Technophobia* is the book to help them move from struggle to sustainability.

Since 1990 Tracy has been involved with 'all things digital'. She is passionate about helping small business owners embrace and use technology to support the growth and productivity within their business.

She's partnered with the Federal Government as an approved advisor to coach and advise small business owners, as well as working with hundreds of business owners directly to overcome technophobia.

With bulk purchases, you can include your own company message in the book and Tracy can work with you to deliver tailored webinars, workshops or training for your clients.

To explore ideas, please reach out to Tracy at: info@thedigitalguide.com.au

# WANT TO INTERVIEW TRACY SHEEN?

When you chat with Tracy you'll realise she's got a story for just about everything, from growing up behind the counter of a country general store to her corporate career in technology and marketing.

Tracy can talk with passion and credibility on any of the following topics:

- How technology has evolved and impacted small business
- The impact of COVID on technology uptake and business adaptation
- Working in a family business
- Podcasting, interviewing and using the medium to build a business
- How technology is changing communication in business
- Technophobia in business
- Most topics around small business

To interview Tracy about these topics, or to discuss her book *The End of Technophobia*, please email info@thedigitalguide.com.au

# LOOKING FOR A DIGITAL GEEK WITH PERSONALITY TO SPEAK AT YOUR LIVE OR VIRTUAL EVENT?

Tracy Sheen has delivered hundreds of workshops, programs, webinars and seminars over the last 25 years. She is known for her humour and ability to cut through the technology jargon so the audience can easily absorb the information.

Tracy leaves her audiences feeling like technology is something they can adopt in their business. She draws upon her 30-year career across regional and metro Australia in corporate life and as a business owner.

As an Australian podcast pioneer and creator of the country's first panel-style podcast 'Not Another Business Show', Tracy loves talking about how technology, communication and marketing combine to create new opportunities for small business.

She is inspiring, quirky, practical and funny (well, her Mum says she is). Best of all, she works with you to make your event the very best it can be.

For more information about having Tracy speak at your next event (face to face or virtually) contact her team directly: info@thedigitalguide.com.au

www.thedigitalguide.com.au

# NEED TO IMPROVE YOUR INTERVIEW SKILLS?

As one of Australia's podcast pioneers with formal training in interview techniques, Tracy has developed a reputation as one of Australia's best small business interviewers.

She has developed a 6-week online program to help you level up your interview skills and learn how to ask better questions.

It doesn't matter if you're an author, podcaster, small business owner or content creator, we all need to be having better conversations and asking better questions.

Want to find out more about the program?
Email the team at info@thedigitalguide.com.au for more details.

www.thedigitalguide.com.au

# I WANT YOUR TECH TIPS

Every month I host a webinar sharing the best tech hacks of the month, and I'd love to hear from you.

In return I'll give you a shout out in the webinar and on social media.

Share your top tip, hack or favourite software platform by scanning the QR code below, or email: info@thedigitalguide.com.au

Want to find out more about the program?
Email the team at info@thedigitalguide.com.au for more details.